The Power
of the Impossible

On Community and the Creative Life

The Power
of the Impossible

On Community and the Creative Life

Erik S. Roraback

BOOKS

Winchester, UK
Washington, USA

First published by iff Books, 2018
iff Books is an imprint of John Hunt Publishing Ltd., No. 3 East Street, Alresford,
Hampshire SO24 9EE, UK
office1@jhpbooks.net
www.johnhuntpublishing.com
www.iff-books.com

For distributor details and how to order please visit the 'Ordering' section on our website.

ISBN: 978 1 78535 149 5
978 1 78535 150 1 (ebook)
Library of Congress Control Number: 2017951271

A CIP catalogue record for this book is available from the British Library.

Design: Stuart Davies

Printed and bound by CPI Group (UK) Ltd, Croydon, CR0 4YY, UK

We operate a distinctive and ethical publishing philosophy in
all areas of our business, from our global network of authors to
production and worldwide distribution.

Contents

Illustrations/Photos

Picture 1, p. 36
(©Photo by Ann Ronan Pictures/Print Collector/Getty Images/
Hulton Archive)
St. Augustine of Hippo, 1460. Artist: Joos van Gent
Collection: Hulton Fine Art Collection
Used by permission

Picture 2, p. 197
Details
Dante and Virgil enter a fortress surmounted by owls. From
Dante's *Divina Commedia*, Cantica del Inferno. Ms. 597/1424,
folio 48. Italian, 14th century.
Location:
Musée Condé, Chantilly, France
Photo Credit:
©Erich Lessing / Art Resource, NY
Used by permission

Picture 3, p. 238
Ivan Lendl (L) Presents the Cup (The Musketeers' Trophy/
La Coupe des Mousquetaires)
(Photograph: ©JOEL ROBINE/AFP/Getty Images)
Used by permission

In Memory of My Father
Steven Roger Roraback
Seattle 1942—Seattle 2013

Preface and Acknowledgments

This volume on community formation and the creative life has been in a general gestation of reading, teaching and thinking transnationally since its author landed in Prague as a newly minted researcher in 1997—having earned a DPhil from the University of Oxford in July of 1997—to begin teaching at Charles University. During this period, I have been shuttling back and forth on average twice a year between my native city of Seattle, Washington and Prague, Czech Republic, which has given me a transatlantic perspective on this volume. Research and visiting scholar or professor stays, conference papers and guest lectures, have contributed to this study on the paradoxical power of the impossible/possible community and creative life.

I wish to express my appreciation to students of the following MA seminars I have taught at Charles, for their cooperation in confronting questions that inform this book: 'Psychoanalysis and Cultural-Studies'; 'Lacan's Seminars and After'; 'Experience, Commodity Culture, and Spectacle Society: Critical Theory and US Fiction'; 'The Philosophical Baroque: Joyce's *Finnegans Wake* and Pynchon's *Gravity's Rainbow*'; 'Transforming Tradition: Baroque Ventures, Identities and Values in Literature and Theory I and II'; 'Joyce's *Finnegans Wake* and Aesthetic Joys'; 'Spinoza and Contemporary Culture'; 'Literary and Philosophical Baroque: Spinoza and Leibniz for the 21st Century'; 'Cultural Baroque: Heidegger, Joyce, Klossowski'; 'Literary and Philosophical Baroque'; 'Explosions of Being'; 'Explosions of Freedom: James, Bataille, Deleuze, Nancy'; 'Aesthetic Pleasure and Authority: Joyce's *Finnegans Wake* and Pynchon's *Gravity's Rainbow*'; 'Desire and Power: Late Novels of James'; 'Artistic Authority: Joyce's *Ulysses*'; 'Theoretical Approaches to Joyce's *Finnegans Wake*'; 'Theoretical Approaches to Henry James'. Treatment of the *Invisible Man* benefits from BA level classes taught at Charles on

1

'US and Canadian Literature III'; further, I have taught relevant texts in courses at the UPCES program at CERGE-EI in Prague.

I have been privileged to benefit from research stays, which have been invaluable for library access to some documents used in the present work. First, as a Visiting Researcher at the University of Constance (Universität Konstanz), Germany between 2004–14 with the academic support of Aleida Assmann, and with the financial contribution of the DAAD foundation (Deutscher Akademischer Austauschdienst / the German Academic Exchange Service). Second, I profited from time spent as a Visiting Scholar at the University of Washington in Seattle, USA from 2015–17, with the academic support of Robert McNamara and Brian Reed. I wish to thank the relevant library staff at Constance and at Washington for their assistance and also faculty there with whom I have spoken about this inter-disciplinary project.

A debt of gratitude is owed to my former department chair and the coordinator of a research grant, Martin Procházka, for his administrative help for many trips abroad for comparative cultural research and lecturing that led to much of what is now before you in this volume, as well as for offering editorial guidance on some of the material in the project. In this context, I wish to acknowledge that through research stays, conference presentations and guest lecture talks, the composition of this book was supported from the "Programme for the Development of Research Areas at Charles University, P09, Literature and Art in Intercultural Relations," subprogram "Transformations of the Cultural History of the Anglophone Countries: Identities, Periods, Canons." / Tato kniha/kapitola / tento článek / toto číslo bylo vydáno v rámci Programu rozvoje vědních oblastí na Univerzitě Karlově č. P09, Literatura a umění v mezikulturních souvislostech, podprogram Proměny kulturních dějin anglofonních zemí identity, periody, kánony.

Added to this, I have benefited from three research visits

to use libraries in Paris, France, including the FFT (Fédération Française de Tennis) Museum Library at Roland-Garros and the École de la cause Freudienne. I also draw inspiration from two research trips to the University of Oxford in Oxford, England to use the Taylor Institution (the Institutio Tayloriana) and the Bodleian Library. A five-year Visiting Research Fellowship that I hold in the Faculty of Arts at the University of Winchester in the UK (2014–19) also aids this endeavor. I extend my gratitude to all who made these visits possible. I also thank Meredith Miller Richards from the International Tennis Hall of Fame research library in Newport, Rhode Island, USA, for her help and advice. I wish too to acknowledge source-matters of this enterprise. A range of material from popular and from élite culture was presented at venues between 2004–12; endnotes provide details. My sincere thanks go to the organizers and audiences who made these academic and cultural events possible. All extracts adduced are for critical human science and literary-critical purposes only, and remain the property of the individual copyright holders. Grateful thanks go to the editors for permission to use material in earlier versions of Chapters 2 and 4. My thanks also go to the three reviewers of this manuscript for Iff Books and for their helpful criticisms, which made the tome better.

The wide panorama of this present volume addresses readers interested in aesthetics, cultural theory, literature, philosophy, world tennis, theoretical psychoanalysis, creativity, the community of a world society and by extension of a world on the scale of the universe. Last not least I want to thank scholars with whom I have discussed or presented on community and the creative life, or who have read my writings on the subject; these include Robert Appelbaum, Marcel Arbeit, Aleida Assmann, Jan Assmann, Annick Duperray, Michael Frank, J. Hillis Miller, Christopher Norris, David Lee Robbins, the late Hugh J. Silverman, Jonathan Webber and Shirley Sharon-Zisser. Paul Michael Levitt is owed a particular acknowledgment for reading and for offering advice and encouragement on how to improve Chapters 8 and 9. Grateful thanks go to all those friends and relatives who showed interest courtside in this textual endeavor. I wish to express a special thank you to Petra for everything along the way! The dedication records a huge privilege and honor.

Erik S. Roraback
Prague, Europe
March, 2018

Abbreviations

COD: Roberto Esposito, *Communitas: The Origin and Destiny of Community*, trans. Timothy Campbell (Stanford: Stanford University Press, 2010).

DS: Susan Buck-Morss, *The Dialectics of Seeing: Walter Benjamin and the Arcades Project* (Cambridge, MA: MIT Press, 1989).

EF: Jean-Luc Nancy, *The Experience of Freedom*, trans. by Bridget McDonald, with a foreword by Peter Fenves (Stanford: Stanford University Press, 1993).

EP: Gilles Deleuze, *Expressionism in Philosophy: Spinoza*, preface and trans. Martin Joughin (New York: Zone, 1990).

FW: James Joyce, *Finnegans Wake*, intro. John Bishop (London: Penguin, 1999).

G: Georges Bataille, *Guilty*, trans. Bruce Boone, intro. Denis Hollier (Venice, CA: Lapis, 1988).

GA: Leland de la Durantaye, *Giorgio Agamben: A Critical Introduction* (Stanford: Stanford University Press, 2009).

GB: Michael Richardson, *Georges Bataille* (London: Routledge, 1994).

IC: Jean-Luc Nancy, preface, *The Inoperative Community: Theory and History of Literature, Volume 76*, foreword Christopher Fynsk, ed. Peter Connor, trans. Peter Connor, Lisa Garbus, Michael Holland, and Simona Sawhney (Minneapolis: University of Minnesota Press, 1991).

IE: Georges Bataille, *Inner Experience*, trans. with an intro. Leslie Anne Boldt (Albany: SUNY Press, 1988).

IL: Mark Hodgkinson, *Ivan Lendl: The Man Who Made Murray* (London: Aurum, 2014).

IM: Ralph Ellison, *Invisible Man* (New York: Vintage, 1952).

IOC: Thomas à Kempis, *The Imitation of Christ*, trans. with an intro. Leo Sherley-Price (London: Penguin, 1952).

LN: Slavoj Žižek, *Less than Nothing: Hegel and the Shadow of Dialectical Materialism* (London: Verso, 2012).

MC: Slavoj Žižek and John Milbank, *The Monstrosity of Christ: Paradox or Dialectic?*, ed. Creston Davis (Cambridge, MA: MIT Press, 2009).

MWD: Antonio Negri and Michael Hardt, *Multitude: War and Democracy in the Age of Empire* (New York: Penguin, 2004).

N: Giorgio Agamben, *Nudities*, trans. David Kishik and Stefan Pedatella (Stanford: Stanford University Press, 2011).

ON: Georges Bataille, *On Nietzsche*, trans. Bruce Boone, intro. Sylvère Lotringer (London: Athlone, 1992).

POAP: Baltasar Gracián, *The Pocket Oracle and Art of Prudence*, trans. with an intro. and notes Jeremy Robbins (London: Penguin, 2011).

SBL: Steven B. Smith, *Spinoza's Book of Life: Freedom and Redemption in the 'Ethics'* (New Haven: Yale University Press, 2003).

SPP: Gilles Deleuze, *Spinoza: Practical Philosophy*, trans. Robert Hurley (San Francisco: City Lights, 1988).

TE: Benedictus de Spinoza, *The 'Ethics'* from *A Spinoza Reader: The 'Ethics' and Other Works*, ed. and trans. Edwin Curley (Princeton: Princeton University Press, 1994).

TTA: Brian Davies, *The Thought of Thomas Aquinas* (Oxford: Clarendon Press, 1992).

WD: Maurice Blanchot, *The Writing of the Disaster*, trans. Ann Smock (Lincoln: University of Nebraska Press, 1995).

YCS: John McEnroe with James Kaplan, *You Cannot Be Serious* (New York: Berkley, 2002).

Note on the Quotations

The linguistic original for extracts in this book are included in an endnote where the author considered it advantageous and relevant.

Introduction

Ways for Thinking Community and (De)creativity

An affect and a thought that something rots in the world of enclosures and borders today for *homo politicus* stimulate this tome. The general antagonism and universality of the market that pervades the neoliberal orientation toward competitivity and large-scale commodity production thwart contemporary forms of cooperation and creativity. I nuance creativity here as decreativity (following Simone Weil, Giorgio Agamben and Simon Critchley). My sense of the term decreativity is more exactly a genuine enterprising creativity at war against false creativity, and so a substantive creativity in our pseudo-creativity times of rampant neoliberalism that mediates a reductionist capitalist universality.

Accordingly, the objective driving this interdisciplinary text concerns the impossible made possible task (the impossible/possible) of how to live as individual knowledge agencies—as active, autonomous, creative, free and spontaneous moral-ethical individual subjects—in forms of togetherness. That these noble activities occur in a world of reductive and destructive 'creative' big capital and power may seem oxymoronic, yet it is exigent that the ideological space and creative conditions enable it to thrive. Each chapter constitutes a case study of a complicated struggle and a picture of agency that construct a line of one generalized struggle in the service of some larger and more potent cultural, economic and geopolitical vision. As against the universality of the market, the universality that we are aiming at is one of (re) thinking and (re)actualizing community and the creative life. This is informed by the universality that informs and defines struggle itself.

To give two provocative and rich thoughts from contemporary culture, consider this from Agamben

> Perhaps the only way to lead them back once again to their common root is by thinking of the work of salvation as that aspect of the power to create that was left unpracticed by the angel and thus can turn back on itself. Just as potentiality anticipates the act and exceeds it, so the work of redemption precedes that of creation. Nevertheless, redemption is nothing other than a potentiality to create that remains pending, that turns on itself and 'saves' itself.[1]

Likewise is there a model that teaches to base oneself on the creative life ("a potentiality to create") may prove salvific for a communal dimension of life including for one's self-identity. This will recur in this work as a way to invent universality. Now ponder this from Peter Sloterdijk

> Aristotle held the view that only someone to whom 'greatness of soul' (*megalopsychia*) had become second nature could be a citizen. Why should this no longer apply to the contemporaries of the global and nation-state era, simply because they now speak of 'creativity' rather than 'greatness of soul'? The creative people, one hears now and again, are those who prevent the whole from being bogged down by harmful routines.[2]

The present text takes stock and extends this high valuation of 'creativity' for our contemporaneity.

Claims Slavoj Žižek, "The 'hard real' of the 'logic of [...] capital' is what is missing in the historicist universe of Cultural Studies, not only at the level of content (the analysis and critique of political economy), but also at the more formal level of the difference between historicism and historicity proper."[3] The present cultural-studies analysis takes capital into account. And the below chapter-length forays flow from a drive to formalize community relations, and modalities of the creative life—athletic, existential, intellectual, political, social, spiritual—as concrete examples of struggle and so too of our shared universality. Universalists of the world, to echo Karl Marx (1818–83) and Friedrich Engels (1820–95), must cease their disunity and unite. Julia Kristeva articulates the importance of instituting an effective creative existence as one output of the Freudian-Lacanian psycho-analytic process: "Isn't the aim of the cure, precisely, to reveal to the analysand his own particular singularity, thereby encouraging this creativity that seems to be the best criterion for ending analysis?"[4] To realize one's creative potentials and impotentials (compare Agamben's decreation on this point below, and so the (im-)potential to not do something) as adventurers of the spirit enable one to claim one's own life project; as classical Greek culture has it, one's individual and unique *daimon*. In this light, this book unfolds emancipatory and exemplary figures and forms as pictures of agency and chapters in the cultural history of the quest to exist, to create, and to commune with others and with one's own self-identity.

Sloterdijk on Friedrich Nietzschean values of creativity and self-discipline, "Nietzsche stands fatally [...] at the start of the modern, non-spiritualistic ascetologies along with their physio- and psychotechnic annexes, with dietologies and self-referential trainings, and hence all the forms of self-referential practising and working on one's own vital form that I bring together in the term 'anthropotechnics'."[5] In another perspicuous passage from Sloterdijk that heralds the value of creative work, "The economic paradox of Nietzsche's good news consists in the indication that the primary, immeasurably bad news must be recompensed by an as yet unproven mobilization of creative counter- energies."[6] Notions of the ascetical, exercising and practicing life and its lineage Sloterdijk teaches in *You Must Change Your*

Life: On Anthropotechnics/Du mußt dein Leben ändern (2009). In this context, unpleasant news or results may also conduct a need for the person to change her exercising and praxis of life by surrendering to the principle of radical necessity. For there is perhaps nothing that conducts the notion of spirit (athletic, intellectual, etcetera) greater than lost opportunities and of a sense of necessity for the human agent. This notion the present study will confront in its encounter with cultural figures ranging from Benedictus de Spinoza to Ivan Lendl.

This book instances a notion from the Hungarian-British polymath Michael Polanyi (1891–1976), "personal knowledge". The contemporary French researcher Bernard Stiegler notes that to write for a scholar enacts "what Husserl calls the communization of knowledge."[7] In this light, the present study aspires to construct "the communization of knowledge" about the power of the impossible, the communal and creative life.

The intractable nature of thinking about let alone of realizing community must be accounted for; contemporary French philosopher Alain Badiou recapitulates theoretical positions in the forefront of contemporary research on the subject,

It is a 'community' whose disposition of being is not available for discovery [...] a community that we will therefore call, with Maurice Blanchot, unavowable.

It is a 'community' that no institution can realize or serve to perpetuate [...] that we will therefore call, with Jean-Luc Nancy, inoperative (*désoeuvrée*).

It is a community with no present or presence [...] that we will therefore call, with Giorgio Agamben, the coming community (*communauté qui vient*).

[...] in this world the community is an impossibility. Since reasonable management, capital and general equilibria are the only things that *exist*.[8]

These contextual and critical lines of vision constitute so many (de)creative lines of light for thinking a multitude of global communities and cultures. While matters that count now in the zone of the economic élites of the world are "reasonable management, capital and general equilibria", this study points a way out of this deadlocked contemporary ideological universe and financial oligarchy. Major US literary scholar J. Hillis Miller (1928–), let it be duly noted, has written two recent books on the problem of community, which itself says something to the present conditions for intellectual work in the critical human sciences.[9]

Classical Spanish baroque era thinker, Baltasar Gracián y Morales, SJ (1601–58) in *The Pocket Oracle and Art of Prudence* sets the cultural stage, "Knowledge and courage contribute in turn to greatness"[10] — which may translate to educated knowledge and courage or global knowledge and courage work. To acquire and deploy knowledge work to progressive effect enacts courage and intelligent creativity. This in turn would institute positive and productive ethical and existential consequences for critical, free, generous, just and liberated forms of individual and collective sociality. Gracián also notes, "self-knowledge is the start of self-correction" (*POAP*, 27). This notion translates too as collective correction in what we term with Sloterdijk "the practicing life" for collective/societal and individual/self-giving cultural creativity and emancipation. Though creativity may prove problematic in being outsourced for uncreative purposes, a remediated use of it is essential. The idea of decreativity taken after Simone Weil among others—as noted—adds a distinct flavor to our against the instrumentalist grain sense of what constitutes genuine creativity.

Not only are courage and self-knowledge important, but so too are movement, *movens*, and the gestation of growth. Historical processes of maturation and movement both then are components of the operative concept of community: whether a self/person or a collective commons. Community as Italian scholar of community studies Roberto Esposito (1950–) argues embodies a "void, that distance, that extraneousness that constitutes them [subjects] as being missing from themselves [...]."[11] In this light, we must traverse and cross that cultural void in the activity that would be the construction and the making of affirmative forms of community. Further, Esposito notes that the concept and practice of community "isn't having, but on the contrary, is a debt, a pledge, a gift that is to be given, and that therefore will establish a lack. The subjects of community are united by an 'obligation,' in the sense that we say 'I owe *you* something,' but not 'you owe *me* something'" (*COD*, 6). This is a crucial distinction. It informs for example the Lendl-Andy Murray relation, as tennis coach/teacher to player/pupil, par excellence a 'gift to be given' as Chapters 8, 9 and 10 will reveal.

Useful for our investigation too concerns what Esposito highlights, that in the etymology of the Latin word *communitas* one finds *munus*: "the specificity of the gift expressed in the word *munus* with respect to the more general use of *donum* has the effect of reducing the initial distance and of realigning this meaning with the semantics of duty." Esposito continues, "The *munus* in fact is to *donum* as 'species is to genus,' because, yes, it means 'gift,' but a particular gift, 'distinguished by its obligatory character, implied by its root *mei-*, which denotes exchange'" (*COD*, 4). What unites our figures and their practices is that in their gift or *munus* they made the impossible possible.

Crucially, to switch back to Gracián, "What use is knowledge, if it isn't practical? And today, knowing how to live is true knowledge" (*POAP*, 88). What could be more salient in our confounded times, of confused existences, in a chaotic economic, political and social reality of beginning, if not of a disintegrative late capitalism, than to speak of the everyday praxis of living meritorious, intelligent and (de)creative lives that would embody "true knowledge"? An enormous and grand topic thus absorbs the present essay, how to exist in common in productive and in beneficial ways for one's daimon and for one's community? Hence a leading matter concerns the subject's modus vivendi and its intersection and constitution of a common life/the creative commons.

Added to this from Gracián: "We have nothing of our own but time, which even the homeless can inhabit" (*POAP*, 93). The wealth and fertile force of time is one true subject, and in the commodity universe potentially the most precious and valuable commodity of all. A respect for time's value informs our paradigm for the construction of forms of the creative life and community. In one of Gracián's searching observations, "Three S's make someone blessed: being saintly, sound and sage" (*POAP*, 112). In spite of contemporary attacks on the notion of sagacity or wisdom, this perdures in our age of the rationality of big finance. Perhaps today we can properly appreciate and sublate such lessons as the foregoing, and so give them their true substance and meaning. Christianity awaits its figures and forms of being. This is also why the notions of creative work, discipline, humility, play and community solidarity require those three procedures—'health, holiness, and wisdom' (mediated by "being saintly, sound and sage"). The subversive potential of such ideas and forms of praxis tap into the revolutionary energies of the Christian heritage: a tradition of meaning that awaits its sublation in a critical transformation, even as it dialectically revisits its foundational paving stones in the twenty-first century. Forms of virtue thus await mobilization and awakening for the basic coordinate of life and for complex truly (de)creative activities.

Key is to vindicate 'health-holiness-wisdom' for another modality of being, sociality and togetherness. That this remains to be brought into existence offers up global hope for (post) human experience in the creative commons and beyond. As for the idea of discipline, Žižek argues "the struggle for the new society of universal freedom should obey the harshest discipline [...]."[12] Rex P. Stevens in his account of Immanuel Kant writes that for the Prussian philosopher, "Discipline erects a series of attitudes toward the world and the persons in it [...]." In another remark from Stevens: "discipline creates a way of life, not just the exercise of some isolated talent or skill. The moral way of life is maintained as an attitude that pervades living first as an unusually unnatural and strained way of looking at the different experiences of life."[13] Wonderful discipline must also be mobilized for the practicing and exercising life in its various configurations, modalities and modes of creative and communal being. Our hypothesis is that disciplined efforts, with a touch of grace and predestination or fate, may lead to miracles. This includes, paradoxically, facility in not being misguidedly effortful in the right contexts and ideological spaces, and so constructing subversive and (de)creative forms of paradoxically radical non-effortfulness that are themselves heterodox kinds of noble and liberal effortfulness and acts of grace.

Consider the following from Žižek, which taps into our conceptual investment in reason and drive to spawn revolutionary figures and practices, and by extension, self-sublating movements, dialectical mediations and forms of life: "Freud proposed as a utopian solution for the deadlocks of humanity, the 'dictatorship of reason'—men should unite and together subordinate and master their irrational unconscious forces. [...] Freud uses the same formulation for both: the voice of reason or of the drive is often silent, slow, but it persists forever. This intersection is our only hope."[14] This offers for human hoping a way of thinking a different conceptual intersection, mediation and economy of reason and drive. In a neo- and post-Žižekian reading there is some death drive in all forms of drive, and the death drive here is the precise opposite of death, for the death drive is all about life, and it is eternal. As a foundational and immortal energy, the death drive survives our biological demise. This repositions us on a different level for thinking the construction of the specific revolutionary subjectivity and figure, and of the precise revolutionary emancipatory achievement and form-of-life as one based on a creative and focused drive. For example, we shall demonstrate how Ivan Lendl's radical athletic strategies embody these ideas.

Moreover, this text includes for analysis a wide band of figures and forms of being. To be sure, the chosen élite and pop-cultural figures range from Spinoza in philosophy, about whom the French scholar Louis Althusser claims "effected a revolution in the history of philosophy unparalleled in the history of philosophy" to a representative from popular and mass culture, Lendl, who likewise as a change agent revolutionizes and subverts the culture and sport of tennis in the 1980s. Lendl does so with the pioneering methods of his unprecedentedly powerful baseline game, intelligent mental and physical fitness and dietetic regime of good nutrition. British author Mark Hodgkinson writes that the early 1980s saw Lendl "reinventing the geometry of a tennis court—somehow, now that Lendl had a composite racket, everything was different, everything was new."[15] Lendl's (de-)creative physical and cognitive talent precisely allows for this re-geometricalization of the tennis universe. Napoleon on the Horse, Lenin on the Train, Lendl on the Court. Lendl emerges as an athletic discoverer and revolutionary of the late twentieth century who brings something new to the table, even if on some level it was already there for the finding.

Hodgkinson also notes how after Lendl's 1984 French Open victory, the French women's singles winner from that year Martina Navratilová's dietician (and author) Dr. Robert Haas, "put together a customized diet for Lendl, based on what the computer was telling him, which would make him lighter, faster and stronger—he would have the muscle-to-fat ratio, and the cholesterol levels, that you would expect from someone with ambitions of tennis greatness" (*IL*, 173). Here the idea of physical training as an instance of emancipatory discipline and self-surrender, if not self-cancellation, emerges for the athletic creation of new tennis truths for the radical tennis imagination. Sloterdijkian-like ideas too of the exercising and practicing life come to the fore in the Lendl experiment that lends wings to the will and a stimulant to the spirit. A certain history of tennis coincides with the Lendl-event, and of his transformation of himself with his tennis discoveries.

The present study promotes a cultural politics that takes tennis as a legitimate object of intellectual focus. Indeed because community is an elusive thing it precisely requires another unorthodox angle. Lendl provides this as one entrance key to our theme. Hodgkinson adds with regard to creative/decreative gastronomy, "Lendl started a revolution at his breakfast table [...]. For all the recent interest in gluten-free Novak Djokovic's eating habits [...] they don't seem as outlandish as Lendl's appeared to be in the 1980s" (IL, 174). This is true for Lendl's resourceful and creative approach to tennis was far-seeing so that he configured another template for the modern game. This was uncommon and provoked the future tennis commons. An imaginative if not an ascetical and monastic form-of-life is incarnate in the creative novelty of Lendl's diet. This was a first among top male players on the professional tennis tour. Lendl's psychic system was also subject to creative scrutiny and adjustment by psychologist Alexis Castorri. Lendl would later enlist Castorri to help his mentee, the contemporary Scottish tennis player, Murray (1987–). Mental and physical training regimes then open up as spiritual practices for establishing revolutionary forms of existence and athletic creation.

It is criterial for French thinker Michel Serres (1930–) that: "High-level sportsmen live like monks, and creators live like these athletes. Do you seek to invent or to produce? Begin with exercise, seven regular hours of sleep, and a strict diet. The hardest life and the most demanding discipline: asceticism and austerity. Resist fiercely the talk around you that claims the opposite."[16] These words on exercises and practices of self-discipline for aspiring creators map on to what Sloterdijk explores in *You Must Change Your Life: On Anthropotechnics*. We thus examine a wide field of cultural attention, which taps into both élite and popular culture energies, and the modes of world-making such energetics and application produce. Thus, the athletic and the scholarly or culture producer office require key habits and a modus vivendi that maps and opens onto new forms and spirits of the (de)creative (future communal) dimension of life.

Merit involves a decision first of all to live your life in a focused, idiosyncratic and so self-particularizing way. Our cultural figures are (de-)creatively revolutionary in how each revolutionizes a field of endeavor and/or an era. Giving a further and fuller account of these persons and their deeds allows us to consider a different community revolution and emancipation yet to come. Any number of female cultural figures might too have been chosen. But given the accidents of interpretive history, and the chances in the compiling of the study, they are not primary sources in surveying configurations of community and the creative life. This is a contingent feature. For another study one could imagine an inclusion of such figures and their deeds as Saint Teresa of Ávila, Emily Dickinson, Kate Chopin, Gertrude Stein, Hannah Arendt, Julia Kristeva, Martina Navratilová and Toni Morrison, inter alia.

Bulgarian-born scholar and psychoanalyst Kristeva writes about what we need more than ever, a developmental culture of revolt: "The question I would like to examine [...] is the necessity of a culture of revolt in a society that is alive and developing, not stagnating. In fact, if such a life did not exist, life would become a life of death, that is, a life of physical and moral violence, barbarity."[17] This cultural study too, takes on board common notions, to detonate cultural figures and their projects, as emancipatory agents for activating Walter Benjamin's revolutionary "now-time" and his conception of experience (in German *erfahrung*), which Lutz Koepnick elucidates:

> Explicitly opposed to scientific or positivistic definitions of experience, Benjamin unfolds his concept along spatial and temporal vectors at once. Experience mediates individual modes of perception with collective patterns of cognition and material modalities of production, transportation, and information; experience articulates conflicting temporalities, including those of utopian promises and historical memory, of conscious and unconscious acts of recollection and remembrance.[18]

This account articulates many issues in our transnational study. It also applies to the different sorts of temporality our chosen figures and their deeds embody. Such forms of temporal experience include "utopian promises and historical memory, of conscious and unconscious acts of recollection and remembrance" for transhistorical and transnational historical exchange and transmission.

David S. Ferris remarks succinctly that for Benjamin, "Experience is the uniform and continuous multiplicity of knowledge."[19] Linking up experience with knowledge remains paramount for Benjamin, and by extension also for this critical project. This Benjaminian knowledge and experience link indexes what may ripen with one's selection procedures in the spectacle societies of hyper-consumerism and commodification in the twentieth and twenty-first centuries. Knowledge fires our faculties of thought and reason and promotes originality, progressiveness and the deployment of radical and subversive imagination or creativity that moves history forward. Revolutionary imagination and creativity (or pioneering innovation) make possible the potential production of new forms, ideas and methods. This idea of potentiality endorses Agamben's commentary on Aristotle's *Metaphysics* "all potential to be or to do something is always also potential not to be or not to do [...]. The 'potential not to' is the cardinal secret of the Aristotelian doctrine of potentiality, which transforms every potentiality in itself into an impotentiality";[20] this makes impotentiality in certain contexts a positive task and attainment. Likewise in this way does the term "decreation" function that Agamben deploys. Leland de la Durantaye teaches us that the idea of decreation for Agamben is "something that brings the contingent—'what could have been but was not'—into view."[21] These ideas give a deeper sense to our reading of creation and impotentiality/potentiality in an Agamben context if not in a Spinoza one, since for the latter the conatus functions in a different way from that of Agamben impotentiality/potentiality. To be clear, we give our own nuance to decreation, namely that it denotes a certain potent creativity as against its subjectification to capitalist instrumentalization.

In another cultural example, the expressive dynamics of French scholar Deleuze's edition of Spinoza is crucial for thinking existence and creation across a multiplicity of vectors of temporality, including present focused goals and forceful memories. This constitutes a productive transposition for a critical conduit for making and remaking individuals and communities of radical agency, via our choices and actions as active and concrete human agents.

Needed also are nontraditional conceptions of subjectivity and of time for revolutions in existence, creation and community operations. Crucial is to rethink subjectivity in the light of models of temporality and of the unconscious. US scholar de la Durantaye notes in Benjamin the German word *Jetztzeit*

'Now-time' is [...] a conception of time focused on the radical opportunity that every moment brings with it [...].
Agamben stressed the need to probe 'the folds and shadows

of the Western cultural tradition' for a critique of the instant [...] Agamben adopted this model of a now-time, giving it the kindred name *kairology* and linking it to a 'catastrophe' that he sees as ongoing [...]. *Kairology* is best understood in opposition to *chronology* [...]. (*GA*, 102–03)

This Benjaminian idea of time we apply where applicable in this text to contest the calamitous and continuing catastrophe that Agamben designates as the polar opposite of "chronology", in the form of a "kairology". This allows us to move from the temporality of the instant, to that of the larger time frame. We need to identify moments of "now-time" for their emancipatory potential for the common good, for an enlarged sense of communal agency and for a paradoxical cultural politics of impossibility as forms and pictures of possibility.

Consider de la Durantaye on what Agamben and Benjamin's thought challenges: "the idea of the end as a model or paradigm for a mode of thinking and living that is not waiting for dialectical completion or messianic fulfillment [...]. Agamben also says that this time of the now as time of the end"

'was Benjamin's idea [...]' (UL, 18) [...]. His idea is not of apocalypse but of *immediacy*; [...] it is acting as though He were already here. [...] Agamben will say not only [...] that the central idea in Benjamin's *Theses* is 'messianic time,' but also that 'the paradigm for understanding the present is messianic time' (UL, 18). Here Agamben makes perfectly explicit that what is at issue is a paradigm—or model—for our action. (*GA*, 103)

This model of time informs the present work. The Moravian born Ivan Lendl's athletism—via his emancipatory, non-fundamentalist, courageous and energetic self-discipline and focus for the revolutionarily changed practical and theoretical knowledge about how to approach tennis, which also instituted higher standards for tennis culture—offers one such "paradigm— or model—for our action". For Lendl models discovery as the creative initiative of a method of intelligent physical training, diet and tennis practice this study finds exemplary for attaining a spirit of the power of the impossible, namely the athletic-creative life to work within and to conduct the achievement of community as a mediating agent for connection on the rotating global stage. Preparational creativity finds a new level of attainment as a form of knowledge in Lendl's athletic praxis. Tennis takes a fateful direction of strides with Lendl's intervention in the 1980s.

In the light of the popular nature of tennis and the universality of mass culture, the Lendlian frame and revolution still provoke and inspire the mass- and pop-cultural heritage and the athletic imagination. With regard to temporality, as for today's deity of mechanical clock time that views time as concordant with space—the time of the big finance banks—there is a messianic temporality that locates paradoxical and radical hope in the past, and that is as against clock time tout court. So, with Benjamin-Agamben in de la Durantaye's account "a *messianic* idea of history [...] in which we act as though the Messiah is already here, or even has already come and gone. [...]. To this [Agamben] adds,"

'[...] the messianic is not [...] the end of time, but the time of the end' (LAM, 51). [...]; and it is through such expressions as 'dialectics at a standstill' and 'means without end' that the two thinkers aim to return our gaze from the distant future to the pressing present.

[...]. The standstill is brief—and opportune. It denotes the fortuitous moment [...] for a new—and very different—start. (*GA*, 120)

These notions of the messianic and of historiography are

valuable resources for individual and for collective change and transformation to reboot our intellectual, moral-ethical and political projects. We may start afresh for the individual and for the community when, "The dialectic in question is at a standstill".

Historical materialism takes into account the class system in sociality, including of human global society, wherein we are responsible for the past. Here is Benjamin scholar, Michael Löwy, on history's victims:

> A secret pact binds us to them [...] if we wish to remain faithful to historical materialism [...] a vision of history as a permanent struggle between the oppressed and the oppressors.
>
> Messianic/revolutionary redemption is a task assigned to us by past generations [...] we are ourselves the Messiah; each generation possesses a small portion of messianic power, which it must strive to exert.[22]

This dynamic would serve justice on behalf of the dead for a collective emancipation and redemption for another public sphere and cultural zone yet to come. The aforementioned modest bit of "messianic power" our figures and their deeds activate in a kairology from the philosopher Spinoza to the tennis icon Lendl, for acts of popular memory and revolt for a radical rethinking of creative/decreative and communal experience. This take on history and justice may seem counterintuitive yet it has content.

Xan Brooks argues, Lendl was "spurred on by an epic sense of injustice." What is more tennis's enigmatic and driven human machine

> played the game in a state of beautiful torment. Stick him on hard courts and the Czech proved all but unbeatable. But it was on the treacherous lawns of SW19 that we saw the man

at his most exciting. Time after time, he would launch himself at the prize, slipping and skidding to the final rounds before going down in flames. Failure, after all, is so much more interesting than success. And the failure of a man who might otherwise be immortal provided a drama that was positively Shakespearean.

[...] Lendl returned to Wimbledon in well upholstered middle-age, with his bright new brief as [Andy] Murray's coach. On this occasion he sat impassive and motionless in the player's box, chivvying his 21st-century avatar towards the one title that had eluded him. That's why I choose to see last year's final as his grand redemptive moment, a roundabout blessing for so many old efforts. [...]. They should put up a statue; they should sit it in the box. It would never move and never speak and it would never crack a smile. It would be like 2013 all over again.[23]

To be sure, many judge that if Wimbledon had rye grass in Lendl's era, he would have won the grass slam multiple times. In any case, it is a paradoxical truth of this broad field of cultural attention that Lendl embodies much of note in this work. That Lendl's individual failure to win Wimbledon in spite of winning it as a junior singles player in 1978 proves a drama "that was positively Shakespearean" conducts the revolutionary energy and conative force (for Spinoza *conatus* signifies a power that any finite thing holds, and that enables it to persist in the power of being including the power to act and the power to exist) that we need in order to take back community and the creative way of life in our current dysfunctional societal landscape of a destructively violent neoliberal globalization that diminishes the social contract; this includes notions of economic justice and basic human rights, as well as forms of truth, community and creativity. This would be to reclaim new forms of critical agency and collectivity as so many forms of solidarity and liberty.

Perhaps in the passionate seeking and striving for the honor of SW19 Wimbledon champion, Lendl somehow located the aim anyway; for example, he constructed an ideological space and laid down the foundations for future coordinates of athletic community and creativity. For the collective agency that Lendl and his creative disciple Murray embody constitute a power of the impossible and of the true interbeing and transferential nature of subjectivity. A transindividual and transnational subjectivity describes their interrelation. Also, the Shakespeareanization of Lendl's historical pop culture career indexes flashes of energies for the construction of forms of radical community, true creativity/decreativity and potentiality/impotentiality.

Figures in this study contain within their mental or physical activities, subjectivity, character, values and basic lessons, historical materialism may tap into for the emancipatory potentials of the past that were (catastrophically) missed. This is where to locate the possibility of achieving our dreams: to rediscover what was lost or neglected in the past. These essential energies lead us to cultural renewal, and to forms of local and global hope. So by going backwards and beginning with a reboot we can move forward. As the foregoing suggests, theorist Fabio Vighi describes how for Žižek an idea such as freedom "has the form of a loop: we have a chance to disconnect and opt for a different cause, i.e. choose a process of subjectivation with a different content."[24] The point above from Benjamin/Löwy is that it is a question of historical memory and of heeding the infinite demand of the deceased. Namely: to do them and their historical plight cultural and economic justice. Thus the vital importance of the potential energy of memory and of a 'kairology'.

The above would constitute and embody the great dignity of the destiny of humanity with this well-grounded historically informed approach to emancipate the revolution in a view of history from the angle of dialectical materialism (class struggle) and by extension from a theological point of view of predestination. Further, Jacques Lacan's frequent asseveration that *il n'y a pas de grand autre* (there is no big Other) that Žižek unmasks in his writings, must be replaced by ourselves, as the true and good authority in this problem of construction and affirmation. In this account of matters for the upcoming efforts 'we are ourselves the Messiah'. The demise of God on the Christian cross makes this eventual form the nonesuch case-study. For a pop-cultural example of this notion of the messianic vision of history, and of the notion of an interventionary force at precisely the right courageous time, consider the song *While You See a Chance* (1980) that was first performed by the British musical artist Steve Winwood. Each moment in time contains a chance, a messianic moment with emancipatory potential.

Löwy adds in a note—which relevantly for our epoch clearly requires a generalized struggle to function with a larger geopolitical vision—"The only possible Messiah is a collective one" upon which Löwy continues and clarifies on what separates Benjamin from Marx, to wit

> not just the theological dimension, but also the extent of the demand coming from [...] the victims of history.
>
> Why is this messianic power *weak* (*schwach*)? As Giorgio Agamben has suggested, we might see this as a reference to the preaching of Christ according to St Paul in 2 Cor 12: 9 for the Messiah 'my strength is made perfect in weakness' [...]. But the expression also—probably—has a present political signification: the melancholy conclusion Benjamin draws from the past and present failures for the struggle for emancipation. Redemption [...] is merely a slim possibility [...].[25]

One thinks here of the athletic struggle that breaks out on the cultural platform and global stage of the 1984 French Open men's singles final between the Homeric-like warriors, antagonists and protagonists, McEnroe from the capitalist West and Lendl from the communist East. One ponders how Lendl in this match and after emerges to create a cut, both in his career, and in the culture of the sport. It was "a slim possibility" that Lendl would win after being down two sets to love and a break in the fourth set (and after losing four prior finals in majors). But the comeback happens because of the courageous and athletic hope, and joyful persistence, the athletic *conatus*, of Lendl to activate his 'self-redemption'. This is the kind that can occur in the first instance for more macro-scale ones to follow. This figure and form of a messianic moment in history can thus be as Benjamin writes, "the small gateway in time through which the Messiah might enter."[26] For this we have to emancipate ourselves. This is our infinite responsibility and possibility, and so an example of the miraculous power of the impossible on the stage of cultural modernity in multiple contexts that deconstruct the opposition between writerly/intellectual and athletic/physical work.

Energies from the cultural memory and evental status of this Cold War tennis combat constitute an unconscious and forgotten messianic monad of emancipatory potential if as Löwy writes, the goal with Benjamin's use of the radical energy of historical memory is "to build 'constellations' linking the present and the past. [...] these moments wrested from empty historical continuity are monads. [...] they are concentrates of historical totality [...]. These moments represent a revolutionary opportunity [...] for the oppressed past, but also, doubtless, for the oppressed present." Löwy continues,

According to the preparatory notes, the universal history of historicism is false; [...]. But there will one day be a true universal history, as there will be a true universal language: in the messianic world, which is the 'world of universal and integral actuality'. This messianic history of delivered humanity will burn like an 'eternal lamp' that includes the totality of the past in an immense *apokatastasis*.[27]

This invites thought about the politics of possibility with which to contest oppressive material, moral-ethical, and spiritual conditions for a "world of universal and integral actuality". An "apokatastasis" then "in the messianic world" in relation to one's individual subjective experience and history promotes thinking on other possible temporalities. In such a frame, the messianic community arrives wherein new forms of individual and collective emancipation emerge in concert with class solidarity and class-struggle to organize the idea of universality that encircles all for "a true universal history". This study mobilizes such transindividual and transnational monads as Deleuze and Spinoza, Nancy and James, or Murray and Lendl and so forth. Another constellated monad could be Spinoza and Lendl insofar as the latter constitutes an embodiment of the former's philosophy in deploying the body and mind to excellent effect for enhanced conditions for a future class-struggle; even if as reductively and superficially conceived, tennis may seem merely to advance class interests and class society, yet this is not essentially the case, for self-discipline both is a universal and builds universality.

Multiple stars of our constellation make another monad and a kairology for another beginning for thinking with and through our common social substance and forms of existence in a cultural struggle for a world society community of radical equals. The stakes of this struggle include the construction of forms of radical freedom and of community. From the sky of ideas, to the earth of daily experience and forms of praxis, this investigation interrogates the true substance of creative existence and the innovative commons. What Polanyi argues with regard to scientists we extend to our producer-creator figures: "We call their work creative because it changes the world as we see it, by deepening our understanding of it."[28]

We hypothesize that persons must act en masse to build on ways of being-in-common (in post-Nancyese) or as forms of a collective social symbolic substance (in post-Žižekese). We need more creativity, more invention and to act on this collectively as a form of solidarity to rejuvenate our general brain and social imagination in the hegemonic era of big finance and digital technology. For one example, this cultural form and ideology comes out of a USA that coats global capital for a mega net profit for the US per day. Enlarged creativity follows on from what Agamben terms below "decreation" or in our take on it, decreativity, another form of potent creativity in an era that talks incessantly about creativity's merits, even if it is often outsourced by hegemonic powers of capital that often militate against creating historical conditions for the positive construction of community. So, far from making things more equitable, weak forms of pseudo creativity end up intensifying injustices and inequities in the world, and obstructing the institution of a community of radical equals.

This writer endorses a more creative and philosophical criticism and critical imagination and intellect. In this light, we incorporate additional notions from de la Durantaye on Agamben including a desire "to find *paradigms*—exemplary figures and forms—through which to conceive a new relationship between part and whole, individuality and community, particularity and universality" (*GA*, 163). Interestingly too, "The *example* [...] is neither a singularity nor a universal. [...] Agamben offers [...] a nondialectical relation in which the singularity or example is at once a member of, and excluded from, the set of things it exemplifies" (*GA*, 163). Furthermore: "*Examples* occupy a seemingly paradoxical relation to universality and particularity [...] Agamben suggests that 'examples' are 'exemplars [*gli esemplari*] of the coming community' (CC, II [14]). They are, however, not the only ones" (*GA*, 163). The paradoxical nature of the individual example's or of the exemplar's relation to the classical connection between universality and particularity, permit us to think something beyond traditional dialectical thinking. Even the dialectical effects of the exemplar's hitherto (mis-)reception, make their historical neglect a necessity given the idea of the return of the repressed from psychoanalytic thought, and also in a dialectical movement a more consonant reception and sublation that might find form and a place with the passage of time for the exemplary cultural figure. This all is crucial for the collective enterprise of the engenderment of a world society of moral-ethical (de)creative-spiritual work, self- and collective-discipline and a community of equals. The individual figure stands for precisely an instance of the dynamic of the dyad, particular/universal. Accordingly this study points to figures and forms as examples of the "coming community" for a futuristic world society.

Agamben suggests forms of temporality to cultivate for redemptive work for individual and communal creativity when he writes that unlike "creation, the work of redemption is eternal. [...] the supreme knowledge is that which comes too late [...] is the last and most precious fruit of our lives [...]. Until humans learn to dedicate to it [...] their eternal Sabbath, this supreme knowledge will remain a personal matter, which one attends to hurriedly and quietly" (N, 9). This formula contains implications for thinking and for being. Each transformative agent in this work mediates an exemplary paradigm for critical and existential steps in the practical reality. However, precisely by deploying the miraculous resources of the impossible, this study argues it may not always be that "the supreme knowledge is that which comes too late".

Inasmuch as miracles are happening all the time, the impossible is after all distinctly possible. Or, as Polanyi instructs us in one of his monumental essays, the designer of the first nuclear reactor, the Italian physicist Enrico Fermi "is reported to have said that a miracle is an event the chances of which are less than one in ten."[29] Those are perhaps surprising odds to actualize the immense force of the impossible/the miraculous. Less than a ten percent chance defines the likelihood of any of the figures and their respective deeds in this book from emerging.

To think more with Agamben, one critical strategy to see through and at our present history: "To perceive [...] this light that strives to reach us but cannot—this is what it means to be contemporary. [...] to be contemporary is [...]"

> a question of courage, because it means being able not only to firmly fix one's gaze on the darkness of the epoch but also to perceive in this darkness a light that, while directed toward us, infinitely distances itself from us. [...] it is like being on time for an appointment that one cannot but miss. (N, 14–15)

Political, intellectual-mental, athletic-physical and creative-cultural agency and courage are sources of value our élite and popular cultural figures embody and what make them our extreme contemporaries. These foregoing properties and a capacity too, to be washed in blood, by sacrificing themselves to their projects and forms of praxis, mark the committed and impassioned cultural figure and their works, which connect self and society in rational ways to build universality.

To Agamben again, "Only those who perceive the indices and signatures of the archaic in the most modern and recent can be contemporary." Agamben continues: "*Archaic* means close to the *arkhē* [...] the origin. But the origin is not only situated in a chronological past: it is contemporary with historical becoming and does not cease to operate within it, just as the embryo continues to be active in the tissues of the mature organism, and the child in the psychic life of the adult" (N, 17). With this light, we focus on a perhaps archaic and anachronistic for some accounts, albeit up to the minute thinker for this study, the courageous and (de)creative Spinoza. Such a paradox would be a structural necessity for thinking the possible emancipatory radicalness of our contemporaneity. Namely, to return to one of its paving stones, Spinoza's weighty project from the early modern seventeenth-century Dutch Republic.

We may go further back to the world of late antiquity to return not only to such figures as Augustine (354–430 CE), who is among the first to construct modern forms of human subjectivity, but also to a project of later antiquity, that of the philosopher Plotinus (205–270 CE) who argues, "All that one sees as a spectacle is still external; one must bring the vision within and see no longer in that mode of separation but as we know ourselves; thus a man filled with a god—possessed by Apollo or by one of the Muses— need no longer look outside for his vision of the divine being; it is but finding the strength to see divinity within."[30] The visual, the seen and the eye, have become dominant in today's cultural landscape. Precisely this conglomerate must be contested to discover what is important and of value, for various forms of individual and collective social agency. Plotinus also notes, "We ourselves possess beauty when we are true to our own being; our ugliness is in going over to another order; our self-knowledge, that is to say, is our beauty; in self-ignorance we are ugly."[31] The ancient Greek culture injunction 'know thyself' and Nietzsche's to "Become who you are" both resonate as stars of incandescent intensity. In this we retain some belief in the self as a person.

In the scramble for the accumulation of earthly commodities, the contemporary subject requires historical, moral-ethical and ontological sensitivity and awareness so that one be not falsely informed and formed. Thereby, we retain that which is 'beautiful' and truly free about ourselves as radical subjects and agents, and so by extension for others whom we mediate. For the price of material commodities often proves catastrophically high and not in our vital interests. Commodities often prove reified forms of hipness that are shallow, if not bankrupt forms and sources of meaning, movement and value; this is especially if a truly free and radical materialism takes the nonexistence of the object, or of the entity, as its premise. That time itself is potentially the most valuable commodity gives another model too of the object universe to realize our potentials and powers as individual and collective agents.

A critical sense perdures that we require for enhanced individual and communal agency a new praxis of self- and communal-discipline as a form of society building universality and religiosity (with which to contest the current society founding religion of money and big capital). This format taps into new figures, moral-ethical forms and practices of creative work, training-discipline and community. In a book coauthored by Žižek and a Croatian philosopher and theologian Boris Gunjević, the latter argues that we must look to Augustine (one of the first modern subjects) to exit from the impasses of today's genuinely punishing militarized capitalism and digital technology whose "understanding of ascetic practice begins with a voluntary renunciation of desire for glory and thirst for power. After that follows the renunciation of submission to pleasure, the renunciation of a weakening of the soul and body, and renunciation of the avaricious aspiration to greater wealth. [...]. To be radical means [...] to accept and adopt a disciplined asceticism as a way of life."[32] So, this idea of spiritual and by extension intellectual discipline would mediate more substantive forms and figures of life as a high value and wellspring of meaning and knowledge. This radical modality of our being would bypass inane and destructive forms of commodified pleasure, which are in super-abundance. Sloterdijk also writes of the need for a "General Ascetology" and a "General Immunology", and concludes *You Must Change Your Life*:

> Although communism was a conglomeration of a few correct ideas and many wrong ones, its reasonable part—the understanding that shared life interests of the highest order

can only be realized within a horizon of universal co-operative asceticisms — will have to assert itself anew sooner or later. It presses for a macrostructure of global immunizations: co-immunism.

Civilization is one such structure.[33]

These notional possibilities and ideas map on to the sense of things in the present account of the formation of forms of radical community and the creative life for "co-immunism" and for another experience of the genuinely civilizational. A praxis and spirit of the ascetical would inform in our present history this gestation, growth and movement to subvert problematic degrees of non-ascetical consumption.

Philosopher and theologian Gunjević claims that today's hegemonic capitalist globality "offers only a binary capitalist taxonomy (included-excluded, outside-inside, the haves and have-nots) there is little room left for improvisation,"

unless we constantly question this division with a certain asceticism, as Augustine suggests. We could understand Augustine's vision [...] as a synthesis of nomadism and asceticism, as a joint 'therapeutic' journey to the City of God. Nomadism and the ascetic exercise of ecclesial practices [...] ground the political subject, interpreting in a new way the desertion and exodus of which Hardt and Negri speak. Such a political subject would be revolutionary, and capitalist rationality would not be able to tame it.[34]

Figures in this book display features of a health-bringing asceticism and nomadism: and this even if a positive and a good Epicureanism subsists as a balancing mechanism, in order to extend the Augustinian revolution of 17 centuries ago for one's deeds and projects.

Reading constitutes one form of creative discipline, exercise and 'practice' for Gunjević to contest our spectacle and mediatized society, "Today the practice of reading embodies a reaction to the terror of the media."[35] Further, the power of virtue needs to be recuperated and remediated. As Gunjević reads in an interpretation of Mark 9:43–50, this biblical passage engages the notion of "a community founded through virtue."[36] While virtue alone may be inadequate to break through any number of power setups, it remains a crucial value-ideal and a practice to transform. Perhaps we need to innovate new forms of virtue for novel kinds of personal and collective-communal experience.

Notes Žižek: "Fredric Jameson has argued that Saint Augustine's most celebrated achievement—his invention of the psychological depth of the believer [...]—is strictly correlative to [...] his legitimization of Christianity as a state religion, as fully compatible with the obliteration of the last remnants of radical politics from the Christian edifice" (*LN*, 278). All the same, Augustine once wrote of "a new heaven and a new earth"[37] and of the need to re-vision and to re-model one's person in a project of improvement. The idea of personal or self-redemption may be gleaned in the portrayal of Saint Augustine by the Dutch painter Joos van Gent (1410–80). Augustine as if has his right hand out to the divine, and his left hand on the good book, as so many

Saint Augustine by Joos van Gent, 1460. (©Photo by Ann Ronan Pictures/Print Collector/ Getty Images/Hulton Archive)

inspirational ways to marshal productive and subversive energies, forces and resources for community and the creative life.

An Augustinian monk Martin Luther extends this Augustinian revolution, in the canon of human practice, of how to lead the proper form-of-life, which this study recognizes for the developmental model of the individual person and communal society. Contemporary Canadian thinker Charles Taylor reminds us that Augustine gives us that first person dimension in writing with his *Autobiography,* and yet even more we may for Taylor turn to the early modern French writer Michel de Montaigne (1533–92) as the one who "is an originator of the search for each person's originality"[38] and how the Montaignean also "requires a deeper engagement in our particularity."[39] This cultural heritage we also incorporate in this project for re-visiting and rethinking from a different depth and height radical creativity and the commons toward figures of emancipatory and genuine freedom both for individual-personal and communal agency.

This would be requisite for thinking the best conditions and interests for creativity and freedom for the person and for the community, including also in another amplification what the French scholar Michel Serres describes, "The new triangle is called: the Sciences—Society—Biogea. It really is a new game for three players: two kinds of humans often battling each other, plus that world that moreover includes us."[40] This we aim at in our engagement of the problem of the creative commons for the politics of possibility, and of the flash in the light of Benjamin's thesis V from "On the Concept of History": "The true image of the past flits by. The past can be seized only as an image that flashes up at the moment of its recognizability, and is never seen again."[41] We now move to a class of indispensable chapter-length studies of the power of *communitas* as a *munus* (gift), and of the creative and intelligent life for the exercise and practice of community and experience. Should we ask for the paradoxical possibility of the impossible we may get it. Otherwise we shall never know. So here with our investigation in comparative cultural research, we reopen the doors for pondering a world society community and the creative life in an adventure that will take us from Spinoza down to the present with professional tennis.

For the reader's knowledge and interests, the chapters here may stand on their own, and so they may be read separately, but together they do make up a complex dynamic whole and an unfolding argument, and so it may be read wall to wall. The argument sharpens in building on the élite cultural energies of philosophical, literary and theoretical culture in Part I and Part II, to mass and pop-cultural energies in Part III, so as to explore the universality that we share with others for community life and radical (de)creativity. The book stands therefore as a set of meditations too on the general theme of the volume: the contrasting cases and spirits of radical community and creativity as examples of the world spirit; and here to be sure in the present study world spirit departs from GWF Hegel's understanding of it (the *Weltgeist*), albeit Hegel remains an inspirator. For us we take world spirit as a form of universality with which to contest neoliberal globalization. Most importantly, the reader is invited to become a part of the text as discoverer and agent of meaning and knowledge. This all serves as a prolegomenon to this study.

Part I

Toward Community with Élite Culture Energies I

Chapter 1

Expression, the Fold and Spinozan Existence *qua* Gilles Deleuze and Slavoj Žižek[1]

In Baltasar Gracián's valuation: "what's to last an eternity, must take an eternity. Only perfection is noted, for success alone endures. A truly deep mind achieves eternity" (*POAP*, 22). This encapsulates basic tenets of the system we shall elucidate of the Dutch philosopher Benedictus de Spinoza (1632–77) of Sephardi/Portuguese descent. The following passage from Žižek articulates the missed opportunity of Spinozan happiness and joy that summarizes a liberated Spinozan modernity, which awaits realization: "the new we are dealing with is not primarily the future New, but *the New of the past itself*, of the thwarted, blocked, or betrayed possibilities ('alternate realities') which have disappeared in the actualization—of the past [...]" (*LN*, 322). In addition, the German-Swiss philosopher Karl Jaspers (1883–1969) writes in a judicious study of Spinoza, "Nowhere has thought raised so vast a claim, nowhere has philosophical thought attained such heights of happiness."[2] The profundity of Spinoza's meditations on existence, creation, and community produce the philosophical 'happiness' to which Jaspers refers. As the present chapter will demonstrate, Spinozan knowledge, desire and values activate the power of the impossible: powerful lives and communities of meaning and value informed by the principles of justice, freedom and democratic equality.

Cheery and ethereal properties pervade Spinoza's work; these affects and effects abide too in Gilles Deleuze's output, including in his coauthored works with French scholar Félix Guattari, and in the intellectual happiness and joy in Žižek's philosophical work. One purpose here is to highlight how the projects of happiness, human flourishing (or eudaemonia) and joy are cardinal aims for the human subject in a Spinozan modernity. The emancipated, generous, humane, open and synthetic human work of the historical baroque music of Johann Sebastian Bach (1685–1750), and its properties of development, modulation, rhythm and tempo offer a similar politics of existence. A commonality on the achievement and experience of joy with Spinoza and Bach would thus inaugurate a creative commons of transpersonal and intercultural mutuality.

The viewpoint of the philosophical baroque's allegorical outlook—and of the historical baroque's aesthetic fingerprint for Deleuze's Leibniz of the aesthetic property and operation of the fold—illuminate Spinoza's work and life.[3] Spinoza was enfolded in a world of power. He is one of the few philosophers who not only contributed to philosophical-civilizational accomplishment, but also was excommunicated in 1656 at age 24 from Amsterdam's Jewish community. This shows how community may also function as a regressive and exclusionary form of enclosure. According to the official history, Spinoza also endured a violent attempt on his life. Deleuze notes, "It is said that Spinoza kept his coat with a hole pierced by a knife thrust as a reminder that thought is not always loved by men."[4] Spinoza's summa the *Ethics* (1677), unpublished in his lifetime, illuminates a perception of his epoch that forges and enfolds the modern world in which incubating, and not yet hegemonic, (neo) baroque configurations of capitalist and religious power and relationships need dealing with in one's daily practices. This praxis would modulate the fold of subjectivity and so activate the enfolding, folding and unfolding of an efficacious existence amidst the kairology of an ongoing cultural modernity.

Reminiscent of Hegel's critical philosophy on the power of negative experience to beget knowledge in a retrospective narration that yields positive self-knowledge (witness for example Hegel's statement, "The owl of Minerva spreads its wings only with the falling of the dusk") consider Spinoza's words on life as a testing period, an opportunity for the politics of possibility, and in Benjaminese a 'weak messianic power':

> I resolved at last to try to find out whether there was anything which would be the true good [...] which [...] would continuously give me the greatest joy, to eternity.
>
> [...] if only I could resolve, wholeheartedly [to change my plan of life], I would be giving up certain evils for a certain good. For I saw that I was in the greatest danger, and that I was forced to seek a remedy with all my strength [...].[5]

Here we discern the impetus of Spinoza's life and deeds: hard-won experience in practical reality, to grasp "the true good" of a flourishing form of life replete with autonomy, courage (*animositas*), freedom, generosity (*generositas*), joy and kindness (*modestia*). Hence the importance of our historicity for our acts of cognition, and for new forms of individual and by extension of the praxis of communal development and being-in-the-world as exercises of joyful immanence; the lattermost constitute a moral-ethical knowledge, as well as liberating forms of cultural and existential capital, and flashes of dynamic energy.

Spinoza sees through the dysfunctions, toxicity and traps of a world of irrealism; his work seeks an active self-starting human agent to live effectively and meaningfully within it by expressing forms of joy as manifestations of eternity, and so too by extension of a certain immateriality as immortality and even as a paradoxical true form of materiality. At stake here is the problematic of the practices and exercises of a powerful creative existence and commons: one must discover that which gives one joy, and moves one, to find one's *clinamen* or swerve, for a line to follow and a platform on which to stand amidst the abstract and chaotic powers of modern life and a perplexing modernity.

Thus, as the fledgling consumerist era of capitalist big finance emerges in seventeenth-century Amsterdam, Spinoza must revolt against a social system that would thwart his projects and aims for an efficacious existence of radical creation (and of a community including that of a self in a spiritual and intellective task). Spinoza hence seeks a self-community in order to immunize himself against the social system, if as Robert Esposito has put the matter, "the category of immunity is inseparable from that of community: as its inverse mode, it cannot be eliminated."[6]

The Spinozan values of substantive authenticity (a notion we have since become skeptical about more generally), of eternity as immortality, of hope, of achieved individuality, of expressive human agency, and of the capacity for meaningful self- and other-and so transindividual transformation through the inventive and mediating agency of the power of virtue as an individual and social praxis inaugurate communal forms. Such activities allow one to hover over the mess of humanity's run of the mill behaviors that are a stack of cards that will fall down. This both inward and outward conversion to a powerful mode of immunized life constitutes the truly precious thing. *Credisne miraculis?* (Latin: Do you believe in miracles?) For one is at a crossroads here, a midpoint, and the future will be decided on the basis of a profound, and even militant stunning power of decision. Self-mediation arises out of a moral-ethical choice. Spinoza describes this quest as 'something' that would be 'acquired' and so the operation of a spiritual knowledge purchase.

To safeguard and to immunize one's self against modern obscurantism, vanity and pomposity within the coordinates of the baroque world of a misguided understanding of what constitutes real power, Spinoza notes that one must "assume certain rules of living as good:"

1. To speak according to the power of understanding of ordinary people, and do whatever does not interfere with

our attaining our purpose. [...].

2. To enjoy pleasures just so far as suffices for safeguarding our health.

3. Finally, to seek money, or anything else, just so far as suffices for sustaining life and health, and conforming to those customs of the community that do not conflict with our aim. (*TE*, 6)

Strikingly, Spinoza claims that clear writing and speaking may operate as a sacramental penance and gesture of solidarity for the category of the truth, and secondly these procedures may establish clear corridors of communication in the construction of communities. For to communicate in a clear language that is accessible to one's contemporaries will yield a greater audience for apprehending the content of one's arguments and the drift of one's intellectual work. To democratize one's capacity to be understood then holds an inestimable value for community relations.

Spinoza's proposals indicate too that pleasure and money should be health-bringing and not extend overkill structures that obstruct equality, justice, liberty and blunt our true interests and productive activities that affirm the power to act and to exist (our *conatus*). For another commons to come, Spinozan battle strategies invent effective forms of existence and creation. A Spinozan form of spiritual discipline captures the magical power of existence and creation. A virtuous practice of human agency itself constitutes also the wellspring of knowledge, meaning, movement, and value. Herein too lies in one flash of the eye (coup d'oeil), the philosopher's aesthetics of existence.

According to one of Spinoza's philosophical disciples, Deleuze, Spinoza's life embodies these foregoing intentions exemplarily. Spinoza practices what he teaches, and this augments the credibility of his message. Deleuze writes of Nietzsche (1844–1900) another key reader and disciple of Spinoza, in *Spinoza:*

Practical Philosophy: "The philosopher appropriates the ascetic virtues—humility, poverty, chastity—and makes them serve [...] extraordinary ends that"

> are not very ascetic [...] a production, a productivity, a potency, in terms of causes and effects. Humility, poverty, chastity are his [...] way of being a *grand vivant*, of making a temple of his own body, for a cause that is all too proud, all too rich, all too sensual. (*SPP*, 3)

This is suitably paradoxical because for all of his highly concentrated abstractional work, Spinoza remains interested in the good life, and in questions of how ought one to live with practical force in practical reality with his practice and exercise of a "General Ascetology" and a "General Immunology" à la Sloterdijk's *You Must Change Your Life*. The image of the philosopher as a transformative agent instances a forceful being able to function on a plane of self-same immanence (of *causa sui*). The milieu and ideological universe/multiverse of a species still living unconsciously to itself is constitutively unable to comprehend the expressive value ideals of 'humility, poverty, and chastity' for the folds of subjectivity and of a producer-creative existence. This is partly because such practices occur in a situation of self-interests mediated by a society built on finance, spectacularization and surveillance. Such Spinozan procedures and selections are necessary as immunizations for the (unlikely) occurrence of cultural production of high achievement for the individual and the community. A love of thinking and philosophy are desirable too in this context in terms of indefatigable work toward a powerful form of existence as an exercise and practice where so much is at stake and rendered possible.

Recall from the Introduction, for comparative purposes, the tennis icon Lendl's relaunching his own post-Spinozan geometrical methodology of the tennis courts in the 1980s.

As Deleuze declares on Spinoza: "The geometric method, the profession of polishing lenses, and the life of Spinoza should be understood as constituting a whole. For Spinoza is one of the *vivants-voyants*. [...] he says that demonstrations are 'the eyes of the mind.'" To this idea of a complex dynamic system neo-Hegelian approach to Spinoza's thought and historical person, his mode of reality and of the production of intellectual work, Deleuze adds, "He is referring to the third eye, which enables one to see life beyond all false appearances, passions and deaths. The virtues—humility, poverty, chastity, frugality—are required for this [...]. Spinoza did not believe in hope or even in courage; he believed only in joy, and in vision" (*SPP*, 14). Crucial is here, "the third eye", which conducts forms of radical creativity for radical democracy and for deeds and work of value and substance. Though, Deleuze is mistaken in that Spinoza did find content in the notions of hope and of courage (we quoted Spinoza above on 'hope', and courage is part and parcel of a Spinozan mode of reality on some level too, which he terms *animositas*). All the same, Deleuze finds in Spinoza's geometric style a way out of both philosophy and theory for a more powerful mediating activity for the creation of a potent expressive aesthetics of existence. Accordingly, Spinoza invests the business of living in capitalist modernity with new knowledge, value and life. It is a question of *an ethic of responsibility*, to a more authentic and moral-ethical form of being, which would find motivating vectors in forms of 'joy' and of 'vision' in one's existence, and in inventive forms of creative production. Thus emerges a Spinozan morality and faculty of reason for the cultivation of good choices of the praxis of existence. In this model, a moral-ethically enlightened and awakened life takes stage center for the delicate and luminous force and prize of the power and miracle of (de)creative existence.

Deleuze also polemicizes for Spinoza's sake, "No philosopher was ever more worthy, but neither was any philosopher more maligned and hated."

[...]. We must start from the practical theses [...]. These theses imply a triple denunciation: of 'consciousness,' of 'values,' and of 'sad passions.' These are the three major resemblances with Nietzsche. And already in Spinoza's lifetime, they are the reasons for his being accused of *materialism, immoralism,* and *atheism.* (*SPP,* 17)

Spinoza bypasses various illusions and confronts reality in the face for a·special sort of knowledge work. The device of Deleuze's reliance on Nietzsche as a way of legitimating his version of Spinoza indexes one signal vector in this dynamic (the scholar Louis Althusser for example in contradistinction uses Karl Marx vis-à-vis Spinoza in this way to accredit his Spinoza). As for the category in Spinoza of the body (model) that entails for Deleuze "a devaluation of consciousness in relation to thought: a discovery of the unconscious, of an *unconscious of thought* just as profound as *the unknown of the body.* [...] consciousness is by nature the locus of an illusion. Its nature is such that it registers effects, but it knows nothing of causes" (*SPP,* 18–19). Again here we remain unconscious. Key is to enact "a discovery of the unconscious, of an *unconscious of thought* just as profound as *the unknown of the body"*. In this Deleuzo-Spinozan sense then our bodily and mental existences wait to be forged with a better notion of this transcendental subjectivity that would be the life and subject of the unconscious. Thereby, we may tap into desire, knowledge and values that would construct forms of community and the creative life to alter oppressive relations of power and violence.

The mind-body identity thesis provides a twofold way for a transformative relation for the modern subject to respond to the dictates of the winner-take-all modern culture of competitivity, power and violence. Additionally, for Deleuze, Spinoza's *Ethics* communicates the specific idea that "only joy is worthwhile [...] bringing us near to action, and to the bliss of action" (*SPP,* 28). For existence, blissful and joyful acts in the practical reality thrive in a Spinozan-inspired plan. Perceptively Deleuze adds that with regard to its formal structure, Spinoza's magnum opus "is a book written twice simultaneously: once in the continuous stream of definitions, propositions,"

> demonstrations, and corollaries […]; another time in the broken chain of scholia, a discontinuous volcanic line, a second version underneath the first, expressing all the angers of the heart and setting forth the practical theses of denunciation and liberation. The entire *Ethics* is a voyage in immanence; but immanence is the unconscious itself, and the conquest of the unconscious. (*SPP*, 28–29)

The concept "immanence is the unconscious itself, and the conquest of the unconscious" remains to be unpacked in Spinoza studies and beyond. Our unconsciousness therefore is where to locate powerful redemptive work. This would mediate a set of individual and collective archaeologies of the future, of a tracing of memories, and of imagining spaces of togetherness for both individual and collective projects and practices of existence, creation and *communitas*. Further the idea of creative joy takes here center stage in a purposive whole for how to compose a genuinely agential human life full of the politics of radical possibility and joy for both individual and communal-civic experience.

Additionally, one discerns that Deleuze has precisely these foregoing powerful senses in reading Spinoza's work. In an exemplary form of transindividual becoming, Deleuze becomes an external alter of Spinoza's in a remediated late twentieth-century key and mode. For the exigencies of academic power and state violence, Deleuze's Spinoza may seem over speculative to the more straight and narrow scholar. Yet in a proper paradoxical manner, I argue it is through an imaginative betrayal of the master that the innovative disciple keeps the faith in the original impetus that was high creativity and so thereby signals solidarity with and remediation of the antecedent figure. I claim that this captures the reality of Deleuze's Spinoza, a figure and mediator of knowledge who is a transformative agent of philosophical and spiritual knowledge, for precisely as against current doxa, the joyful cultivation of one's individual soul or inner being and moral-ethical development.

In addition, for Deleuze and his sometime coauthor Guattari in the late-style *What is Philosophy?*, the following suggests the idea of the need for both a notion and a praxis of the paradoxically fruitful concept of the impossible: "*THE* plane of immanence is [...] that which must be thought and that which cannot be thought. [...]—the incessant to-ing and fro-ing of the plane, infinite movement." Guattari and Deleuze continue thus on what they hypothesize may be the most philosophical happening of all

> not so much to think *THE* plane of immanence as to show that it is there [...] which was thought once, as Christ was incarnated once, in order to show [...] the possibility of the impossible. [...]. Spinoza [...] thought the 'best' plane of immanence [...] the one that does not hand itself over to the transcendent or restore any transcendent, the one that inspires the fewest illusions, bad feelings and erroneous perceptions.[7]

"[T]he possibility of the impossible" resonates with *The Power of the Impossible*. And up to a point, 'The not-external outside and the not-internal inside' constitutes the plane of immanence. Note here also the inherent dynamism and complexity of movement and so process. This indexes the flashes of profound dynamism in Spinoza's metaphysics. In the light of Žižek's orientation of sorts to the Christian heritage at one point (in his move away from paradox and toward mystery or enigmaticalness as a leading trope in his critical philosophy) it is also notable that in *Organs without Bodies: On Deleuze and Consequences* (2004) he makes the categorical claim, "It is only with Kant (with his notion of the transcendental) that true philosophy begins. What we had before was a simply global ontology, the knowledge about All, and yet not the notion of the transcendental-hermeneutic horizon of the World."[8] I claim that contrariwise it is precisely Spinozan immanence that accords in a certain way to Kant's transcendental noumenal realm. If for Žižek's Kant, *"Our freedom persists only in a space IN BETWEEN the phenomenal and the noumenal"*[9] is this not also the Spinozan lesson that we are forever mediating immanence, but never quite reaching it? Is this precisely not reminiscent of Guattari and Deleuze's notion too of "the body without organs"? Spinoza's point is the brutal necessity of freedom, and of the need of an enlarged sense of what real freedom means than merely to be free from certain strictures or constraints. For with a plane of immanence on board freedom will be a reclaiming and remediation of the power of life's force, innocence and joy; this teaches us to know that operating on the threshold and edge structures offers up a creative space.

The notion that the cross of the project and of the conceptual persona of Spinoza attract more outside hallowed and specialized academe than those within it Deleuze suggests on the thinker whose knowledge work aspired to transform the individual and the community: "Writers, poets, musicians, filmmakers—painters too, even chance readers—may find that they are Spinozists; [...] he is the quintessential object of an immediate, unprepared encounter, such that a nonphilosopher, or even someone without any formal education, can receive a sudden illumination from him, a 'flash'" (*SPP*, 129).

This would combat the generalized police state repression of an ironclad capitalist baroque modernity. Indeed, Spinoza's own decision to eschew a conservative and co-opted academia with capitalist/religious power during his lifetime made possible the individual historical conditions for his radical intellectual work. Such intellectual labor might produce in the reader thoughts of expression and existence. For the human situation, a Spinozan politics of the *flash* contains commonality with and anticipates Benjamin's politics of the *flash*. Both forms mobilize insight for new forms of being, and so of existing and creating-producing. This also pertains to other figures and their deeds in our study, for discovery maps onto this idea of flash.

Spinoza invites us to reassess forms of immortality as pertaining to our self-enhancement as subjects with a soul or an inner life that augur and signal generous spirits of even-handedness and magnanimousness. These characteristics spring from a tenacious and powerful human subject who taps into passages of the eternal. Deleuze reminds us with regard to Spinoza's relation to objects, "What defines Spinoza as a traveler is [...] his inclination to stay in boarding houses, his lack of attachment, of possessions and property, after his renunciation of the paternal inheritance. He continues to work on the *Ethics*" (*SPP*, 8–9). Spinoza thus lives according to the twin themes of reason and drive that Žižek espouses in our Introduction as a radical hope for individual and by extension collective betterment. Spinoza immunizes himself against false albeit prevalent value ideals of his day, such as a valorized capital and power reductively defined, as against beneficent power and capital.

There is a further point. In a Deleuze of basic modesty, "We have not yet begun to understand Spinoza, and I myself no more than others."[10] This stands as a clarion call and an injunction to comprehend and to read Spinoza, however difficult if not baffling and discombobulating his project remains. Deleuze on the historical baroque thinker: "there is no living corpse who raises the lid of his coffin so powerfully, crying so loudly 'I am not one of yours.'"[11] So Spinoza emerges as a chameleonic and polyvocal being for his conceptual-philosophical persona and project, which resists sectorally interested appropriation within today's hegemonic cultural capitalism and digital technology. Spinoza serves as a prime example of a thinker who dealt with the harried baroque configuration of centripetal power. In this context, the double problem of existence and expression for the fold of the self is important for the birth of a new subjectivity, and so too for creative activities.

Let us move to Deleuze on Spinoza. Here we shall gain a complex theoretical account of the network of the intersecting values of expression and immanence; the latter "is inseparable from the concept of expression [...] Spinozism [...] asserts immanence as a principle and frees expression from any subordination to emanative or exemplary causality. *Expression itself no longer emanates, no longer resembles anything.* And such a result can be obtained only within a perspective of univocity."[12] Therefore, 'immanence is the very vertigo of philosophy' because it denotes the highest concept to which an individual human life may aspire and attain. It means also to be in touch with (to have conjectural knowledge of) one's particular unconscious and so singularity and possible specific creativity. In a statement that underlines the agreement between 'expression' and the negative or the 'inexpressible' Deleuze claims in his account of Spinozan radical expressive agency, "The inexpressible is, then, maintained at the heart of expression itself" (*EP*, 178). This makes the concept of expression a more potent carrier of meaning and of a power of existence from what may first strike the eye. Moreover, for Deleuze in another illuminating formulation, "Expressive immanence is grafted onto the theme of emanation, which in part encourages it, and in part represses it" (*EP*, 178). In these lights, a radicalization of immanence makes it more expressive in a symphony of multiple movements, wherein each fragment from an expressive human subject constitutes a larger global movement of potential revolutionary becoming and radical creativity that conducts equality, justice and liberty.

As for the early modern epoch and our keyword of existence, in Deleuze's important and strong creative reading of Spinoza's *Ethics*

(1) The capacity to exist [...] is a power; (2) Now, a finite being already exists necessarily [...]; (3) If absolutely infinite Being did not itself exist necessarily, it would have less power than finite beings, which is absurd; (4) But the necessary existence of the absolutely infinite cannot obtain by virtue of an external cause; so that it is through itself that the absolutely infinite being necessarily exists. (*EP*, 89)

This claim is intriguing. For power since the late seventeenth-century ceases in many contexts to be associated with 'existence' or life per se and more with hegemony (Jean-Paul Sartre, et al.) and control (Michel Foucault, et al.), and for some commentators today even for the out-of-control society (Bernard Stiegler, Nicolás Salazar Sutil, et al.). In the first glimmers of Spinoza's early modern period one observes a different point of view toward power, even if the notion was warily approached too in Spinoza's time.

Rather Spinoza's tack on the concept of power has congruence with what Žižek terms "power-potentials" in *Organs without Bodies: On Deleuze and Consequences*. In truth, this proactive stance toward force is also suggested, in how both thinkers disfavor the notion of resistance, for it presupposes a dominant structure that should not even be intersubjectively recognized; or that is how I read this power setup, however much the present writer retains some belief in the idea of *creative resistance*. Further, for Deleuze's Spinoza, *"the quantity of reality is always grounded in a power identical to an essence"* (*EP*, 94). That is, an immunizing modality of being embodies the form of a powerful virtue, such as to be endowed with fortitude and resourceful tenacity to one's projects, regardless of the consequences and antagonisms such enterprises may encounter, and without a need to make explicitly known one's creative resistance to the non-sympathy of the world and its antagonistic values.

As for ways of being, Deleuze articulates that "modes themselves present us with the following triad: a mode's essence as a power; an existing mode defined by its quantity of reality or perfection; the capacity to be affected in a *great number* of ways. Thus Part One of the *Ethics* may be seen as the unfolding of three triads, which all find in expression their principle: those of substance, of absolute and of power" (*EP*, 95). What are 'expressions' for Deleuze? "Expressions are always explications. But the explications of the understanding are only perceptions. It is not understanding that explicates substance, but the explications of substance refer necessarily to an understanding that understands them. God necessarily understands himself, just as he explicates or expresses himself" (*EP*, 102). And since for one intellectual tradition God exists as much as the human self or subject, this serves as an example of a cooperative movement of expressive becoming and unfolding, of inventing and of creating-producing during our existence.

The 24-karat gold Spinozan task and quest from the *Ethics* is as follows: "What must we do in order to be affected by a maximum of joyful passions?" (*EP*, 273). The problem of expression, of the fold and of the (de)creative opportunity of existence thus remains a subtending operation of primal importance for the event of existence (wherein movement occurs as a sequence of acts). Herein the value of joy prevails over the dominant one of sadness that is—in the light of the material base of capitalist universalism that obstructs thought about and emancipatory forms of praxis of the impossible/possible community and creative life—so present in the world and determined by so-called necessity and resignation. This is a problem for Spinoza's understanding of evil, wherein the affects of sadness or sense of impotence prevail. In contradistinction, the affects of joy and the sense of one's agency, flourishing, power and well-being are on the side of the good. Correlatively choices of existence here occupy the true domain of life.

On the shaping of forms of the creative life, for Deleuze "a common notion is an adequate idea; an adequate idea is an idea that is expressive; and what it expresses is God's essence" (*EP*, 297). Here all forms of being come under one social unit. Also, in Deleuze's account of Spinoza's philosophy, "Our essence is a part of God, and the idea of our essence a part of the idea of God, only to the extent that God's essence explicates itself through ours" (*EP*, 309–10). In this light, it is through the idea of traversing immanent modes of being that our individual and collective lives may remediate the divine. It is a question of responsibility opening out onto mutual indebtedness. Accordingly, the variety of virtues are themselves individually forms of good human power and expressive agency. Furthermore, for Deleuze on the value of knowledge work in Spinoza's edifice, and of the strategic intentions and structures one encounters in a life

1. We begin with inadequate ideas which come to us, and passive affections which flow from them, some increasing our power of action, others diminishing it; 2. We then form common notions [...]; active joys of the second kind follow from common notions, and an active love follows from the idea of God as it relates to common notions; 3. We then form adequate ideas of the third kind, and the active joys and active love that follow from these ideas (beatitude). (*EP*, 310)

In a sliding scale of value, active passions are the ultimate source of value in Spinoza's project. In this account, such passions serve a powerful form of life, and a capacity to conduct effective forms of a creative commons in the wake of active joys of the second and third kind. So as Deleuze describes, the construction of forms of joyful passions such as thought itself as a form of blissful passion may be deemed a joy of the third sort. A crisis of knowledge that we are now experiencing also percusses the individual as a bearer of meaning and knowledge in our information age of digital technology.

Care is needed to understand this take on human agency and the human subject. For this is a crucial point about knowledge from Deleuze on his philosophical master: "To feel and experience that we are eternal, it is enough to enter into the third kind of knowledge [...] Death is a subtraction, a cutting-back. [...]."

> The part of us that remains [...] is in any case more perfect than all the extensive parts which perish [...]. The ideas we have are necessarily adequate ideas of the third kind, as they are in God. Our essence adequately expresses God's essence, and the affections of our essence adequately express our essence. *We become completely expressive* [...]. (*EP*, 314–15)

With the democratic institution of bodily death for one of the most democratic of all philosophers Spinoza in his belief in rule of all by all "we become completely expressive". Perhaps this is because we have ceased to be unconscious, if as one age-old adage goes, life is but a dream. In this model our physical death gives us access to the transcendental subject and subjectivity of the unconscious. This is our kernel drive and our sense for conative being. Herewith the third kind of knowledge attains authority in one's life project, an accomplishment that vindicates a particular conception of immortality.

Centrally, for Deleuze's Spinoza, given that only while living do we have the opportunity to enact active affections, joys and so knowledge too of the second and of the third sort, it is life before we die that truly counts, "[Spinoza] entirely preserves the positive content of the notion of salvation. Existence itself is still conceived as a test. Not, it is true, a moral one, but a physical or chemical test [...]" (*EP*, 317). So the special chance of one's existence provides the circuit for folding and for ennobling the second and third kinds of knowledge, the latter of which is intuitive, and both of which are salvific. Thus life is a supereminent task to be fulfilled within human time in an eternal world for each individual's self-redemption. Yet Deleuze is on one critical reading mistaken, for it is a moral and not only an ethical problem with Spinoza. Again, from a practical viewpoint, Deleuze's interpretive claim on Spinoza's philosophy supervalorizes the opportunity of our concrete existence as a special exam given that

> while existing we must select joyful passions, for they alone introduce us to common notions and to the active joys that flow from them; and we must make use of common notions as the principle [...] to ideas and joys of the third kind. [...]. Such is the difficult path of salvation. [...] to be oneself an idea through which the essence of God explicates itself [...]. (*EP*, 319–20)

This is pivotal to Deleuze's conception of Spinoza's project, and a valid reading on the superpower of joy in Spinoza's philosophical cathedral. In this manner, the central part of our human agency, in the dynamic movement that is the project of existence, becomes the redemptive project too of the God or equivalent concept, as may be the case within each individual, each of whom is more internal to the void at the heart of our selves than we ourselves are; this is all ascribable to that aforesaid void. Spectacle society and seductive forms of visual and material commodity culture vanish here for our individual and collective projects. This constitutes a redemptive passage for the experience of existence and of the commons. The expressive register would contour a self- and other-transformation from the position of servitude, to one of a richer and freer humanity. Through our active joys and visions, our friendship and love feelings, we live on transpersonally in others. This is a suitably Spinozan paradox to note for the construction of the creative commons. In this paradigm life is a joyous and complex intersubjective communal process and space with sites for the articulation of active and moral-ethical agency. To this we add expressivist agency saturated with purposiveness. Hegel's project would deem it the concordance and concomitance of spirit and substance.

Spinoza himself makes this crucial claim, in which he has something important to say about religion, morality and friendship,

> whatever we desire and do of which we are the cause insofar as we have the idea of God, *or* insofar as we know God, I relate to religion. The desire to do good [...] by our living according to the guidance of reason, I call morality. The desire by which a man who lives according to the guidance of reason is bound to join others to himself in friendship, I call being honorable [...] what is contrary to the formation of friendship, I call dishonorable. (*TE*, 218–19)

The beings of intelligence of expression and of the fold outfit institutions such as friendship, morality and reason to increasingly intense effect for the universality that we all share with and for one another. Reason, morality and friendship are wellsprings for the folds of community, existence and expressive creativity. These are open to folds, to that which as Deleuze writes of Leibniz, "*the soul is what has folds and is full of folds.*"[13] So, the idea of a soul or of an inward life, remain to be developed and radicalized for Spinoza-Deleuze and for radical creativity/ decreativity studies and forms of praxis. In this way, an inwardizing activity of the mind allows the truth to peek through for forms of immortality and truthfulness. Aristotle's idea of 'greatness of soul' comes center stage here in a reassessment of one's inner being for creative life and community.

The importance of 'modes' as a God-like power appears thus in Deleuze's critical account, "the reduction of creatures to the status of modes appears as the condition of their essence being a power [...] an irreducible part of God's power. Thus modes are in their essence expressive: they express God's essence [...]" (*EP*, 199). Thus the power potentials of human living may be jump-started with the subtending force of a divine being. By becoming active through our expressive activity at the level of individual and collective life, our individual peculiarities and idiosyncrasies emerge in collective forms of experience and thought; indeed, according to the US scholar Steven B. Smith, for Spinoza: "Freedom is only achieved inside a community of rational persons."[14] This ascribes a high valuation to the achievement of reason from human agents in accomplishing the task of community. What is more, Smith writes of Spinoza as an expert in the art of living whereby the philosopher's most masterful masterpiece is not a

collectivist morality in its 'epicurean' endorsement of joy, especially the pleasure of laughing and joking. There is nothing of either Spartan austerity or Christian asceticism in the *Ethics*. It is a work devoted to the celebration of the self. Self-esteem is thus said to be the highest thing we can hope for. [...]. It is entirely self-generated or grows out of the good opinion we hold of ourselves. (*SBL*, 148–49)

A community of self and other then is one of endless movement, of intersubjective nourishment, and of a generative capacity with its paving stones in the individual self for a good self-estimation that derives from a mediating sense of self-identity and value. While there may not be a certain "Christian asceticism in the *Ethics*" for Smith, this is not to say that there is not a "General Ascetology" at play in what Sloterdijk considers necessary for our contemporaneity. Nor does this mean that other forms of asceticism do not sparkle in Spinoza's work. Also Smith rather too easily ignores how identity is a present bestowed on us by others, however much one's self-esteem may be self-generated. The self is not as atomized as all that; it is shared and collective, indeed even incompossible (different or divergent and yet coexistent or common) with other selves to use the GW Leibnizian concept.

What of the power of a God agent, or of such a related agency? For Deleuze, Spinoza

> seeks specifically modal principles, whether arguing from the unity of substance to the ontological unity of modes differing in attribute, or arguing from the unity of substance to the systematic unity of the modes contained in one and the same attribute. [...] mode is [...] according to Spinoza, the only way of showing how things 'participate' in God's power [...]. (*EP*, 227)

These are suggestive claims about how the person partakes in the radical force and agency of a God function. The goodness and power of the practice of existence may come into being, and become complete in itself, by the life project that mobilizes a spiritualized community of the self that includes in Deleuze's Spinoza the narrative of God not as the 'big Other' but as a source of flashes of energy, meaning and value for one's self-elaboration and movement.

With regard to Spinoza's proof 33 from the *Ethics*, "*He who is guided by fear, and does good to avoid evil, is not guided by reason*" (*TE*, 233). Is this not one big problem today, how we are guided by the sad passion of fear and the principle of unreason? And how that makes us incapable of a true culture of revolt, in the way Julia Kristeva describes in multiple publications? One on behalf of a soul, be it of an individual, shared or beyond form?

The soul contains folds in the tradition of Deleuze's *The Fold: Leibniz and the Baroque*. Smith writes in *Spinoza's Book of Life*

> The peak of the virtues [...] is given by Spinoza the name of *Fortitudo* or strength of character.
>
> [...] *fortitudo* is intended to convey something like a form of inner strength or moral integrity [...]. It is akin to the aristocratic virtue of greatness of soul (*megalopsychia*) described by Aristotle in the *Nicomachean Ethics* and carries the implications of generosity and high-mindedness. (*SBL*, 114)

This noble broad-mindedness, in a Spinozan pathway of life, subtends one's modus vivendi for another science of life, and for a new understanding of the world. 'Moral integrity' and 'fortitude' stand out as two big attributes. Perseverance or steadfastness are part and parcel of a quality of fortitude that may serve the power of life and the deployment of radical creativity in one's field or project. A subtraction of the reified self into a form of spirit or joy also applies. The self engages in a sacrifice to something greater than itself, by disconnecting from the ruling value ideals of the day in order to become a potent and agential sovereign if finitely individual being. Mari Ruti writes, "creation is a delicate blend of self-surrender and an almost cruel degree of perseverance" so that, "The art of living I have been promoting can be said to require a similar combination of self-surrender and discipline."[15] These ideas have a strong resonance with this study that valorizes creative discipline and work for the construction of forms of the equal, free and just communal life; practices of fortitude aid and abet the foregoing. As a key notion in Spinoza's philosophy, fortitude communicates energy for a cosmology that points toward the future for the power of virtue in the construction of creative and communal being.

Of central importance for Spinoza is his notion that "the more the body is capable of affections, and being affected by, external bodies in a great many ways, the more the mind is capable of thinking" (*TE*, 243). This communicates the idea that the more others may affect an individual the more powerful she is, and also the more capacity for thought she possesses to enact and produce. And Spinoza in some key claims states the following, setting him against generally accepted public opinion both during his era, and our own neoliberal one, in which capitalist universalism prevails as modernity's bottom line:

> XXVIII. [...] the powers of each man would hardly be sufficient if men did not help one another. But money has provided a convenient instrument for acquiring all these aids. That is why its image usually occupies the mind of the multitude more than anything else. [...].
>
> XXIX. But this is a vice only in those who [...] pride themselves on it very much. [...]. Those, however, who know the true use of money, and set bounds to their wealth according to need, live contentedly with little. (*TE*, 243)

One's outlook should incorporate the question of the use-value of money in one's relation to it. Money capital should not be over-valorized. Spinoza continues with élan:

> XXX. Since those things are good which assist the parts of the body to perform their function, and joy consists in the fact that man's power, insofar as he consists of mind and body, is aided or increased, all things which bring joy are good. Nevertheless [...] most affects of joy are excessive (unless reason and alertness are present). Hence, the desires generated by them are also excessive. (*TE*, 243)

These are important items on the Spinozan menu for an unscripted existence by any external agent, a dynamic process of the positive and productive creation of value, through the particular nature of our specific agency to construct experiences and forms of joy in the investments of our life project. This in turn mediates spirit for the production of community relations. Money is to be taken as a bounteous gift, but also with its own limitations that include the notion of function and use, and not of overdone structure and deployment. Joys should also be accompanied by 'reason' or 'alertness' lest they become overdeveloped to destructive effect.

Spinoza's acute and provocative words in a passage from proof 23 mediate an amazing universalist sensibility: *"The human mind cannot be absolutely destroyed with the body, but something of it remains which is eternal. […]."* Spinoza continues thus,

> Schol.: […]. And though it is impossible that we should recollect that we existed before the body […] we feel and know by experience that we are eternal. For the mind feels those things that it conceives in understanding no less than those it has in the memory. For the eyes of the mind, by which it sees and observes things, are the demonstrations themselves. (*TE*, 256)

However, some readers may claim that though 'impossible' for Spinoza they do remember existing before they were born. US writer Gore Vidal (1925–2012) for one claims precisely this. Overall though this remains a tenable and possible reading, and an example of tacit knowledge à la Michael Polanyi from Spinoza, who continues from the same section, "though we do not recollect that we existed before the body, we nevertheless feel that our mind, insofar as it involves the essence of the body under a species of eternity, is eternal, and that this existence it has cannot be defined by time *or* explained through duration" (*TE*, 256). Proof 23 is notable for its sparkling brilliance and practical rationality in our age dominated by the regime of optical visuality (not what Deleuze articulates as the Spinozan 'third eye'), a faculty that lines up that which will not reach its posited development and fulfillment. Instead Spinoza underlines "the eyes of the mind". If the foregoing from Spinoza were taken seriously, we could cultivate a general cultural sensibility that many now call for, including Jean-Pierre Dupuy and the present author. This we need to save our imperiled (post-) human situation and the deadlocks and impasses to which we are subject. On multiple fronts equality, justice and liberty are under violent attack, in Spinoza's day and in our own. So by extension are real spirits and living examples of the communal and creative life under a brutal assault.

In Spinoza's proof number 25 the thinker makes a vital claim that recurs on the particular knowledge work to esteem: *"The greatest striving of the mind, and its greatest virtue is understanding things by the third kind of knowledge"* (TE, 257). This brings us to the crux of the matter, and is a basic idea we have covered elsewhere. A desire or conative drive for knowledge informs the quester in search of knowledge of the third kind. In proof 26 from Spinoza on knowledge exercises: *"The more the mind is capable of understanding things by the third kind of knowledge, the more it desires to understand them by this kind of knowledge"* (TE, 257). The more the third sort of knowledge we have, the more we desire. Forms of the third kind of knowledge will yield more forms of the same. To build on this notion of a valorization of third types of knowledge from the originally published in 1677 Latin text, *Ethica, ordine geometrico demonstrata Ethica,* "P27: *The greatest satisfaction of mind there can be arises from this third kind of knowledge"* (TE, 257). In a statement of the first importance, for Spinoza in "P29: *Whatever the mind understands under a species of eternity, it understands not from the fact that it conceives the body's present actual existence, but from the fact that it conceives the body's essence under a species of eternity"* (TE, 258). In philosophical interpretation, an eternalization of the mind may be discerned, insofar as it occurs concomitantly with a consideration of "the body's essence under a species of eternity". With such a mode of being a general cultural sensibility may follow in its wake, as well as an encounter with the politics of possibility.

In another major point, for Spinoza's proof number 34, "*Only while the body endures is the mind subject to affects which are related to the passions*" (TE, 260). So, affects connected with the passions take place when the biological body is extant. Last not least for us here in the present context, Spinoza formulates the claim in proof 38: "*The more the mind understands things by the second and third kind of knowledge, the less it is acted on by affects which are evil, and the less it fears death*" (TE, 261). This shows that a fearless power accompanies knowledge of the second and third kind. These foregoing citations stand as summits on Spinoza's mountainous conceptual edifice and describe that which would account for a subject's journey to the creative life. In this light we must discard prior false values, and fasten on to more advanced and refined ones, to achieve a form of immortality. In this way, the subject stares down biological death for the cultural and spiritual goods of existence, creation/creativity and the commons. Resources of time and so power too are limited, which is why we need to use our time and our power well, and this especially given how the unreality of the world will prove your opponent in the pursuit of such things as Spinoza invites the human agent to achieve: a life process of knowledge, meaning and creative value.

Concerning the penultimate proof 41 to Spinoza's chef d'oeuvre, the *Ethics*, which crashes as a reef on the modern world to illuminate and to awaken it: "*Even if we did not know that our mind is eternal, we would still regard as of the first importance morality, religion, and absolutely all the things we have shown (in Part IV) to be related to tenacity and nobility.*"

> Dem.: The first and only foundation of virtue [...] is the seeking of our own advantage. But to determine what reason prescribes as useful, we took no account of the eternity of

the mind, which we only came to know in the Fifth Part. Therefore, though we did not know then that the mind is eternal, we still regarded as of the first importance the things we showed to be related to tenacity and nobility. (*TE*, 263)

Spinoza's claims comprise a realization of how to compose the practice and exercise of an authentic potent existence; this too in a contemporary age suspicious of the idea of authenticity, hence our endorsement of a spirit of the contrived inauthentic à la the musical artist David Bowie's (1947–2016) use of the notion as a way paradoxically to attain the truly authentic, because of the corruption of the latter concept since Spinoza's period. Here Spinoza's deep and original revolution in thought evokes a sense of radical possibility and hope for breaking new ground for the developmental potential of the individual and of the community. Human beings in this context have a divine potentiality to deploy their reason and to bring into existence forms of mental and intellective joy of great power. This may be achieved by employing in one's individual sensibility what Spinoza calls "the eternity of the mind" to which "tenacity and nobility" are devoted.

As for the last proof of the *Ethics*, which constructs a philosophical perspective, a goad and a guide for how to construct the modality of a powerful and virtuous life immunized against fakery and falsity: "*Blessedness is not the reward of virtue, but virtue itself; nor do we enjoy it because we restrain our lusts; on the contrary, because we enjoy it, we are able to restrain them*" (*TE*, 264). After these important thoughts on the power of existence as seen in the operation of 'blessedness', the *Ethics* concludes with this memorable coda, "If the way I have shown to lead to these things now seems very hard, still, it can be found. And of course, what is found so rarely must be hard. For if salvation were at hand, and could be found without great effort, how could nearly everyone neglect it? But all things excellent are as difficult as they are rare" (*TE*, 265). These broader claims make up an extraordinary achievement in philosophical culture for creative domains of thinking about how one ought to live; namely, by inverting one's self into something different in an altered human individual and social life. The cardinal virtue is to transform one's self in a project of self-enlightenment and self-redemption. Could this provide an ethics for individual invention and autonomy, and a blueprint for folding and for thinking archaeologies, for imagining spaces, and for tracing memories of the future, however bizarre and bewildering such memories of the future? Even as if like something from the Book of Ezekiel from the Hebrew Bible? Here for Spinoza, as also for Immanuel Kant, virtue is its own reward, and needs no other. We may always enjoy the exercise of our virtue no matter what else befalls us. The power of virtue is an active and expressive fold. A massive effort of willpower also here finds a place for the hard attainments to which Spinoza summons the subject to aspire. An injunction and directional force for a more spiritual modality of living is the aim, as well as a new understanding of what should be taken as the source of meaning and value: the exercise and practice of joyful forms, modes and passions of knowledge both local and global. This would mediate a general and a redemptive cultural sensibility.

In a 1999 literary-philosophical Spinoza analysis, US scholar Warren Montag observes, "The last thirty years [...] have witnessed a renaissance of Spinoza studies [...]." Montag ascribes this to how in the 1960s a period

of mass action against the despotism of 'civil society' as well as the state, a time when [...] our 'democratic' states feared their own people more than any external enemy and periodically required armed force to maintain 'domestic security', and even more that the material, corporal practices of everyday life determined even those who saw the better to do the worse that the previously overlooked concepts in Spinoza's philosophy became suddenly, stunningly visible and his critique of servitude reappeared [...].[16]

That Deleuze is a part of this movement in cultural history both in and outside of the academic heritage in the last 50 years therefore is hardly surprising. However, the lack of in-depth looks and critical analyses at this cultural pair relationship of Spinoza-Deleuze Deleuze-studies should heed for multi-disciplinary critical-theory studies and for cultural-studies. This would be consequential and of considerable fascination. The link between Spinoza and Deleuze is a powerful one full of examples of 'now-time'.

As life becomes more subject to neoliberal globalization, Spinoza's ontology becomes more noticed. Also, as advanced capitalism and technology intensify their grip on power, the problems that Spinoza's philosophy addresses become more apparent and relevant. In addition, Montag adds, "the new theodicies [...] are those of the market and its spiritual expression, the public sphere, the mechanisms [...] by which the best of all possible worlds will be selected." Thus we know not how much "the 'new' Spinoza can disturb these political somnambulisms. [...] in the absence of active, mass resistance to servitude and domination, his critique of theodicy both divine and secular cannot remain actual and will almost certainly recede into obscurity as it has so often in the past."[17] The extent to which critical- and cultural-studies could engage these "new theodicies" of the market or of the Economy, would be a Spinozan enlightenment of revolutionary becomings. Here history can get in the way. For what is often necessary to understand Spinoza is to engage in a decontextualization of matters or texts at hand for them to be encountered for their substantial and radically emancipatory future-oriented content. Historical materialism nevertheless persists as an approach to understand and to use the theoretical resources found in Spinoza's work for "mass resistance to servitude and domination". Yet the relative oblivion that Spinoza has experienced, as well as the great publicity, will as Montag argues, likely continue its oscillative course. What is problematic in Montag's formulation above is the idea of "the public sphere" for that precisely is collapsing into the private sphere, and this is something that a newfangled Spinozism could contest.

Even more, Montag writes with the power of suggestion: "the absence of resolution, the accumulation of unfinished theses, suspended arguments and even certain images [...] give Spinoza's philosophy its immense force. [...] a liberation of the mind that depends upon the liberation of the body and a liberation of the individual the condition of which is collective liberation."[18] Spinoza needs a cultural era that genuinely believes in making the impossible possible. This is something for which Žižek and Jacques Derrida, inter alia, for example too have called. In a personal communication in 2012 at a conference in Tallinn, Estonia, Jacques Rancière expressed the same concern to me that as against the period of time of a few decades ago today we no longer have this sense that anything is possible. We may start in Spinoza's lights with the idea that an emancipation of the body and mind both are required for a collective emancipation. This praxis will key the construction of forms of the community of creative life.

Further to the foregoing, for the Deleuze and Guattari of *What is Philosophy?* Spinoza's principal achievement is that he "knew full well that immanence was only immanent to itself and therefore that it was a plane traversed by movements of the infinite, filled with intensive ordinates. He is therefore the prince of philosophers." Also Spinoza "discovered that freedom exists only within immanence. [...]. Spinoza is the vertigo of immanence from which so many philosophers try in vain to escape. Will we ever be mature enough for a Spinozist inspiration?"[19] Again:

movement is a spiritual phenomenon and helps construct forms of the third sort of knowledge in Spinoza's dynamist metaphysics. This is an injunction for the contemporary world and for the future of creativity, community and Deleuze studies. The key ideas here are 'power of being and power of thinking' for the construction of forms of community and the creative life, and thus a making possible of the erroneously conceived impossible. And as Guattari and Deleuze note in a phrase pregnant with meaning: "Will we ever be mature enough for a Spinozist inspiration?" instructs that it is a question of maturity here for Spinoza's readers if we are to effectuate a revolution in being that would be worthy of Spinoza's pioneering work.

The problem, the task and the gift of expression, of the fold and of existence, offer a way of tracing memories and imagining spaces for an archaeology of the future in both thought and in experience, between common content, creation, freedom and space. By establishing a sensitivity to these issues, Spinoza lays the basis for these foregoing developments; this all would constitute a process of maturation that would take Spinozan injunctions closer to heart in what is done out there, and here in the academy, for the practical reality. The problem also remains as Deleuze notes one of a gestating process of development. In our reconstructive account of Spinoza's philosophy, we take this movement as a pattern of possible self- and other-realization and knowledge. This also includes forms of knowledge of the third kind that open the door to courage, generosity, hope, vision and the powers of creativity and community.

The mind is eternal for Spinoza. Or as Smith elaborates: "the eternity of the mind is based on the recognition that the contents of our minds cease to be ours alone and become the common property of mind in general. At some level our ideas are not simply our ideas but belong to the common stock of knowledge" (*SBL*, 174). Therefore, our minds have the status of a form of immortality for minds are shared and part and parcel of forms of community togetherness after one's demise. Indeed, a mind constitutes the most true because collective form of immortality. This is a perhaps surprising and truthful paradox. Yet in a paradoxical challenge Smith underlines, "Despite Spinoza's 'proof' of the eternity of the mind, the *Ethics* provides no clear or compelling account of how we can bootstrap ourselves into eternity" (*SBL*, 174). This is only partly true, for the idea of achieving our intrinsic as opposed to merely extrinsic joyful passions could be one such battle strategy to take on board. Still this is a problem for each reader of Spinoza: to make out for one's own self for the process of folding and of existing the individual life narrative, whose truth would be that story with one's self the critical agent to enact in a way that one's ostensible impossibility as an eternal change agent becomes instead possible because shared and collective.

Žižek gives a disavowed accent to that Deleuzoguattarian Christ-figure among philosophers Spinoza, "is not the 'theological' dimension without which, for Benjamin, revolution cannot win, the very dimension of the excess of drive, of its 'too-muchness'? In other words, is not our task—the properly *Christological one*—to change the modality of our being—stuck in a mode that allows, solicits even, the activity of sublimation."[20] The injunction "to change the modality of our being" echoes the classical and miraculous idea of being born to a new existence. This is the task also for Spinoza's aesthetics of existence. There is more, theologian Marcus Pound notes, "as Augustine understood it, the creative God is *Deus interior intimomeo*, 'the God who is more interior to me than I am myself.'"[21] Thus as Pound aptly puts it, "The unconscious operates as a thief who hides a diamond in a chandelier."[22] And also of note is that for Žižek, "as Lacan put it in the last pages of *Seminar XI*: after the subject traverses the fantasy, desire is transformed into drive)" (*LN*, 131). These as such then may constitute some hints on how to deal with this matter of the engenderment or of the folding, and of the expressing, of multiple forms of immortality. One must first construct a self able to exist without the crutch of the fantasy of "the big Other" as Lacanian psychoanalysis instructs us to think for another alliance of solidarity, and for decking onto another possible world, one where impossible equality, justice and liberty would be possible.

To argue in tandem with Smith, as for the intellectual love of God, which maps onto what we point at here, "If all things are in God, then to love God is to love those things that participate in God."

> [...] the more we understand nature, the better we understand ourselves, and the more we understand ourselves, the better we understand nature. The *Ethics* likens this kind of self-knowledge to a form of salvation or blessedness because it liberates the knower from dependence on unrefined passions and emotions and puts the mind in touch with something eternal. (*SBL*, 175)

So, a process of individual self-enlightenment is necessary, for these sorts of self-transformative events to occur for this conative power of life. Thus will a singular life achieve ownhood, the power of the fold of being and singularity. Self-identity thus will see through and rise above an appearance/reality distinction; or, as we read in Smith, "Spinoza describes this type of love as affecting a kind of Platonic turning of the soul away from the transient toward the absolute" (*SBL*, 175–76). To challenge the authority of the world for Spinoza, changes meaning and gives us hidden reverences and layers that release energy for a new basis of human existence: the hope and passion of individual and collective virtue, knowledge and redemption.

Spinoza's philosophy constructs a doctrine of life as the highest value. For Spinoza to live well, is to be active, expressive and joyful toward another experience of a realized self that begins again every day as well as with one's own death. This is the pedagogic function of Spinoza's life and work. Aimed at here then is to attain a well if not a great souled subjective praxis of life, and so of subjectivity yet to be begun, for another experience and exercise of the self as ennobling and virtuous modality of being in knowledge. Smith writes, "self-esteem is not a vice, but is related to a kind of noble ambition for recognition and distinction. Although [Spinoza] defines ambition as an *'excessive* desire for esteem,' he also acknowledges that it is the desire 'by which all the affects are encouraged and strengthened' [...]" (*SBL*, 178). This idea of self-esteem as the highest aim and status to which one may aspire, goes hand in glove with the notion that the focus of one's existence should be toward such self-knowledge, self-perception and self-understanding. The symbolic revolution and recognition in oneself must first occur for a moral-ethical regeneration of the economic, intellectual and spiritual goods of creativity and community.

The well worth reading *Ethics* to quote Smith's concluding words on the powers of virtue and of redemption "encourages the qualities of joy, friendship, sociability, and love. The free individual [...] is fearless before death, resolute in action, and fiercely independent in mind and judgment. [...] Spinoza could not help but transform everything that he touched. The point of his philosophy is not just to interpret the world, but to redeem it" (*SBL*, 201). By way of these lights, we conclude that one shortcoming of current discussions is how little more than lip service is paid to the transformative radicality of Spinoza's ground-breaking and redemptive philosophical work. A more focused attempt to engage his philosophy in the light of such figures as Deleuze and Žižek, by way of example, argues that the true essence of Spinoza's philosophy would precisely be the real possibility of that philosophy, one that awaits a process based engenderment for practices and projects of self and collective redemption. This redemption would be a more developed figure of interpretation, reception and proper transformation of such institutions as active love, eternity, friendship, joy, passion and sociality. This would mediate the genuinely immortal and express that which deserves attention and recognition: services rendered to the value ideals of radical creativity or of a creatively transposed variant of the Aristotle-inspired notion of 'greatness of soul' or *megalopsychia*. If this were to occur, our pre-modernity would melt into history, and our modernity will have begun. For the loss of ideological battles, from the seventeenth to the twenty-first centuries, would be turned around in a movement that would indicate something weighty is happening in the revolutionary methods that emerge, via the mystery of redemption in Spinoza's wake, to wit, signature figures and forms for powerful practices of the commons, creativity, existence, freedom, friendship, knowledge and virtue.

The (decreative) commons would engage the power dynamic of what Michel Serres calls to be sure: "The new triangle is called: the Sciences—Society—Biogea. It really is a new game for three players: two kinds of humans often battling each other, plus the world that moreover includes us."[23] Our twenty-first century Spinozism concurs, even while it transforms what Žižek rightly identifies as the 'Christological' endeavor. In the present reading, self- and community-realization grounded in daily life activities will for an ongoing 'kairology' communicate the invigoration of positive values and powerful forms of life. Moreover, via hard-won experience these forms of existence would mobilize the *munus* (the gift) of *jetztzeit* (now-time) for a hard-earned agential existence and co-creative commons.

To conclude Chapter 1 on Spinoza, a foundational figure for this study, all of the foregoing matters constitute a movement, struggle and task for the conative (the striving) force in the impossible/possible construction of community and the creative-intelligent life. Spinoza's geometric science thus still instructs us toward the production of these modalities of being as so many indexes of the force of the impossible. For forms of virtue as forms of being also remain to be discovered as so many instances of 'now-time' embodied and folded in our experience of the everyday and of the politics of possibility. In this way we step a little bit outside of the enclosure of ideology by treating the impossible in a more objective and realistic way about what is actually possible, even if it appears untenable: namely, the complex achievement of meaning and knowledge of an incipient and still open radical and substantial community and creative life.

Chapter 2

Jean-Luc Nancy, Being-In-Common and the Absent Semantics of Myth[1]

This chapter interrogates the problem and rôle of myth in establishing a collective symbolic body and an enlarged sense of community. Accordingly, we move from Spinoza, Deleuze and Žižek, to a contemporary French theorist, Jean-Luc Nancy, inter alia, in our adventure and exploration of the notions of community solidarity, and of forms of free creative cultures of democratic coexistence. This extract from Maurice Blanchot, who blends literature and philosophy to spawn a new community and creative form of writing, accords to our conception of 'absent semantics' in our chapter title: "To write is perhaps to bring to the surface something like absent meaning, to welcome the passive pressure which is not yet what we call thought, for it is already the disastrous ruin of thought. Thought's patience. Between the disaster and the other there would be the contact, the disjunction of absent meaning—friendship."[2] Consider too this passage from the Strasbourg School thinker Nancy (1940–)

> I shall be speaking […] of a bond that unbinds by binding, that reunites through the infinite exposition of an irreducible finitude. […].
>
> […]. the intensity of the word 'revolution' names […] a word […] whose meaning has perhaps still to be revolutionized.
>
> […] if we do not face up to such questions, the political will soon desert us completely […]. It will abandon us to political and technological economies […]. And this will be the end of our communities […].[3]

This states unequivocally the exigency of the task to re-engage the political and the communal, lest we forfeit any positive access to them and so too by implication the 'meaning' of our shared lives for any impossible/possible movement of community relations to come. This includes radically rethinking and re-conceptualizing the unfashionable concept of revolution in an age of digital finance and technology.

In the twenty-first century, Antonio Negri and Michael Hardt argue in their jointly authored *Multitude: War and Democracy in the Age of Empire*, "The World Bank reports that almost half of the people in the world live on under two dollars a day and a fifth on less than a dollar a day"[4] and in which I would add beyond this material hardship one country among over two hundred sovereign nation-states, the USA, spends more on violence than the rest combined. It is inconclusive that this state of affairs has improved one iota as I write this in 2017. Negri and Hardt add, "The average income of the richest 20 countries is thirty-seven times greater than the average in the poorest twenty—a gap that has doubled in the past forty years. Even when these figures are adjusted for purchasing power—since some basic commodities cost more in rich countries than in poor—the gap is astonishing" (*MWD*, 278). But the loss of substantial community relations is now so ostensible that such data rarely enter official public discourse. There will be no discussion, for there is still no community or being-in-common to make such a conversation desirable or necessary.

Cultures of digital technology, financial capitalism and globalization instead predominate. The current discussion is—in its framing of the problem—an oppositional one to the dominant academic discourse whereby myth may be seen to flourish in any sense at all in the West without acknowledgment of myth's complicity with the abuse of some form of ideological, institutional or political power and prejudice. Moreover, it submits that Western myth no longer functions effectively, nor can it under current conditions without community solidarity, and another experience of the economic and of the social. The present ongoing 'kairology' teaches us too to heed such matters.

Nancy remains among the notable French-language thinkers writing today along with Alain Badiou (1937–), Luce Irigaray (1932–), Kristeva (1940–), and Jacques Rancière (1940–) to cite four figures among an attenuated list of others, now that since the rise of populist capitalism and digital technology in 1980, Althusser (1918–90), Roland Barthes (1915–80), Jean Baudrillard (1929–2007), Simone de Beauvoir (1908–86), Maurice Blanchot (1907–2003), Pierre Bourdieu (1930–2002), Guy Debord (1931–94), Deleuze (1925–95), Jacques Derrida (1930–2004), Foucault (1926-84), Guattari (1930–92), Jacques Lacan (1901–81), Philippe Lacoue-Labarthe (1940–2007), Emmanuel Lévinas (1906–95), Jean-François Lyotard (1924–98) and Sartre (1905–80) have all passed on. These foregoing authors constitute a thinking world of minds; indeed, in a recent text authored by Alain Badiou on *The Adventure of French Philosophy* (2012) he argues that postwar French philosophy belongs with the eras of German Idealism and of ancient Greece in its world-historical import. The death of so many major thinkers as a form of community has confluence with one basic thesis here, namely that with Nancy's Georges Bataillean-inspired directive, death ignites and stamps conditions of possibility for instituting a commons.

Beyond its polemical aims, this chapter's argumentative strategy thinks with, through and in Nancy's path-breaking essays, "The Inoperative Community" and "Myth Interrupted" from *La communauté désoeuvré* (1986)/*The Inoperative Community* (2000) and quite cursorily a later work that owes much to Martin Heidegger, *Être singulier pluriel* (1996)/*Being Singular Plural* (2000). In so doing, the chapter will build on Nancy's investigations as a point of orientation and departure, for other meditations and arguments. By interrogating Nancy's essays, we shall conceptualize some new ways of thinking the mythic function and of how it intersects with notions of community and of Being-in-Common and by extension of Being-With (Being-*cum*); or, even more, of how these forms do not thrive today, and of what that means for a future myth and communal form.

In an introduction to *The Inoperative Community*, Heidegger and Nancy scholar Christopher Fynsk writes the intriguing claim: "Nancy is attempting to expose what still speaks in [...] 'community' when we assume the closure of the metaphysics of subjectivity [...]."[5] Hence, Nancy is trying to re-semanticize 'community' (or to re-subjectivize its current infantile form of meaning), by thinking its possible meanings and potentialities as a 'subject' or rather a movement in a post-metaphysical, post-modern, post-representational and post-signifying age. In pellucid prose, Fynsk also submits that what is fatal for Nancy regarding our contemporary situation "lies in the isolation of the individual in its very death and thus the impoverishment of that which resists any appropriation or objectification. [...]. when death presents itself as *not ours* [... it] exposes us to our finitude. Nancy argues with Bataille [...] that this exposure is also an opening to community: outside ourselves, we first encounter the other."[6] So, it is then the fact of death, and thus our ontological status as ephemeral biological subjects, that might serve as special resources for Nancean and Bataillean social change, and for another community to supersede the current neoliberal one. Such factual bases function as a special refutation of the notion that the current twenty-first century situation mediates acceptable community relations. For Nancy it is a shared abandonment that resists a fascist form of fusional and immanent power that is required of its subjects to unleash a proper, 'non- or un-community', one could neologize, in actuality; that is, a community without the destructive and evil contours that regressive immanent forms of community bring with it (unlike the good form of immanence as defined by Deleuze and Spinoza); a community open to the innovative new in a good, positive and non-coercive way.

In Nancy, "community does not consist in the transcendence [...] of a being supposedly immanent to community. It consists on the contrary in the immanence of a 'transcendence' — that of finite existence as such [...] its 'exposition'" (preface, *IC*, xxxix). This *'exposition'* of community needs an astonishing imaginative achievement to theorize and to actualize it, a protagonist and intellectual hero of the speculative social theoretical imagination of the twenty-first century. In the event though, it is the 'exposition' or 'exposure' of our finitude that constitutes a fact, a happening of sufficient strength of 'transcendental immanence' to spawn a so-called community as process or as procedure instead of as immanent substance or entity for in Deleuze and Guattari-inspired terms a "molecular" (flowing, multiplying, deterritorializing) sharing and community. Again the basic coordinates of the contemporary social and economic situation of financial capitalism and digital technology would need here considerable overhaul for the effective realization of an innovative experience of the communal.

In "The Inoperative Community", which also constitutes in part a meditation and extension of some ideas and arguments of the French thinker Georges Bataille (1897–1962) on the community concept, Nancy notes that genealogically "the true consciousness of the loss of community is Christian:"

> the community desired or pined for by Rousseau, Schlegel, Hegel, then Bak-ouine, Marx, Wagner, or Mallarmé is understood as communion [...]. At the same time as it is the most ancient myth of the Western world, community might well be the altogether modern thought of humanity's partaking of divine life: the thought of a human being penetrating into pure immanence. (*IC*, 10)

So not only is community the most longstanding myth of Occidental culture, but also it today constitutes nothing less than the divine. Necessary today then would be to mobilize a certain re-Christianization of the world in a good Hegelian way. That Christianity is something worth salvaging Žižek teaches including in *The Fragile Absolute: Or, Why Is The Christian Legacy Worth Fighting For?* Unfortunately though, as Nancy reminds us: "Fascism was the grotesque or abject resurgence of an obsession with communion; it crystallized the motif of its supposed loss and the nostalgia for its images of fusion. In this respect, it was the convulsion of Christianity [...]" (*IC*, 17). Clearly the dangers remain of a certain regressive Christian sort of communal fascism, and so it is necessary to improve understanding to this sensitive fact, and at least potentially, catastrophic danger under late populist capitalism.[7] Yet the Christian heritage does offer precious resources for individual and for collective social, economic, political and cultural-spiritual transformation.

As an accomplished post-Heideggerian and post-Derridean thinker whose work *Being Singular Plural* preeminently reads the Black Forest/Freiburg thinker Heidegger, Nancy records already in an earlier 1986 text, "The Inoperative Community": "All of Heidegger's research into 'being-for (or toward)-death' was nothing other than an attempt to state this: *I* is not — *am* not — a subject."

(Although, when it came to the question of community as such, the same Heidegger also went astray with his vision of a people and a destiny conceived at least in part as a subject, which proves no doubt that Dasein's 'being-toward-death' was never radically implicated in its being-with — in *Mitsein* — and that it is this implication that remains to be thought.) (*IC*, 14)

Hence the suggestion that while Heidegger is a revolutionary philosopher of Being, he is not one iota of Being-with, which is in fact not posterior to, but anterior to the question of Being, insofar as for Nancy "ontology itself [is] a 'sacrality' or an 'association' more originary than all 'society,' more originary than 'individuality' and every 'essence of Being'. Being is *with* [...]."[8] This lamentable lacuna Nancy's 1996 tome seeks to fill in, by interrogating into more detail about the nature of the word "with" in Heidegger's incomplete ontology of Being.

As for the concept of death for Nancy's philosophical edifice: "Community is calibrated on death as on that of which it is precisely impossible to *make a work* [...]" (*IC*, 15). Death's surplus value derives from Bataille's conceptual edifice of whom Blanchot comments in *The Unavowable Community*, which was a direct published response to Nancy's "The Inoperative Community": "Mortal substitution is what replaces communion. [...] Bataille writes: '... It is necessary for communal life to maintain itself at the *height of death*.'"[9] Hence 'communal life' must be a self-sustained quest for blocks and movements of energy forces that register continuously mortality, for a new community dynamics and psychic communal space of community relations.

Centrally too, for Nancy, "A community is the presentation to its members of their mortal truth (which amounts to saying that there is no community of immortal beings: one can imagine either a society or a communion of immortal beings, but not a community)" (*IC*, 15). Accordingly, it is the fact and experience of our shared mortalities that stamp a plausible historical condition for a community to come. Once we expire as organisms, we cease with our new ontological status to belong to any Nancean community. However, as against Nancy, I claim one continues transindividually to live in a community if one's own life mediates a source of nonorganic energies of inter-animating energy forces for other subjects.

In a pointed provocation, Nancy composes, "Perhaps we should [...] recognize in the thought of community a theoretical excess [...] that would oblige us to adopt another *praxis* of discourse and community" (*IC*, 25–26). The inexpressible or the inarticulable prevail. This occurs amidst the disaster that is the failed expression of the communal, which remains to be thought for 'another *praxis*' by human beings wherein hitherto greed is the law, the principle and the rule of the social universe. Negri and Hardt's coauthored volume *Multitude: War and Democracy in the Age of Empire* has something to remark about "another *praxis* of discourse and community" when they ask for a re-minting of the concepts of the 'multitude' and of the 'common' to activate the 'singularities' animating the globe. This would be to achieve another community to arrive, another becoming global of the global community, which would tap into its true operations that are already ongoing yet need the institutional structures to support their activities; for they are in dire need of a newly fashioned locus, with which to contest the agents of the crushing powers and juggernauts that be of digital technology, big finance and bureaucratic capitalism.

For the Italian teacher-scholar Negri (who has written a book on Spinoza while in jail as a political prisoner in Italy that was translated as *The Savage Anomaly: The Power of Spinoza's Metaphysics and Politics*) and the US scholar Hardt who has written a volume on Deleuze, "the network struggle of the multitude [...] takes place on the biopolitical terrain [...] it directly produces new subjectivities and new forms of life. [...] creativity, communication, and self-organized cooperation are its primary values" (*MWD*, 83). 'New subjectivity effects' for a new global. That global values include "creativity, communication and self-organized cooperation" serve singularities that might thrive in an unmutilated community. French philosopher Étienne Balibar's (1942–) felicitous formulation, "*expanding subjectivity*"[10] captures what I wish to convey for this notion captures new movements and events of existence, creation and community for a world society.

Also, we read the Negri-Hardt injunction: "Political action aimed at transformation and liberation today can only be conducted on the basis of the multitude" (*MWD*, 99). Lest one think the multitude an unwieldy social unit "it remains multiple, is not fragmented, anarchical, or incoherent" (*MWD*, 99). In Deleuzoguattarian terms the proof of the pudding is in the eating. Or: namely, how the multitude effectuates a "molecularization" (a term inspired by Deleuze and Guattari's usage of "molecular") of the social (and so of molecularized, which is to say in Guattari and Deleuze parlance "deterritorialized", bodies) for a social space open to a more just and free communal encounter and process. This would service a dynamic movement of a cultural reality of an autopoietic world society.

Now, for Negri and Hardt the concept of the 'common' occupies the place of certain functions or notions of community: "The common [...] is based on the *communication* among singularities and emerges through the collaborative social processes of production. Whereas the individual dissolves in the unity of the community, singularities are not diminished but express themselves freely in the common" (*MWD*, 204). So in this paradigm community does not function as a transcendent moral or tendential figure that intimidates if not emotionally, existentially and temporally appropriates the other, but operates as an ethically sound becoming or a process of the living and labor activities of the key concept of the common. What makes the common an effective weapon against oppressive and potent biopowers is that "it breaks the continuity of modern state sovereignty and attacks biopower at its heart, demystifying its sacred core." Further, "This concept of the common not only marks a definitive rupture with the republican tradition of the Jacobin and/or socialist state but also signals a metamorphosis in the law [...]" (*MWD*, 206–07).

The common will thus confront head-on and diminish, if not negate, various biopowers (bio-power comes originally from Foucault) as well as Bernard Stiegler's notion of "psychopower", toward an historical shift. As for this chapter's position, it is 'post-Jacobin and post-socialist' and so it is a third pathway beyond the two dominant paradigms of post-1980 neoliberal-capitalism and twentieth-century socialism-communism, even while learning from the experiential information, which both offer us to think with, through, beyond and against for a new social and economic experience and communication for communal experience.

To again adduce Nancy from "The Inoperative Community": "As an individual, I am closed off from all community, and [...] the individual—if an absolutely individual being could ever exist—is infinite. [...]. However, the *singular being*, which is not the individual, is the finite being. [...]. There is no process of 'singularization,' [...]" (*IC*, 27). This accords to the lesson of modern and postmodern/late modern art and thought, which teaches that the docile individual is an ideological ruse that serves the military-industrial-digital complex. Such conceptual fetishes as the individual serve to lay the groundwork for the hegemony of military, financial, state and technological power.

The crucial idea of finitude links up with Nancean "compearance", a word that denotes *"co-appears"* (*IC*, 28) wherein, for instance, "Communication consists [...] in this compearance (*com-parution*) of finitude [...] constitutive of being-in-common [...] inasmuch as being-in-common is not a common being" (*IC*, 29). Meanwhile, for Negri-Hardt too the common "is not a common being" but rather a multitudinous becoming non-organic global body or "global common". As Negri and Hardt claim of the multitude, "The fracturing of modern identities [...] does not prevent the singularities from acting in common" (*MWD*, 105) that henceforth work in tandem if given the proper institutional support for movement, growth and development. True singularity requires true commonality, and vice versa. This is because they are inherently and in practice if not always in theory hitherto, transversal or trans-connected entities. The further point is that "we are a multiplicity of singular forms of life and *at the same time* share a common global existence. The anthropology of the multitude is an anthropology of singularity and commonality" (*MWD*, 127)—a new anthropology for a new contemporary human that can finally comprehend singularity for, "*Once we recognize singularity, the common begins to emerge. [...]. We share bodies with two eyes, ten fingers, ten toes; we share life on this earth; we share capitalist regimes of production and exploitation; we share common dreams of a better future*" (*MWD*, 128). There are therefore in the first instance only singularities.

If we register singularity/particularity the common will reach its own molecular or molecularized and event-oriented form of non-organic being; that is, of true being beyond the totalitarian and hierarchicalizing tendencies of normalizing or naturalizing procedures that serve human rapacity. Crucially if not alarmingly, "All of the multitude is productive and all of it is poor" (*MWD*, 134) because it services the well-heeled more than the other way around. Justice and true wealth remain to be accomplished or experienced for the 'productive multitude' whose own value surpluses are super-appropriated by a heteronomous current barbaric and repressive form of immoral negative community precisely because community as such does not exist in any substantive geopolitical way in a neoliberal age of late capitalism. Regrettably, community is contemporaneaously a fraudulent concept to invoke. Closer to the heart of real creative power for Negri-Hardt: "Today we create as active singularities, cooperating in the networks of the multitude [...] in the common" (*MWD*, 135). Serving the Immanuel Kantian ethics of the universal good here emerges with force. Myth does not filter singularity for Nancy when he writes in "Literary Communism" from *The Inoperative Community*: "In myth [...] existences are not offered in their singularity [...]" (*IC*, 78). That myth attaches itself to generality causes it to brutalize singular forms, movements and structures. For myth authoritatively naturalizes, discriminates, normalizes and thus sets up strictures for what it means to be a human agent.

As for true contemporary power for the economic sphere of experience, for Negri and Hardt "immaterial labor" ('knowledges', skills, information, 'ideas', what they term "affective relationships" and much more), is now ascendant for, "immaterial labor [...] has imposed a tendency on all other forms of labor [...]" (*MWD*, 141). This is partly the information age updated. And: "Just as we must understand the production of value in terms of the common, so too must we try to conceive exploitation as *the expropriation of the common*. The common [...] has become the locus of surplus value. [...] for example, of the profit extracted from affective labor" (*MWD*, 150). But to go beyond, if not against Hardt and Negri, "affective labor", be it educational, health and suchlike remains subject to not merely exploitation but to what Balibar terms about capitalism more generally *"super-exploitation"*.[11] This is also my own position on so-called soft or simple exploitation, for it is in actual fact 'super', if not perverse and grotesque. In sum for Negri-Hardt, *"For economics to function today it has to be formed around the common, the global, and social cooperation"* (*MWD*, 157). This inter-connective and inter-cooperative state of affairs might then engender a more mindful social and financial economic system, one which would not truckle down to brute capitalist power that keeps the would-be-multitude in the dark and 'super-exploited', but instead would assert studied fairness with respect to notions of economic justice and of a plausible true community-moving-forward-in-progress.

Negri-Hardt in another claim, "A democratic multitude cannot be a political body [...]. The multitude is something like singular flesh that refuses the organic unity of the body" (*MWD*, 162). In this way, it accords to the Spinozan-inspired, Antonin Artaudian and Deleuzoguattarian non-organic Body without Organs that establishes an unfettered body and free life from social forms of representation in the world for what the latter term the 'New Earth';[12] in Nancy: "community cannot arise from the domain of *work*. [...] one experiences or one is constituted by it as the experience of finitude" (*IC*, 31). This again underlines the import of death. This study, however, retains a strong value also in discipline and 'unwork'/work for community production, even while remaining sympathetic to the importance of death. To explain this idea of 'unwork', "Community [...] takes place in what Blanchot has called 'unworking,' [...]. Communication is the unworking of work that is social, economic, technical, and institutional" (*IC*, 31). So 'communication' then would be a de-codification or deterritorialization of the dominant straitjackets, codifications and territorialities of the world's mighty "social, economic, technical, ideological, and institutional" powers. This 'communication' would be in the service for other counter-forces, counter-ideologies, counter-institutions, or counter-powers still to be invented for another true communal event of *"the common, the global, and social cooperation"*. Such counter-logics may seem impossible, yet prove one site after another of possible individual/personal and commons experience.

Intriguingly for Nancy, whom I quote so as not to oversimplify his thought, "community itself now occupies [...] the sacred stripped of the sacred. [...] the 'unleashing of passions,' the sharing of singular beings, and the communication of finitude." More Nancy, "community is transcendence [...] which no longer has any 'sacred' meaning, signifying precisely a resistance to immanence [...]" (*IC*, 34–35). Therefore an absent or interrupted sacred would be one function of the non-pathological community: a sort of re-transcendentalization of the transcendent vis-à-vis the concept and praxis of community that would not brutally flesh subjectivities into one dough, but would instead multiply possible subjectivity effects for our 'compearance' (Nancy's term). This may minimize the injustices and the corruptions of that world's vulgar insistence on uniformizations and normative capitalist structures for subjectivity. Discredited forms of community in the twentieth century might thereby be chalked up as false starts of what was to come for a more just and desirable community form without various communitarianisms. For to look for non-pathological forms of large scale community, without communitarianism in the twentieth century, is to look in vain. Yet from the perspective of Hegel's 'logical temporality' of which Žižek has written, only these wrong choices open up the space for the good choices: "a paradoxical axiom which concerns logical temporality: the first choice has to be the wrong choice. [...] there is a choice, but in two stages" (*LN*, 290). This contains hope for a return of meaning or of the gift, the *munus*, that constructs community-relations.

I wish now to highlight a few salient points of Nancy's "Myth Interrupted". Firstly, we read that:

> We shall never return to the mythic humanity of the primal scene, no more than we shall ever recover what was signified by the word 'humanity' before the fire of the Aryan myth. [...].
> Myth [...] is always 'popular' and 'millenary' [...] according to our version. [...].
> In this sense, we no longer have anything to do with myth. (*IC*, 46)

'Millenary' and 'popular' myth then are in this cultural and political paradigm unacceptable areas of inquiry for the dangers they offer of furthering forms of fascism, ideological, social, super, micro, technical or otherwise. In a word, Nancy adduces a radical de-Nazification of myth. This noted, Nancy adds, "Bataille named this state, to which we are doomed, *the absence of myth*. [...] I will substitute for this [...] *the interruption* of myth" (*IC*, 47). In this way, myth would be 'interrupted' in our current period of being between the modern (indeed in some regards pre-modern) and the post-modern world in which ostensibly a fraudulent economic myth of global capital serves as today's false myth for partly the reason that myth can no longer exist; yet we need myth; this identifies one paradox and impasse today. For lack of anything better with which to invest existence with meaning, the lowest common denominators of money/capital and power win.

To give a wider sense of reference, for Nancy "romanticism, communism, and structuralism, through their [...] precise community, constitute the last tradition of myth [...]" (*IC*, 51). After "structuralism" (and after modernism one might add) we are left with post-structuralism and post-modernism, and now even post-post-structuralism and post-post-modernism in our age, with its attempts to re-mythologize the last Nancean myth of structuralism (and I add here again, of modernism). In truth for Nancy "all that remains of myth is its fulfillment or its will. We no longer live in mythic life [...]" (*IC*, 52). This is perhaps convincing, especially if one agrees that we live now within a shallow economic myth.

Again Nancy makes a point that buttresses one's sense of myth's self-same and tautological understanding of itself and so self-presentation for general consumption: "As Schelling put it, myth is '*tautegorical*' (borrowing the word from Coleridge) and not 'allegorical' [...]. Thus, it does not need to be interpreted [...]" (*IC*, 49). Hence myth's foundational power to which other structures and meanings must adhere. Importantly also, "Myth communicates the common, the *being-common*" (*IC*, 50) maps onto Hardt and Negri's notion of the common. Accordingly this opens new vistas for myth, once the 'common' has been much more consolidated, as a positive force in actuality. One can conceive a myth of the planet, as a certain sort of new non-organic being (beyond large, 'molar', or macro powers of representation) with which a non-organic human might identify, for example, thereby allowing a more positive task of the creation of community via myth to come out of Nancy's negative philosophy of myth and negative philosophy of community. Of course, this may take a century or more, for example, for myth and for community relations to return, but that it remains a possibility gives one pause that such a movement might not repeat the mistakes of the historical past in a *dynamic instant* full of *jetztzeit* for an emancipatory event of community participation.

In Nancy, we no longer desire myth in a classical or in a traditional sense because, "Mythic will is totalitarian, for its content is [...] of man with nature, of man with God, of man with himself, of men among themselves" (*IC*, 57). Moreover for Nancy, "the idea of a 'new mythology' is not only dangerous, it is futile [...]" (*IC*, 56). It seems, correspondingly, that any classical notion of a new community would also be 'dangerous and futile' if "there can be [...] no community outside of myth" (*IC*, 57). It is again a form of the inherently immanent transcendence of our co-mortalities whose exposure might spawn a good form of community. In a movement of extension, Nancy alludes to Blanchot's *The Unavowable Community*, "in the interrupted myth, community turns out to be what Blanchot has named, '*the unavowable community*'" (*IC*, 58). So, we need a new sense of myth but cannot ostensibly have it; and, we need a new comportment toward community, but cannot avowably experience that either, at least not as classically conceptualized: this is again a current double bind and tension.

The Nancy concept of compearance sits well with Hardt-Negri singularity, and by extension of the common and of the multitude. Nancy on compearance: "It is a contact, it is a contagion: a touching, the transmission of a trembling at the edge of being [...]" (*IC*, 61). This is as close as we get to togetherness, "a touching". Relatedly, Derrida titles one of the longest and last productions of his writing career (a 350-page work) partly on this topic area in *Le toucher, Jean-Luc Nancy*.[13]

Crucially again "death as the unworking [...] unites us because it interrupts our communication and our communion" (*IC*, 67) for it disbands us from the Deleuzoguattarian molar (large-scale political and territorial) machines of the social, the technical or the organic. Or: as Pierre Joris avers in regard to Blanchot, "for Blanchot friendship is profoundly linked to the possibility of community. That death, disaster, absence are at the core of this possibility of community — mak[es] it always an impossible, absent community [...]."[14] Therefore, it is an absent semantics of myth that will allow for the possibility of a being-in-common, to adduce two components within the triptych of the title of this Chapter 2. And it is "the disjunction of absent meaning" that convokes the concept of 'friendship' to allude to the extract from Blanchot that opened this unit, both of which follow the 'disasters' of community of the past, and of a new respect for the 'other', with the conceptual aid of notions of the common, of the multitude and of singularity.

If we are in an undeveloped state it will then be a new regime of affects and intensities that forge if not a new human, then a new social, and perhaps even a new perspective toward or modality of myth or community; or, as Negri and Hardt state: "The intensification of the common, finally, brings about an anthropological transformation such that out of the struggle come a new humanity" (*MWD*, 213). Such a conceptual scheme seeks to re-conceptualize a new human that would register more true to the reality of things as "molecularized" singularities for a new being-in-common. Or: as Nancy puts it in "Literary Communism": "'Community' means [...] the presence of a being-together whose immanence is impossible except as its death-work" (*IC*, 80). This by itself suggests that a paradoxical joyful myth of the hard and indefatigable unworking work of death, which squarely faces the impossibility of immanence without transcendence within it, namely, a perpetual exposure to our finitude, would jump-start the bringing into existence of a new non-fascist, non-totalitarian, non-organic and mature event and figure of a redemptive community. This too is how we are exposed to the possibility of friendship, to the 'New

Earth', to being-in-common, to myth and so by extension to a new developing form of community, existence and creation of radical autonomy in a purposive whole.

The present author (and others including Žižek) believe we need something more radical from that to which the multitude points. We need to universalize things at the level of the unconscious, for example, to create a more efficacious political culture. This makes it necessary to engage the above investigations as something to build upon as so many foundational paving stones for a retrospective and a true Hegel-informed understanding of existence, creation and the commons within the framework of a more genuine and true dialectical materialism; this would accommodate big structures for community and self transformation at a global level of cooperation.

Added to all this, consider these thoughtful words from the political philosopher Esposito

> The fact that we are all debtors, or are becoming ones, means that there are no more real creditors. [...]. The problem we are facing is to transform the oppressive chain into a circuit of solidarity. [...]. What flickers briefly, in the reverse of political theology, is the law of jubilee, which dictated that in sabbatical years, all debts were forgiven and all debt slaves were freed. If we revised this law, we would go from sovereign debt to a common debt, to a community of debt, such that the immunitary grip in which the world is suffocating would be broken. Only then would the ancient *nexum* be shattered and the *servus* return to being completely *liber*.[15]

In this context, the hypothetical construction of a transformative common world debt would attain a new subject position for the world itself. Here the *munus* (the gift) of *jetztzeit* (now-time) finds a place for the practices and exercises in cooperative community, and for disciplined and radical creativity as good examples of the power of the impossible.

The problem of intersubjectivity or of the global commons precisely remains a key problem in this study, especially in Chapter 9 on the antagonists from physical culture Ivan Lendl and John McEnroe. For to connect the self to society in moral-ethical and rational ways constitutes one aim and effect of the forthcoming creative life that offers multiple examples of 'now-time' for the commons. We shall return to the notion of the inoperative in Chapter 7.

Chapter 3

Freedom, Nancy and Henry James's *The Ambassadors* (1903)[1]

In this chapter I further deploy Jean-Luc Nancy's thought in our developing and thickening argument and presentation on modalities and modes of experimental (democratic) community and the flourishing creative life. In this case, Nancy's groundbreaking work on the focal concept of freedom that contains insight and chiasmatic foresight for Henry James's (1843–1916) literary art, a corpus of texts that as the US critic Leo Bersani (1931–) argues, "[James's] subject is freedom".[2] The heterodox mode and genre here of high speculativity may seem unorthodox for a more conventional generic tack. Yet I am fascinated by the complementarizations and possibilities for cross-fertilizations in the construction of a monad or a culturally charged 'dynamic instant' or example of 'now-time' between James and Nancy. A thought from Žižek aids our reflections moving forward

> It is a properly Nietzschean paradox that the greatest loser in this apparent assertion of Life against all transcendent Causes is actual life itself. What makes life 'worth living' is the very *excess of life*: the awareness that there is something for which we are ready to risk our life (we may call this excess 'freedom,' 'honor,' 'dignity,' 'autonomy,' etc.).[3]

Following on the coattails of Benjamin, Adorno, Sartre, Pierre Macherey, Raymond Williams, Blanchot, Lacan, Derrida, Rancière, Lacoue-Labarthe, Nancy, Agamben, Judith Butler, Žižek, Sloterdijk, inter alia, teaches that the oppositional logic of philosophy and literature is as much an effect of ideological disciplinarization, as it is of essentialist differences between the two discourses. Also, retaining the distinction of the philosophical and the literary does not negate the key fact that literature often makes philosophy more comprehensible through the former's inherent dramatic quality or that literature needs, as Adorno argues in *Aesthetic Theory*, precisely philosophy in order to be apprehended in a conceptual way. Further, as Macherey puts it in *A Theory of Literary Production*, "it remains obvious that although the work is self-sufficient it does not contain or engender its own theory; it does not *know* itself."[4]

Strategically I shall illuminate this cultural conjunction of the Nancy-James dyad by adducing passages from Nancy's pioneering *The Experience of Freedom*, to challenge if not to provoke my fellow readers in thinking in both abstract, and concrete terms, about James's labors in narrative art. In so doing, I cut against the going dogma and typical postmodern/late modern stance that takes neither analogy nor creative analogical operations particularly seriously, because so many versions of postmodernism/late modern do not acknowledge privileged representational forms. Originally Nancy's French doctoral thesis written under the supervision of Paul Ricoeur, one reads on the back cover of *The Experience of Freedom*: "One could call it a fundamental ontology of freedom, if freedom, according to the author, did not entail liberation from foundational acts and the overcoming of any logic that determines, in the way ontology does, by positing being either as self-sufficient position or as subjected to strictly immanent laws" (back cover of Nancy text).[5] These words may increase understanding of what follows.

In our experimental and interdisciplinary crossing and comparative treatment of the literary via James, and the social-theoretical-philosophical by way of Nancy, I take this chapter in the spirit of Nancy's own way of thinking: "the essential 'good' of a freedom in which the human existence of human beings would be affirmed, that is, exposed and transcended, has become totally indeterminate, stripped of all divine, heroic, Promethean, or communitarian splendor, and is now barely defined, except negatively, and in relation to evil" (*EF*, 2). I hypothesize that James's work on language precisely defines freedom in ways beyond the dialectical enfolding and sublation of good and evil, of the positive and the negative. So accordingly James is beyond Nancy's tack. Yet the foregoing Nancy passage remains relevant for James's literary imagination and compositional labors. For James does engage largely in a negative de-semanticizing task as far the well-nigh bankrupt concept of authentic freedom in a false social world for the public good and for social relevance.

Still, my initial critical point as a response to the Nancy extract is that a sense of intercultural "communitarian splendor" pervades the subtext of such a novel as *The Ambassadors* (1903). For the communitarian aspect of the artistic world of James's Francophone book of his mature third-period style cannot remain unremarked for the long-suffering reader of James's previous works that exist structurally, one may submit, as a strategic intention for, in James's half-century long writing career, the ten hour and fifty minute-mark-release florid publication of *The Ambassadors*. James's writing career is as if structured to allow for the unfurling of the dramatic development of his late-period style, which include *The Ambassadors*, *The Wings of the Dove* (1902) and *The Golden Bowl* (1904).

Consider also this extract from Nancy: "if freedom is to be verified [...] the very meaning of existence, then this vacancy would be nothing other than the vacancy of meaning [...]" (*EF*, 2). In James's "novel-worlds" (to my knowledge, the Badiou of *L'être et l'événement* 1988/*Being and Event* 2006, and the Rancière of *La parole muette: essais sur les contradictions de la littérature* 1998/*Mute Speech: Literature, Critical Theory, and Politics* 2011, are the first to use the notion of 'novel-world'), an "absent freedom" that would accord to Blanchot's notion of 'absent meaning' and Nancy's later one here of "the vacancy of meaning" reside in the life stories of the Jamesian protagonist. For the devil controls and dominates the world of a cultural imaginary in James's fiction. In this light, one's best hope is to create one's own special possibility and unique loyal form of meaning of vacancy, negation, refusal and resistance be it material/ideological, individual/social or psychic/individual to dominant and false values. Time and again this happens in James's work. Consider the female empowerment and proto-feminist progressivity of Catherine Sloper in *Washington Square* (1881), the anarchistic burden taken on board by the suicided Hyacinth Robinson in *The Princess Casamassima* (1886), the real sacrifice at the material level by the dying Milly Theale in *The Wings of the Dove*, the charity displayed by the 50-something US bourgeois, Lambert Strether, in *The Ambassadors* and that paradoxical under the surface radical bourgeois, Henry James himself, as a figure who also populates his texts, and informs their texture and pattern. To create such individual realities of effective singularization of the self in James's work is for the said characters, the very height and vortice of luxury.

Proposes Nancy in another speculative claim, "Perhaps we must [...] draw freedom back to itself, or withdraw it from itself, or even withdraw it in itself [...] to relate both the necessary thought of existence as such *and* an ethic of freedoms that would no longer be merely negative or defensive,"

> to another concept or another motif whose name or idea we do not yet have. [...] we would [then] have the task of delivering ourselves from the thought of 'freedom' as a property of the subjective constitution of being, and as the property of an individual 'subject.' (*EF*, 6–7)

Nothing better describes the conceptuality of freedom beyond ownership that James's early modernist desubjectifying (that is, de-stabilizing and de-semanticizing) fictional work hints at, but cannot conceptualize, since it is not literature's task to do so directly, even if a subject such as Strether instances what the foregoing extract communicates. James's work with language asks for another conception of freedom beyond his negative critique of the notion, for it is the objective precisely of such a negative operation to open a window onto a positive form of conceiving the notion of freedom for the human subject to fashion possible futures. Strether serves as a good example of this phenomenon, for he essentially possesses a desire to experience vicariously the freedom of others as his own, and hence asks for another ascertainment of the freedom problem as essentially shared.

Furthermore, for all the formal proportionality and complexity of James's major three late-style novels, I submit the thesis that they nevertheless constitute a literary failure insofar as they fail both individually, and as a collective unit of composition, to actualize in fictional form instances of authentic freedom in the Nancean problematic abovementioned. But this does not diminish the potent capacity of James's three great late novels to meditate on the momentous problem of community and the creative life: for in fact James's failure constitute and promote these late novels to a special sort of success as provocative agents that produce new thoughts in their readers.

Moreover, that each of the three final late period novels broach the question of freedom, and give little glimmers of it, via characters such as Strether, Milly and Maggie Verver, remains a considerable accomplishment and a true meaning and value of these fictions. For is it not for the novel-world to straighten things out so much as to ask for a critical recovery of ennobling and valuable question areas? And to ask: what is valuable? As for precisely such subject areas, Anselm Jappé (1962–) writes of the French revolutionary thinker, Guy Debord, "In his film *Critique of Separation* (1961), Debord notes that the problem is not that people live more or less poorly; but that they live in a way that is always beyond their control (OCC, 45; *Films* 45)."[6] This is the point also for James's fiction. On some level it is a question of existence, creation and the commons that will ensue that truly matters. It is a matter of immunizing the subject against a control-oriented culture that one encounters in James's work.

Once more Nancy stage center "the theme of freedom brings us to a liberation with regard to its (re)presentation, in such a way that the resources of this liberation are not yet available to us. The thinking of freedom can only be seized, surprised, and taken from elsewhere by the very thing it thinks" (*EF*, 8). Again, insofar as James's textual art seeks to think the negative, the unthought, the unknown, the un-articulated and to use Heideggeresque parlance, "the un-understood", it is precisely what Nancy's thought requires for the concept of freedom to be thought, per se. In this way, there is a certain concordance between the two authors, James-Nancy, under our interdisciplinary consideration and inquiry. Another Nancean aperçu on which to reflect, "Freedom can no longer be either 'essential' or 'existential,' but is implicated in the chiasmus of these concepts: we have to consider what makes existence, which is in its essence abandoned to a freedom, free for this abandonment [...]. Perhaps it will not be possible to preserve the very name and concept of freedom" (*EF*, 9). However unorthodox this remark, Nancy's theoretical point here inches at what really interests James's art, and what it is on about concerning existence and freedom, for it is not clear that Jamesian freedom is other than Franz Kafka's proverbial "way out" more than freedom per se, at least as the notion is classically conceived. So, in this light, it is more a question of how to get out between two grindstones when required, rather than composing a so-called "free" existence. To have a more dialectical notion of freedom, both a negative and a positive understanding of the concept, and for what that would mean for new possibilities for living, for material reality, and for human consciousness, may even require a radical deconstitution or deconstruction of the concept of freedom. This would be for another more pertinent one for contemporary forms of civic life and active agency. A negative freedom would be the point, a freedom for those without freedom, and yet wanting to attain a degree of autopoietic autonomy.

Meanwhile, for the dialectical functioning that would distinguish a more humane, just and rational conception of freedom, for Nancy, freedom constitutes "the fact of existence as the essence of itself. The factuality of this fact [...] makes itself known [...] by the generativity or generosity of the new, which gives and gives itself to thinking: for all existence is new, in its birth and in its death to the world" (*EF*, 11). The pure factuality of freedom accords to James's version of fictionalized American pragmatism, and to its preoccupation with basic molecules of fact such as life, death, community, conversation, drama and individual choices for being, which are again in James, often choices for disavowment and the redoubtable power of negation. For in James's fictional work denunciation, negation, and renunciation of the cynical, materialist, uncultured and brutality of a capitalist system in a 'kairology' remains a paramount interest. In the wake of the old hierarchies and powers/controls that be, whether bureaucratic, class/material, gender, intellectual, national, race or sex-based ones, James's characters are so often negationists because they struggle for a more firm figure of freedom as of yet to arrive.

To put the object of our theoretical concern otherwise, in Nancy's late twentieth-century text: "Freedom perhaps designates nothing more and nothing less than existence itself. And *ex-istence* [...] signifies simply the freedom of being, that is, *the infinite inessentiality of its being-finite, which delivers it to the singularity wherein it is 'itself'"* (*EF*, 14). The foregoing critical statement puts James and another modernist writer, Kafka (1883–1924), on the same plane concerning the notion of freedom. For in the final tally it is the notion of finitude and of the life coefficient that matter most both to James and to one of James's alter egos, Strether, in his corpus of texts, regarding any line of approach to the question of life and freedom in their intermingling and interpenetrating. Kafka once wrote that, "Life is perhaps truth itself" and James also remarked in one of his letters that, "Life is the most valuable thing that we know of". These sorts of value investments reverberate with ideas of the subjective and immunizing practices of existence, creation and the commons.

With Nancy, and to our object of theoretical interest, freedom "is renounced where the essence [...] of a process, of an institution [...] prevents existence [...] from acceding to its proper essence" (*EF*, 17). This dense remark pertains to James's work, which time and again flags the pole of finding one's center of gravity, and so singular strengths in order to compose an effective existence toward *true success*. Witness for example the remarks to this effect in the James novel *The Tragic Muse* (1890). Let it not go unmentioned too that when Nancy writes, "*discourse* [...] exposes itself as *passion*" (*EF*, 18), it summarizes James's passional writing life. For on the level of psychic facts, James's life-story, even as a solid bourgeois, was one of the meaning and passion of the process of literary writing, over against the accumulation of money capital and falsely sacral worldly power and fame, albeit one spirit of the Master (Henry James) also had a certain grandiose conception of himself and of his conceptual persona. The passionately absorbed Jamesian protagonists in their quest to attain achievements of meaning and knowledge including Lambert Strether in *The Ambassadors* index this phenomenon Nancy describes.

In addition, when Nancy writes that freedom "is a fact of reason" (*EF*, 21), it correlates to James's practical sense that the valuable and ennobling ontic reality of freedom is part of an enlightenment based humanism to which he more or less subscribed. On another register, when Nancy notes of "the abandonment of existence to an obligation" (*EF*, 26) it accords to James's sacral sense of duty in a Kantian sense. This is played out by James himself in his anti-conformist and aesthetically revolutionary compositional career. James micropolitically in his writing praxis was able to revolutionize the revolution. Further, when Nancy composes of "the energy of a power of realization" (*EF*, 28) it agrees with James's profound sense of the importance of invigoration and energy for situations in his narratives including for his own steadfast writing praxis. In point of fact, in the end, James for some wrote too much, but who is to say for sure? If he had not been so prolific, we may not possess the poetic late-period novels.

Furthermore, in Nancy's critical purview: "Freedom is the transcendence of the self toward the self, or from the self to the self—which […] requires […] that the 'self' not be understood as subjectivity, if subjectivity designates the relation *of a substance* to itself; and which requires at the same time […] that this 'self' only takes place according to a being-in-common of singularities" (*EF*, 30). This underscores one's sense that, in James's writings, there is a utopian subtext that asks for another sociality, existence, creation and community yet to arrive wherein 'self' would be irreducible to subjectivity. Strether embodies this in his desire to exist for others as a goad if not a guide to freedom. In the final accounting, the vast majority if not all of his characters are in their innermost essence incomprehensible and enigmatic. We cannot really understand them, nor should we attempt to comprehend them in reductivist ways that are commonplace. Instead, "a being-in-common of singularities" extends our sense of things and of the ideological-creative space James's writings construct. Nancy's point above concerns *The Ambassadors* wherein the intersubjecive aspects of an always moving and dynamic subjectivity 'of singularities' are indispensable to the construction of (self-)identity and (self-)objectification.

In James's artistic worlds too the tip of the hat is given to freedom as the counter-agent over against the totalitarian modern power of capitulative, defeatist and quietist false forms of modern life; also, with James's work, to have or to become freedom is to avoid becoming a mere epiphenomenon, and instead to serve as an example of a revivification of forceful selfhood or identity; or, as Heidegger famously puts it in *Sein und Zeit* (*Being and Time*), the point is to achieve an "owned existence".

Witness Strether from *The Ambassadors*, and his declaration to Little Bilham, which I take as a vortice text for this Chapter 3: "'Better early than late! […]. Live all you can; it's a mistake not to. It doesn't so much matter what you do in particular, so long as you have your life. If you haven't had that what *have* you had? […]. What one loses one loses; make no mistake about that. […]. Do what you like so long as you don't make *my* mistake. For it was a mistake. Live!'"[7] These words constitute an acme for *The Ambassadors* about the importance, opportunity and value of the exercise and praxis of life, and of its caretaking. It shows another way for human subjectivity to function.

With Nancy: "metaphysical freedom designates the capacity to be a cause by and of oneself. Now causality belongs to beingness [*étantité*], not to existence, as does subjectivity insofar as it is the for-itself of the foundation" (*EF*, 38). In James's cultural work, to self-immanentize one's trajectory of 'beingness' to create an existential reality and chain of events of class balance and harmony with oneself, is another way of instancing "metaphysical freedom". This posited event and situation of harmony may be constituted by any number of other simultaneous and traversing affects, ranging from serenity to agitation, yet such happenings remain an ennobling and valuable mode of comportment and outflow onto the world both in fiction and beyond those parameters.

Nancy's charged words, "Freedom then designates the 'resistance' thanks to which beings are allowed to be what they are" (*EF*, 40), well describes culturally symbolic, ideological/ material and imaginary forms of naysaying that James's characters initiate and enact over against the power of an entrenched, imperial and patriarchal economic world. That James as producer-creator has eyes in the back of his head for his observational powers for such social facts and topics as the foregoing illumines his multi-accentual and complex tack on freedom. Furthermore, for Nancy in his investigation: "it is no longer a question here of *freedom* as a property or as a power in whatever sense, but of a specific element, 'the free,' [...]" (*EF*, 43). In James's fiction, then, freedom as a sort of 'element' means that to exist in one's element is to attain a special courageous and cunning loyalty to one's particularized, because singularized, form, and figure of creative freedom. Freedom is accordingly a sacral way of being for James's art, even as the decomposition of the sacred remains a cultural fact of the mass and popular sell-out nature of Occidental modernity/ies.

When Nancy writes that emancipation or, "Freedom is thus understood not only as a particular type of causality in the production of its effects [and] on the model of physical causality, as lawful succession. The specific mode of freedom's causality [...] *is the incomprehensible* [...]" (*EF*, 45). The foregoing theoretical statement from Nancy delineates why James's fictional work instances one powerful manifestation of these fictionally singularized, individuated and unrepeatable laws and types. The notion "lawful succession" informs the politics and the textual subtleties of human interrelations in James's fictional universe. Also, 'succession' agrees with the notion that for the life-story of the individual character, to keep the process going, to continue the concentric dialectical circles of self-continuation, enables by extension to reboot cultural freedom, existence and community.

With critical finesse Nancy notes in another claim: "freedom is causality that has achieved self-knowledge" (*EF*, 45). If so, then James's *The Ambassadors* mobilizes the notion of a topmost force of human agency, for only through a certain agency can one accomplish causality that attains a positive and classical form of self-knowledge: this happens time and again in James's fictional work. The example of Strether here will serve. So, the James-Nancy cultural formation and dialectical dyad adds yet again to the wealth of invention for thinking issues of creative existence and freedom. To hang further upon this essayistic encounter between James and Nancy, we read in *The Experience of Freedom* that freedom entails "a heterogeneous dissemination of states, concepts, motivations, or affects, which could compose [...] an infinity of figures or modes of a unique freedom, but [...] are offered as [...] *bursts* whose 'freedom' is [...] their bursting. [...] there is no freedom without some drunkenness or dizziness, however slight" (*EF*, 57). The same could be said about James's narrative characters, for the individual "bursts" of freedom that they experience at certain privileged fictional moments re-articulate and relaunch what Nancy announces. For freedom in James, as also in Nancy, constitutes not a reified condition, but rather an explosion of being. In this light, consider what Milly of *The Wings of the Dove* (1902) or Strether of *The Ambassadors* (1903) invoke if not exactly instance, although on some register they do embody an ontological explosion. Also, the Nancean notions of "states, concepts, motivations, or affects" communicating different experiential instances of freedom, well delineate what happens during the cultural event and praxis that is reading James. For in James, the possibilities of our consciousness as readers are amplified to include new "states, concepts, motivations, and affects". As an index of the adventure of liberty, one may speculate productively on a good quality of charitable and mental dizziness in Strether's mode of reality.

To accentuate our essayistic whirligig on the philosophical concept of freedom, and how it pertains to *The Ambassadors*, Nancy declaims:

we are done with 'philosophy' because it has enclosed freedom in the empire of its necessity and thus stripped itself of [...] the freedom in thinking. In this way, philosophy has constituted freedom as a *problem*, whereas [...] that which addresses itself to thought and addresses thought to itself cannot constitute a 'problem': it is a 'fact,' or a 'gift,' or a 'task.' (*EF*, 60)

On the one hand, Nancy seems a middle of the economic road affirmative (however much a philosophically advance guard) cultural person and thinker in refusing to accept the notion of the huge "problem" of freedom in the domain of 'thought' in casting it as 'fact, gift or task' (we may add the word *munus*) yet in James too it can be said that the same thing persists. For James appears above all interested in upper middle-class bourgeois strata and their multitasking opportunities for freedom over against the contradictions and treacheries of a social milieu of a materialist, ideological and nationalist drift and focus. In addition, Nancy's parting with philosophy resonates with the interdisciplinary methodological investments of the present theoretical and cultural-studies investigation. Conversely, the above criticism may be reductive and if so, it is laudable to claim as Nancy does that freedom "is a 'fact,' or a 'gift,' or a 'task.'"

Crucial is again Nancy on how "freedom precedes singularity [...]. Freedom *is* the withdrawal of being, but the withdrawal of being is the nothingness of this being, which is the being of freedom. This is why freedom *is not, but it frees being and frees from being* [...] *freedom withdraws being and gives relation*" (*EF*, 68). The complex idea that "*freedom withdraws being and gives relation*" defines Strether's modus vivendi. Better still, in James's writings, freedom negates being, because it opens up new emerging events, forms, and movements and structures of relation and of togetherness: witness for example the coda of *The Wings of the Dove* or of *The Golden Bowl*, for both books invoke states of affairs for emergent forms of human community or human commons at the end of their narratives. In Maggie Verver's triumphant reclaiming of her husband Prince Amerigo at the close of James's summa *The Golden Bowl* the impossible community becomes possible.

Importantly, for Nancy in a quite intricate point: "freedom is [...] the step of my com-pearance which is *our* com-pearance. Freedom is properly the mode of the discrete and insistent existence of others in my existence, as originary for my existence" (*EF*, 69). This emphasis on relationality and on space accords to James's sense that freedom entails a certain new togetherness and spaciosity for the individual fragmented subject to negotiate as herself an ensemble of singularities that would act in concert with other singularities for any (individual, collective or otherwise) gathering event and movement of freedom and by extension of community.

Therefore, that personal and public identity both consist of more than merely a self is a truism of Jamesian subjectivity. Nancy's notion of 'compearance' denotes and affirms our shared appearing and dying unto the world. In this sense, we compear by default, for it is unavoidable. Also, in the foregoing light, Nancy notes: "Freedom is the specific logic of the access to the self outside of itself in a spacing, each time singular, of being. [...]. Ontological sharing, or the singularity of being, opens the space that only freedom is able, not to 'fill,' but properly to space" (*EF*, 70). Again the spaciosity involved in re-spatializing one's individual possibilities—within the larger domain of temporality/spatiality—embeds the Jamesian character's life-narrative. Witness the numerous transatlantic intercultural characters in *The Ambassadors*, whose international quality and modality of life snappily and snazzily enable a given character to test new contexts and extend her choices for 'being-in-the-world'.

In Nancy the value and concept of "freedom *measures itself against nothing* [...] no way [...] will one avoid the excess of freedom—for which heroism and ecstasy are in fact also figures and names, but these must not obscure other examples [...] serenity, grace, forgiveness, or the surprises of language [...]" (*EF*, 71). The emphasis on "nothing" from Strether in *The Ambassadors* serves as a good example of what Nancy launches; further, that Strether is so serenely and even enormously forgiving at novel's end (for instance toward Chad's decision to return to Woollett, Massachusetts) instances a powerful Nancean figure and form of freedom. The nothingness of which Strether discourses allows him to create a certain immanence in his own self-experience, for such experience is liberated from ways of thinking bound up with the logic of the profit motive, at least in reductive materialist terms. The reference here also to 'excess' points to the quote from Žižek with which we began this chapter, as well to this chapter's title. Also, when Nancy writes, "Freedom is therefore singular/common before being in any way individual or collective" (*EF*, 74) it accords to how the Jamesian character does not exist in a vacuum, but instead operates in a dynamic social field rife with social agents, concerns and a movement of energies that outfit the subjectivity of the 'individual or collective' so that all existences are on some level inherently part and parcel of one another as forms of interbeing or transindividual cross-resonance. Against Nancy though, in James's fiction at another register we are in our innermost essence alone, and that at such moments human existence is precisely that which remains unappropriated and uninvaded by the other or a would-be expropriator. This is not to endorse identitarian slavery to atomistic capitalist ways of thinking, but rather to think through the quite singular nature of human experience in fiction at privileged moments of literary-philosophical importance.

In Nancy's radical interrogation too, "Freedom can only be *taken*: this is what the *revolutionary* tradition represents." Not only this, "No one begins *to be* free, but freedom *is* the beginning and endlessly remains the beginning" (*EF*, 77). Something comparable could be said about the reader of James's narrative texts, in the sense that we are always at the beginning of the Jamesian work on language in every page of his writing that block the profit motive, of straight and narrow standardized and regularized exegetical capital. James upsets the bottom line of normative interpretive meaning.

Again Nancy declares that the domain of politics mainly involves "the opening of a space. This space is opened by freedom [...]. Freedom [...] only comes to produce itself there [...] in the sense that an actor [...] produces himself on stage" (*EF*, 78). This theatricalization of the self as a form of individual/ existential praxis in the mode of a relation in the foregoing Nancean problematic seems part and parcel of the Jamesian personage and scenario in his dramatic form of fiction. It is crucial for freedom in James that the individual identity 'produce himself on stage'; this is what Robinson fails to accomplish given his suicide in the misprized middle-style novel, *The Princess Casamassima* (1886). Conversely, as against Nancy, for James it appears that the political involves the interanimation of spaces and powers alike. As to the micropolitical, James's emphasis in the artistic world of *The Ambassadors* on the gestural/the look, the micro-flows and the micro-ethics for communal forms and modes of social organization illustrate the center of his concerns as a fabulist of the social universe.

In a distinction for Nancy, "Power has an origin, freedom is a beginning. Freedom does not cause coming-to-being, it is *an initiality of being*. Freedom is what is initially, or (singularly) *self-initiating* being" (*EF*, 78). Over against originating power obsessed with origins would then be the freedom that the reader of James encounters, when reading what I have already argued is the always-beginning Jamesian page, and Jamesian-text, for the individual reader's 'self-initiating', which is to say a self-starting consciousness. This quality of James's fiction may be said another instance of an inauguratory self-starting freedom. Is this idea of *"an initiality of being"* not one lesson of the coda of *The Ambassadors*? In another Nancy aperçu: "Freedom: event and advent of existence as the being-in-common of singularity. [...]. What is lacking today [...] is the thought of this initiality [...] revolutionary thinking has always acceded [...] not so much to the overturning of power relations as to the arising of a freedom untainted by any power, though all powers conceal it" (*EF*, 78–79). James's compositional work including *The Ambassadors* accords to both parts of this statement of Nancean freedom. First off, the courage of "initiality" on behalf of the individual personage in all her forces of negation is quite key for James's artistic world as instanced by *The Ambassadors*; as again for the first half in this two-part argument by Nancy, on some level, I also remain unconvinced that neither the biographical James, nor his work in language, would endorse the notion that the human subject is anything other than "existence as the being-in-common of singularity". However, as against Nancy, I argue with respect to the second point here that in James's art, it would prove impossible to get to some stage where power relations would not require overturning, but rather eschewing. For in James's work power is indeed rather ubiquitous and even lives on, so that the challenge is perhaps to change the semantics of power to something like "un-power" or "non-power", which are visionary forms of soft power so to say (or even to transform and alter its corrupted semantic status) of which the present author discusses at some length in *The Dialectics of Late Capital and Power: James, Balzac and Critical Theory*. Of course, it is perhaps the case that the actual true is not locatable in James's fiction on this matter, but rather in daily experience; we do well here to remember Jacques Lacan's statement, "Truth has the structure of a fiction". For it is perhaps in the fiction of Henry James that the tome truth opens out movingly onto the practical reality truth.

To move on, in another Nancy disclosure for reflection,

"A politics [...] of initial freedom would be a politics putting freedom at the surface of beginning, of allowing to arise, in [...] allowing to be realized [...] *what cannot be finished*. Like sharing, freedom cannot be finished" (*EF*, 80). This is true. In James too freedom and sharing cannot reach an endpoint, for then both risk lapsing into a state of reification. Jamesian freedom and sharing thus are process-based agencies and activities. And when Nancy writes that, "Freedom=the self-deepening nothingness" (*EF*, 81) one may counter that the notion of nothingness crops up on the Jamesian page, in how so many of the protagonists that populate his work become again a freedom via being themselves as individual social agents and social actors, negationists, in their personal missions. James too would concur that experience is the great thing in one's lifeworld, rather as Nancy claims, "The experience of freedom is therefore the experience that freedom *is* experience. It is the experience of experience" (*EF*, 86–87). This gets down to semantic details, but Nancy remains pellucid in a rhetorically stylized text. Simply put, experience then is freedom. This is an insight and gain for our sensibility in engaging the textual and ideological space of *The Ambassadors*. This philosophical remark by Nancy, "experience's self-without-subjectivity—which experience singularizes—is attained in full force by *its* freedom" (*EF*, 89) approximates what happens in James when some of his characters, such as in one valid reading Milly Theale whose real sacrifice of a gift for love to Merton Densher in *The Wings of the Dove* creates a fictional situation in which she is given freedom as singular activity and urgent action. For on some level, she has as possessor of money capital taken a pick and axe to her profit driven subjectivity.

Consider Nancy in another astute claim, "because freedom is not the subject of an action, freedom *surprises itself*" (*EF*, 115). This may be said to happen as a general thing in the overall ambient fictional milieu, as well as the ending of, *The Ambassadors*. Even more, the centrality of experience as the experience of our finitude in James is a concern; in this light, consider the following aperçu from Nancy on the *munus* of time and more: "existence [...] is [...] offered to time" so thus "Its surprise" for Nancy "exposes existence as an infinite generosity to time's finitude [...]" (*EF*, 117). In another Nancy-like key, one feature in James's narrative plots for his character as radical active agent involves an awareness of life as a series of finite existences and by extension fully to recognize one's finitude. This creates the conditions to affirm the affirmative power of judgment for one's specially possible form of a creative, free, powerful and sovereign form of being. Further, in another cross-fertilizing point, Nancy's quip, "Wickedness [...] hates singularity as such and the singular relation of singularities. It hates freedom, equality, and fraternity; it hates sharing" (*EF*, 128) recaps features in Jamesian ethics, and his long nineteenth-century/early modernist preoccupation with diabolical evil. The problem of evil is important in James, and so this confluence with Nancy is worth underlining in thinking about forms of singular creativity and the communal life as so many forms of moral-ethical and communal intersubjectivization.

With Nancy on the concept of the ongoing crisis and overriding importance of and access to space, "freedom is [...] the freedom of a free space" (*EF*, 145). Space is the friend of freedom. In like fashion, James would be in agreement in the spirit of Virginia Woolf that we all need 'a room of our own' to play on the title of Woolf's high modernist British novel. Nancy here then would be James and Woolf's cultural-spiritual heir. James's copious texts would also find helpful Nancy's words on freedom, "This spatiality is not so much a given free space [...] as it is the gift of a spatio-temporality [...]" (*EF*, 145). In James, the present of "a spatio-temporality" life well instances itself in the culturally and socially vibrant Francophone, if not even the internationalist and Kantian "world-civil-society" of *The Ambassadors*. And for Nancy, he writes "freedom does not receive a space [...] but it gives [...] space to itself as the incalculable spacing of singularities. [...] it is also 'habitation' —habitation in the open [...]" (*EF*, 145–46). James's work on fabulating language bears out the same lesson of the webwork of our co-appearances, co-habitations and co-spaces, in fictional reality. In this regard, consider the importance in the narratives of James's universe of the individual cultural power of habitation, not necessarily as a sign of territoriality, or of economic competitiveness, but rather as an instance of freedom giving itself the entitlement of habitation as action and as doing a practice of resonance and of dynamic movement; this occurs in a lively perceiving individual world, irreducible to the physical space of a house, as a militaristic bastion for its inhabitant. What concerns us here is the space-time that James's characters inter-penetrate and traverse as active agents of creative subjectivity, freedom and mutual community togetherness.

In the following, Nancy offers a half-tone to his social theory of freedom that has congruence with James's dialectical tack on the subject, doubly so given the US-born novelist's emphasis on strategic perspicacity and process in the groundless ground of what is the simultaneous ethereality and materiality of the life-process in James's artistic worlds: "The senses of [freedom] matter little to me (but its strategic position, much)" (*EF*, 154). This is important to pause and to consider. In addition, Nancy poses the difficult and necessary open-ended question: "What other semantic is there, which would not be the complete program of the philosophy of freedom?" (*EF*, 154): this is precisely the complicated point, and why James's provocative and searching prose writings continuously explore the unanswerable, yet necessary question of freedom. The ending of *The Ambassadors* in which Lambert Strether and Chad Newsome both go back to North America has congruence in its forceful and productive obscurity to the enormous problem and question of freedom. With skepticism, Nancy adds the following disclaimer, "the sentence 'Freedom, how many crimes are committed in your name!,' whose author I have forgotten, has become a disabused adage of modern times" (*EF*, 161). This is one reason why James's literary engagement with the notion of freedom is an unorthodox one that does not cry out the name, per se, for to do so would compromise the artistic integrity and force of literary-critical investigations into it.

Consider now Nancy's incisive locution for our *kairology* (history as unfolding catastrophe à la Agamben's Benjamin-inspired use of the term) that needs courageous confrontation for what it is: "Freedom Manipulated (by powers, by capital): this could be the title of our half-century. Thinking freedom should mean: freeing freedom from manipulations, including, first of all, those of thinking." (*EF*, 164). This has analogical exactness with the innermost elements and structures, and external aspects too, of James's affectual, perceptual and thinking cultural work in narrative language. The ideological content of *The Ambassadors* addresses the problem of manipulation in its portrayal of Mrs. Newsome and of a superegoization of things that one spirit of the North American mentality conveys and decrees in the novel-world. James is preoccupied with the concept and praxis of forms of manipulation; recall also Ezra Pound's famous remark on "Henry James" as a prime example of an author who should be viewed as a "hater of tyranny; book after early book against oppression, against all the sordid petty personal crushing oppression, the domination of modern life; [...] human liberty, personal liberty, the rights of the individual against all sorts of intangible bondage! The passion of it [...] in this man who, fools said, didn't 'feel' [...]."[8] The brutality visited upon others comprises what James's artistic work including *The Ambassadors* continuously contests, and to which he gives vivid representational form in all its destructive power, indifference and malice.

The dual Nancean and Jamesian point is to create new forms

of freedom beyond identitarian logics in order to give non-identity and non-self identical based forms of subjectivity a chance. This would be for our developing and growing world of big finance that does not entirely eliminate other possible futures including when thought in concert with the artistic world of *The Ambassadors* whose aesthetic power may teach us to know that we ourselves may embody an idea, an ideal or a possibility. Consider Strether's mode of reality that communicates a metaphysical and moral generosity of mind and spirit. It is not impossible that another concomitance of community and the creative life may yet be begun and inaugurated in spite of the negative judgments in the cultural imaginary including in the aesthetic heritages of fiction and theory/philosophy.

Nancy's barefaced cultural injunction, "Philosophers have made theses on being: now the question has to do with the fact of its freedom" (*EF*, 167) communicates his own post-Heideggerian interpretive stance on things for Henry James, a champagne bottle of prose literature, to be imbibed and read. This Nancy claim too accords to Strether's sentiments and worldview in the second half of *The Ambassadors*. These words also map onto James's own becalming and agitated intelligence and courageously unflinching consideration of such paramount concerns in his writing career.

There is another striking parallel to note for our cultural dyad of mutual togetherness if not transtemporal indebtedness. From Nancy: "To depend on nothing—to give oneself one's own law—to be the opening of a beginning [...]."

> It is thus solely a question of [...] having no foundation—accordingly having 'one's own' law always this side of beyond 'oneself'—being as removed from oneself as an opening is, and grasping no more of oneself than can be a beginning. (*EF*, 171)

This approximates to James's own understanding on issues regarding individual and collective failures or successes for freedom. For the password in James is to tap into one's own center of gravity, and to create an unrepeatable narrative for oneself, and for those around one, for forms of community that would not be demarcated by foundationalist notions or coordinates. Instead such forms would tap into the revolutionary energies, events, excitement and movements of shared passions and meanings, in which one makes "one's own law". It is for Henry James, a key noirish sensibility novelist of the USA of unhappy endings in literary text after literary text, even before the key authors that were part and parcel of the 1944–58 classic US film noir movement, Dashiell Hammett (1894–1961) and Raymond Chandler (1888–1959), our lucky chance and destiny to make 'one's own law' in order to immunize ourselves against the cruelty and treachery of a standardized and petty human world absorbed in power interests and power plays for the juggernaut of big capital.

Let us shift backwards in time to the 1960s, to a moment in volume one of Sartre's monumental *Critique of Dialectical Reason*. For this text of philosophical culture has a certain concordance with much of the foregoing, as it pertains to Lambert Strether, and to the community of characters in what this author takes as James's alpha and omega text on the topic of freedom, *The Ambassadors*. Here is the relevant passage from Sartre: "objective exteriority turns out to be lived and transcended in the interiority of my *praxis*, and to indicate an *elsewhere* which escapes me and escapes all totalisation because it is itself a developing totalisation. […]"

this negative rudiment of the human relation is an objective and constituent interiority for everyone in so far as I find myself in the subjective moment of *praxis* to be objectively characterized by this interiority. [Hence] the individual's movement from the subjective to the objective no longer involves knowing his *being* from the point of view of matter [...] it now involves realizing *his human objectivity* as the unity of all the negations which connect it internally to the interior of others, and of his project as the positive unification of these negations. It is impossible *to exist amongst men* without their becoming objects both for me and for them through me, without my being an object for them, and without my subjectivity getting its objective reality through them as the interiorisation of my human objectivity.[9]

Careful analysis of Lambert Strether's position would reveal him an exemplary figure for unpacking Sartre's arguments. For in some ways nothing could better describe Strether's life situation with regard to neutralizing the castrating and manipulating power of Mrs. Newsome, even while helping to re-articulate another community of meaning to come in *The Ambassadors*. I close here somewhat abruptly in this chiasmatic moment of going from Nancy to Sartre, so as to indicate something of the merit of this age-old topic of freedom, a subject that proves a special fascination for the James of the late nineteenth and early twentieth centuries, and for the Nancy of our contemporaneity of populist late capitalism dating roughly from 1980.

Accordingly, the interregnum between mid-to-late-style James and Nancy remains a false problem. For the real issue at hand is the unexamined Nancean nature of James's passional investigations into the power of the gross materiality of the world, and of the problem for the individual to compose an effective modus vivendi within it vis-à-vis another experience of the commons. Such would be a revolution in the order of creative being. This is the case, not despite, but rather because James is one of the most radically materialist of literary authors. For as in Nancy, so in James too, to emphasize what was argued above, freedom is not a reified state of being, but instead an invigorating explosion of being of cardinal events. Better still, since for both of our target authors the absolutely spiritual and the absolutely material are two divides at one and the same time (that is, opposites unite), it makes James so good at formalizing and giving dramatic form to Nancy's conceptualizations of the simultaneously sacral and secular concept of genuine freedom.

This is not to say though that the discovered James-Nancy conjunction, 'dynamic instant', and cultural monad does not remain unexplained, and still ahead of us, however much we tried to put some light in this complex topic area. If Rancière is correct when he writes in *The Ignorant Schoolmaster*, "People are united because they are people, that is to say, *distant* beings. Language doesn't unite them. On the contrary, it is the arbitrariness of language that makes them try to communicate by forcing them to translate—but also puts them in a community of intelligence",[10] this is not in order to forswear the entrenched orthodoxy and sacred cow of today about language. Rather, this is to note that the surprising and replenishing cultural work in language by Nancy and James remains a way of creating new forms of relational connectivity in spaces and in situations, toward corrective forms of freedom for a community of emancipatory agents and figures of creative existence and commons-relations that would liberate and enlarge forms and figures of subjective agency and human autonomy. This is so that agency and autonomy can be rebuilt, as leading edge indexes of what was mentioned in an extract toward the start of this chapter, "the very *excess of life*". This may all be in the service of both fresh creativity and of what Aristotle called "greatness of soul" or what we may simply term a life of nobleness on behalf of creativity, and so by extension of discovering the larger community in a more capacious stance on things and the enabling powers and energies of the impossible. This is more than ever necessary under the current regime of an advanced capitalist catastrophe and culture of crisis.

Consider these words on how to approach the question of

freedom from French thinker Jean-Pierre Dupuy (1941–):

> Its reliance on the metaphysical fiction of fate amounts to a kind of detour in the spirit of Leibniz, who was fond of quoting the old French proverb that often it is necessary to take a step back in order to leap forward (*reculer pour mieux sauter*). In this case one steps back from a weak conception of freedom in order to leap over it and attain true freedom, a freedom that is strong enough to overcome necessity.[11]

Thinking experimentally with *The Ambassadors* and Nancy has given us to consider what it would mean "to take a step back" and pause and reflect to reconceive what we mean by freedom "in order to leap forward". This merits a try. Perhaps it would be the logic of a double go that would make here the crucial difference to create a true sense of world and of community on a larger geopolitical scale.

The axial model of life that we inherit, which teaches us to imagine life as a creative journey from surfaces to actuality, allows us too to reconsider these sorts of basic coordinates as the opportunity to actualize our powers as agents and by extension as communities. In this way revolution may be emancipated from its decayed status. But this emancipation of liberation will require a good deal more struggle in this direction if it is to be effectuated for the achievement of meaning that would be the heralding community of genuine mutuality. Our engagement with the "James and Nancy problem and gift" comes to a close, and with it Part I of the present analysis. Part II will drive home the double idea of community and the experimental creative life as a form of flourishing with further exemplary cases from so-called high culture: texts and examples of the animating world spirit by Walter Benjamin, James Joyce, Georges Bataille, Ralph Ellison and Dante Alighieri.

Part II

Toward Community with Élite Culture
Energies II

Chapter 4

Walter Benjamin's Status in Interpretive Communities[1]

Continuing on from our prior readings, this écrit provides an advanced survey view of the cultic status and symbolic existence that Walter Benjamin (1892–1940) holds since the mid-twentieth century in the academic community of literary and cultural theory, and of philosophical aesthetics and culture. This chapter thus examines the "Benjamin problem" or "Benjamin gift" (and by way of implication the impossible/possible community of the "improbable Benjamin" or "Benjamin miracle") in the context of Theodor Adorno and Hannah Arendt. We shall also consider such later producer-creators as the US scholars Carol Jacobs (*In the Language of Walter Benjamin*), Beatrice Hanssen (*Walter Benjamin's Other History: Of Stones, Animals, Human Beings, and Angels*, Pierre Missac (trans. *Walter Benjamin's Passages*), Susan Buck-Morss (*The Dialectics of Seeing*), Leo Bersani ("Boundaries of Time and Being" from *The Culture of Redemption*), Richard Wolin (*Walter Benjamin: An Aesthetic of Redemption*) and Martin Jay (*Refractions of Violence*). The foregoing have increased Benjamin's valuation in the academic and cultural social systems and professional reading communities. If there was ever a critic/philosopher who embodied creative and experimental criticism, and the concomitant aspiration that the radical experimentalism of such cultural products might conduct a form of community as a sign of the power of the impossible or if you prefer of 'now-time', it is Benjamin.

The theoretical orientation here will draw inspiration and its general cultural and critical sensibility from Pierre Bourdieu's writings on forms of capital, including cultural capital, and also more distantly and subterraneously from Niklas Luhmann's writings on aesthetics and on systems theory. Questions of Benjamin's work and conceptual persona in the canon formation of cultural and literary theory will thus be brought to the fore by adducing a band of the foregoing reactions to Benjamin for a more inclusive trans-disciplinary and transnational understanding of his reception that has reached heretical and cultic heights in the academic community.

Benjamin, Sigmund Freud, Martin Heidegger and Ludwig Wittgenstein form a hit parade of four influential twentieth-century figures in the Western humanities. Of this quartet, Benjamin was the one who never found a place in establishment academic power structures. In an historical dialectic, the skyrocketing aspect of Benjamin's renown is a sublation to make reparations for the neglect his work received while he was alive. Benjamin's intellectual disciple, Adorno, puts it thus,

> His capacity for continually bringing out new aspects [...] by organizing himself so as to be able to relate to his subject-matter in a way that seemed beyond all convention—this capacity can hardly be adequately described by the concept of 'originality'. [...]. Benjamin, who as subject actually lived all the 'originary' experiences that official contemporary philosophy merely talks about, seemed at the same time utterly detached from them.[2]

Adorno's first point about how Benjamin had an unusual ability in "organizing himself so as to be able to relate to his subject-matter in a way that seemed beyond all convention—this capacity can hardly be adequately described by the concept of 'originality'" contains implications for philosophical-literary criticism. For this instructs us to know that this precise mode of operation was the secret miracle of Benjamin's writing career that on some level was itself a metahistory that had to wait for its true meaning and intersubjective form of communal recognition.

The last point here under Adorno's pen gives Benjamin a certain capital form of dignity. For Benjamin "actually lived all the 'originary' experiences that official contemporary philosophy merely talks about" thereby a necessary response would be to contest his ideas with experiential information. No doubt this all made Benjamin's critical creations more potent and substantial, inviting in due course a community of readers that would find his creative work attractive and interesting. This temporality of becoming Benjamin and his community of readers continue.

The dream of happiness for Adorno too underwrites Benjamin's intellectual integrity when he composes of "a quality which intellectual departmentalization otherwise reserves for art, but which sheds all semblance when transposed into the realm of theory and assumes incomparable dignity—"

> the promise of happiness. [...]. In his philosophical topography, renunciation is totally repudiated. Anyone who was drawn to him was bound to feel like the child who catches a glimpse of the lighted Christmas tree through a crack in the closed door. [...] Benjamin's thought [...] had the generosity of abundance; it sought to make good everything, all the pleasure prohibited by adjustment and self-preservation, pleasure which is both sensual and intellectual.[3]

This speaks to the effects of Benjamin's oeuvre, and signals how he got the best out of his pupil Adorno. That Benjamin "sought to make good everything" shows his proclivity to effectuate a cultural redemption for things in the service of justice, if not of cultural salvation. And that Benjamin sought "the promise of happiness" echoes Benjamin's own thoughts on the French novelist Marcel Proust's similar general and aesthetic quest. Adorno explicitly draws here a comparison between the work of Benjamin with that of Heidegger,

The provocative assertion that an essay on the Paris arcades is of greater interest philosophically than are ponderous observations on the Being of beings is more attuned to the meaning of his work than the quest for that unchanging, self-identical conceptual skeleton which he relegated to the dustbin. [...]. To their disgrace the universities refused him, while the antiquarian in him felt itself drawn to academic life in much the same ironic manner as Kafka felt drawn to insurance companies.[4]

Thus, Benjamin's anatomization of cultures of shopping and much more in *The Arcades Project* when compared with Heidegger's influential philosophy of Being in *Being and Time* (*Sein und Zeit*) reveals itself for Adorno as more salient to objective reality and to objective truth. Benjamin, too, was simply uncategorizable in regard to his own particular areas of cultural and intellectual inquiry.

Hence, too, the malignancy of Benjamin's critical neglect by the academies of central Europe from whom notoriously he failed to secure an academic post. As for the supreme flexibility and wide-ranging nature of Benjamin's investigations, Adorno suggests that it is precisely the misrecognition and maltreatment his imaginative teacher receives from a community of universities that forge his interdisciplinary critical bite, for Benjamin wins "his living as an essayist, on his own and unprotected. That greatly developed the agility of his profound mind. He learned how to convict the prodigious and ponderous claims of the prima philosophia of their hollowness, with a silent chuckle."[5] Benjamin, in a word, has the critical intelligence to see through the sometimes overly self-congratulatory, and well-nigh, if not out-and-out, wrong-minded quality of the rather overblown claims of some schools of thought, such as certain spirits of Heideggerianism. This, however, is not to place Heidegger's thought anywhere outside of the first rank of importance, for it continues to inspire studies of the greatest interest.

Benjamin's isolation from the structure of academic power likely contributes to this ability to de-mythologize the dominant academic mythmakers of his era. Adorno on Benjamin as essayist: "The essay as form consists in the ability to regard historical monuments, manifestations of the objective spirit, 'culture', as though they were natural."

> Benjamin could do this as no one else. [...]. He was drawn to the petrified, frozen or obsolete elements of civilization, to everything in it devoid of domestic vitality no less irresistibly than is the collector to fossiles [sic] or to the plant in the herbarium. Small glass balls containing a landscape upon which snow fell when shook were among his favourite objects.[6]

Adorno's incisive words, "Small glass balls containing a landscape upon which snow fell when shook" remind one of the cinematic extract of Charles Foster Kane's towering rage at the end of the 1941 film *Citizen Kane*, in which, after he tears up his spouse Susan's apartment because she leaves him, he clutches just such a glass sphere that is a snow globe as sign of hope, innocence and paradise lost.

Furthermore, for Adorno in his astute essay: "Benjamin overexposes the objects for the sake of the hidden contours which one day, in the state of reconciliation, will become evident, but in so doing he reveals the chasm separating that day and life as it is."

> The price of hope is life. 'Nature is messianic in its eternal and total transience', and happiness according to a late fragment which risks everything, is its 'intrinsic rhythm'. Hence the core of Benjamin's philosophy is the idea of the salvation of the dead as the restitution of distorted life through the

consummation of its own reification down to the inorganic level. 'Only for the sake of the hopeless are we given hope', is the conclusion of the study of Goethe's *Elective Affinities*. In the paradox of the impossible possibility, mysticism and enlightenment are joined for the last time in him.[7]

That, "The price of hope is life" and that, "Only for the sake of the hopeless are we given hope" taps into the revolutionary energies of a theological cast of mind that was Benjamin's own cultural sensibility. To combine theology with philosophy was for Benjamin a revolution in domains of (de)creative and critical thinking. Also that for Adorno, "'Nature is messianic in its eternal and total transience', and happiness according to a late fragment which risks everything, is its 'intrinsic rhythm'" inches at what is among the most profound of Benjamin's critical legacies. Therefore, Adorno's razor-sharp pinpointing that "the core of Benjamin's philosophy is the idea of the salvation of the dead as the restitution of distorted life through the consummation of its own reification down to the inorganic level" cuts to what is of high value for his intellectual master and for the aesthetic, cultural, political, and social effects of the cult value of Benjamin for intellectual, reading, and thinking communities. The immense power of the impossible may also be found in Adorno's last sentence on Benjamin in the above-indicated extract.

German-born Jewish-American authoress Hannah Arendt (1906–75) complicates the issue of Benjamin's delayed and so retroactive acknowledgment among the community of professional scholars when she notes that "posthumous fame is usually preceded by the highest recognition among one's peers."[8] Such was the case with Benjamin at least concerning members of the Institute of Social Research in New York City, which underwrote Benjamin's precarious material situation in the last years of his existence. For those in the know knew the extraordinary nature of Benjamin's project. Arendt then touches upon something we noted Adorno hints at above, which is that it was Benjamin's creative particularity and vocational singularity in his intellectual existence that was not taken on board by the inoperative/negative community of academic, social, and economic reality, "The trouble with everything Benjamin wrote was that it always turned out to be *sui generis*. Posthumous fame seems, then, to be the lot of the unclassifiable ones… those whose work neither fits the existing order nor introduces a new genre that lends itself to future classification."[9] So, in this frame, Benjamin emerges a scholar of coruscating intelligence. However, Benjamin just did not fit into the existing academic and literary communitarian structures: an understandable fate given how structured mental experience and activity are in the control-oriented late modern era including in the businesses of thinking and of writing. Benjamin's mode of thinking and writing cause too much classificatory interference for his own lifetime success in a straitjacketed academic social system. Arendt comments on another aspect attached to Benjamin, "It is the element of bad luck, and this factor, very prominent in Benjamin's life, cannot be ignored here because he himself, who probably never thought or dreamed about posthumous fame, was so extraordinarily aware of it."[10] As an instituter and establisher of actuality, this places high value on radical contingency.

An additional feature of the cultural effect of Benjamin's cultic status derives from what Arendt designates here: "in Benjamin the element of culture combined in such a unique way with the element of the revolutionary and rebellious."

It was as though shortly before its disappearance the figure of the homme de lettres was destined to show itself once more in the fullness of its possibilities, although—or, possibly, because—it had lost its material basis in such a catastrophic way, so that the purely intellectual passion which makes this figure so lovable might unfold in all its most telling and impressive possibilities.[11]

With the facta bruta of the onslaught of advanced capitalism and digital technology the person of letters of independent means becomes a cultural anachronism. Yet Benjamin does offer a revolution in thinking, one to which the intellectual world increasingly today wishes to come to terms as a model for how to imagine forms of creative and community-building interdisciplinary intellectual work. The seizure and brutalization of the academic body and brain Benjamin eschewed to the benefit of his readers. Arendt argues, too, with regard to the cult that "the fetish character which Benjamin explicitly claimed for the collector as well as for the market determined by him has replaced the 'cult value' and is its secularization."[12] Therefore, in this schematic one may speak not of Benjamin cults but of fetishizations of Benjamin. Our sense of the cultic function here has congruence with how New Testament scholars speak of various competing Christ-cults in the first century of our era after the death of the Jewish prophet and sage figure, Jesus.

In Susan Buck-Morss's *The Dialectics of Seeing*: "After the initial, politically charged reception that greeted the first volumes of Benjamin's complete works in the early 1970s, he has quite rapidly gained respectability within universities [...]."[13] This objective situation is partly because the cultural community of the humanities has become more flexible in its own self-understandings and self-descriptions. One may argue that Benjamin's critical reception benefits from the cross-fertilization of disciplines of the last forty years within the academic community. On Benjamin's form of philosophical-critical sanity, Buck-Morss remarks, "if Benjamin threw the traditional language of Western metaphysics into the junkroom, it was to rescue the metaphysical experience of the objective world, not to see philosophy dissolve into the play of language itself" (*DS*, 223). Hence, de profundis a certain linguistic-literary playfulness Benjamin's thought exposes as part of a shallow culture in a world of power.

In a line of business that could only intensify Benjamin as a change agent of countercultural and thus heretical or counter-capital on the Bourdieu inspired notion here of the stock exchange of cultural capital, Buck-Morss espouses Benjamin's own vocation with these words regarding his "comments on the figure of the flâneur, the nineteenth-century stroller on the city streets [...] the 'ur-form' of the modern intellectual."

> The flâneur's object of inquiry is modernity itself. Unlike the academic who reflects in his room, he walks the streets and 'studies' the crowd. [...] his economic base shifts [...] no longer protected by the academic's mandarin status. [...] Baudelaire embodies the qualities of the flâneur. Indeed, his acute awareness of his highly ambivalent situation—at once socially rebellious bohemian and producer of commodities for the literary market [...] accounts for Baudelaire's ability to 'teach' Benjamin's generation of intellectual producers about their own objective circumstances, in which their interests in fact converge with those of the proletariat. (*DS*, 304)

Benjamin's publication activities and creative work dovetail with those that have more to do with working class forms of presentation and expression. The same may be said of certain agents of counter-capital within proletarianized quarters of academia. In this sense then Benjamin might be described as an emancipated autodidact outside of the academy whose function is to emancipate other scholars. In this model, Benjamin may help to produce a different academic community, for he shakes up the established academic power structures. In this model, Benjamin functions as an agent of class balance.

Whether due to being shot by Stalin's agents as some argue

such as Žižek, or in the more standard account being forced to commit suicide through fear of the abuses of totalitarian Nazi power, and a need to flee from where it might find and thus obliterate him, Buck-Morss recounts an eyewitness on the slide Benjamin took downhill into his physical expiration:

> I noticed that Benjamin was carrying a large black briefcase [...] It looked heavy and I offered to help him carry it. 'This is my new manuscript,' he explained. 'But why did you take it for this walk?' 'You must understand that this briefcase is the most important thing to me,' he said. 'I cannot risk losing it. It is the manuscript that must be saved. It is more important than I am.' (*DS*, 332)

This seems an archetypal sacrificial gesture from the German Jewish writer Benjamin, which could only augment the moral effects of his cult status for future generations for the overall shape of our continuing 'kairology'. Further, we read:

> Now back to the steep vineyard. [...] Here for the first and only time Benjamin faltered. More precisely, he tried, failed, and then gave formal notice that this climb was beyond his capability. José and I took him between us, with his arms on our shoulders we dragged him and the bag up the hill. He breathed heavily, yet he made no complaint, not even a sigh. He only kept squinting in the direction of the black bag. (*DS*, 332; ellipsis here in brackets in original)

With this powerful account, Buck-Morss underwrites what could contribute to Benjamin as a heroic figure deserving of every single iota of social, cultural and philosophical capital that would, in turn, service the moral-ethical effects of the cultic quality of his conceptual persona and creative work for intellectual workers across the community of scholars in the humanities and beyond.

Nevertheless, we read the following disclaimer about Benjamin's fate: "In October 1940, Horkheimer requested detailed information from the Spanish border police."

He was told Benjamin's death was 'not suicide but from natural causes,' and that his personal effects taken into custody consisted of

[...] a leather briefcase of the type used by businessmen, a man's watch, a pipe, six photographs, an X-ray photograph (radiografia), glasses, various letters, periodicals and a few other papers, the contents of which are not noted, as well as some money [....].

No mention of a 'heavy' manuscript. The 'few other papers' have not been preserved. Nor was his grave marked or tended. (DS, 334)

Perhaps we shall never know with surety what happened to Benjamin's text on that mountain (if there was one) and how he perished. For this hero of the impossible/possible critical intelligence and imagination, the mystery multiplies geometrically.

Furthermore, Buck-Morss makes a political point when warning those who work in Benjamin's wake not to ignore and betray his community-driven motivations: "Benjamin's dialectical images are neither aesthetic nor arbitrary."

He understood historical 'perspective' as a focus on the past that made the present, as revolutionary 'now-time,' its vanishing point. He kept his eyes on this beacon, and his interpreters would do well to follow suit. Without its constant beam, they risk becoming starry-eyed by the flashes of brilliance in Benjamin's writings (or in their own), and blinded to the point. (DS, 339)

Such incisive criticism appears goaded on by Benjamin's own form of being and writing. More importantly, Buck-Morss implies a danger that teachers and students hijacked by advanced capitalism and digital technology forget that the impetus for Benjamin's investigations is more than flashy literary/philosophical credentials profound social change on behalf of forms of community.

In a turn of the screw to the cultic functioning of Benjamin, Buck-Morss notes, "'One should never trust what an author himself says about his work,' wrote Benjamin."

Nor can we, because if Benjamin is correct, the truth content of a literary work is released only after the fact, and is a function of what happens in that reality which becomes the medium for its survival. It follows that in interpreting the *Passagen-Werk* our attitude should [...] be [...] reverence for the very mortal and precarious reality that forms our own 'present,' through which Benjamin's work is now telescoped. (*DS*, 339–40)

This hits the nail on the head. A creative and participatory cultural criticism therefore is required. That "the truth content of a literary work is released only after the fact" accords also to popular and to élite cultural figures and their deeds and projects in this study such as our own lineage of the philosophical icon Spinoza all the way down to the iconographical pop culture tennis figure Ivan Lendl.

Buck-Morss adds, "In the flâneur, concretely, we recognize our own consumerist mode of being-in-the-world. (The same can be argued for all of Benjamin's historical figures. In commodity society all of us are prostitutes, selling ourselves to strangers; all of us are collectors of things)" (*DS*, 345). This may seem a harsh judgment and yet one can see the logic; at a systemic level we are all to some degree part and parcel of the commodity universe and system. This is theoretically valuable. We also read from Buck-Morss, "The *Passagen-Werk* suggests that it makes no sense to divide the era of capitalism into formalist 'modernism' and historically eclectic 'postmodernism,' as these tendencies have been there from the start of industrial culture."

> The paradoxical dynamics of novelty and repetition simply repeat themselves anew.
>
> Modernism and postmodernism are not chronological eras, but political positions in the century-long struggle between art and technology. If modernism expresses utopian longing by anticipating the reconciliation of social function and aesthetic form, postmodernism acknowledges their nonidentity and keeps fantasy alive. Each position thus represents a partial truth; each will recur 'anew,' so long as the contradictions of commodity society are not overcome. (*DS*, 359)

Beyond the din of critical voices that argue for one or the other of the two positions of modernism or postmodernism, Buck-Morss's conceptual cartography articulates a more nuanced and just approach to the question; by way of analogy, this may also illuminate the contradiction of Benjamin's own objective intellectual and life situation at odds with an enclosed academy and beyond that one still attuned to a general community and sensibility.

In another instance of Benjamin's capacity to live on as a writer for the cultural and academic community, Martin Jay declares in *Refractions of Violence*: "Benjamin's intransigent resistance to symbolic healing and positive commemoration merits continued respect."

> [...] he gave the lie to the assumption that the victims of the war—or more profoundly, of the society ruled by myth and

injustice that could have allowed it to happen—could be best understood as heroic warriors who died for a noble cause. This is a lesson that ironically can be learned as well from the fate Benjamin himself suffered on the eve of the Second World War. For his suicide on the French/Spanish border also defied symbolic closure.[14]

This extract highlights Benjamin's power to defetishize and to demystify the social, which augments his credibility as a major figure, and to his specifically social and moral-ethical effects. With a certain spirit of American positivity, Jay enriches our argument by offering another example which posits that Benjamin's suffering does not contribute to his intellectual profundity "a plaintive letter Walter Benjamin sent to Gershom Scholem from Berlin in 1931 [...]. 'I have reached an extreme,' he wrote,"

'Someone shipwrecked, who climbs the crumbling mast of his boat's wreckage.' And then he added with desperate hope: 'But he has the chance from there to signal for his rescue.' Benjamin's signals were, as we know, not heard [...]. Benjamin was in a real wreck, hopelessly tossed to and fro on the waves that Pascal and Nietzsche said were the precarious human condition itself.[15]

Given the above diagnosis of Jay's North American positivism, one may nuance his assertion by saying it may precisely be Benjamin's 'shipwreck' that gave him the purchasing power to obtain special insight of the objects of his studies in all their catholicity of scope. Also, this extract reminds us that the classic baroque trope of the precariousness of human existence marks and re-marks Benjamin existentially and intellectually in significant and multifarious ways.

In a claim from Beatrice Hanssen, consider a deflation of

Benjamin's intellectual currency: "If Gershom Scholem was one of Benjamin's early companions in his study of the cabala, he also often turned into one of his harshest critics, chiding his friend for engaging in a dialogue with conservative or protofascist authors whose politics defied redemption."[16] Further, in a remark meant to put center stage Benjamin's real subversive and heretical value as a thinker, Hanssen argues:

> [...] Benjamin boldly subverted philosophical tradition when he suggested that Kant's cognitive, empirical consciousness was itself no more than 'a type of insane consciousness.' In so doing, he not only turned the Kantian tradition inside out but in fact meant to expand the notion of experience to include religious experience and the phenomenon of madness.[17]

Furthermore, for Hanssen, "the iconoclastic potential of Benjamin's notions of allegory and the fragment has been well established [...]"

> But less attention has been devoted to the way in which the categories of decay and transience, at the center of the *Trauerspiel* study, anticipate the later materialistic theory of the work of art in an age of mechanical reproduction [...] Benjamin's preoccupation with transience was not simply motivated by the baroque's obsession with things in decay but equally concerned the temporal, historical, and processlike nature of the modern artwork.[18]

The three latter-most aspects cited here of the work of art for Benjamin remain topical for the community of current critical and academic debates. This includes matters to do with the philosophical baroque.

Consider the powerful specter of another cult figure, Friedrich Nietzsche, who so often in the current century proves the elephant in the room. By extension, in certain perhaps even often superficial and unjust ways Nietzsche's work is paradoxically similar to that of the twentieth-century apologist of capitalism, competitivity and selfishness, Ayn Rand. We read from Hanssen: "Benjamin carefully distinguished the *Unmensch* from the hedonism of Nietzsche's *Übermensch*, who was to overcome the 'Krankheit Mensch' (the illness of being human). [...]."

Instead of celebrating Nietzsche, Benjamin saw his own theory of the *Unmensch*, which he claimed to have taken from Salomo Friedländer, as a corrective to the over-man. Benjamin's desire to expel the specter of Nietzschean politics can also be gleaned from one of the notes to a draft version of the Kraus essay, which stated, 'deepest opposition to Nietzsche: the relation of the inhuman to the over-man' (*GS* 2: I, 103). Perhaps Benjamin aspired to hold the disturbing shadow of Nietzsche's over-man at bay by means of the category of sobriety, which was to dispel the irrationalism of Nietzschean intoxication.[19]

Hanssen adds to the effects of Benjamin's cult status in selective intellectual and academic communities. These two are not always the same sorts of groups.

In Carol Jacobs's well-tuned study of Benjamin, "reading Benjamin is inevitably an attempt to redeem him—though, certainly, to rearticulate his work does not mean "to recognize 'it as it really was' (I.2.695;TH, 255). Much in Benjamin speaks to the contrary."[20] The critical motivation that Jacobs articulates reminds one of Kafka's famous injunction, which US writer Gregg Lambert spotlights, "The categorical imperative of modernity's unfinished project can be found in a formula that Benjamin first ascribes to Kafka: '*Act in such a way that you give the gods something to do.*'"

The principle reference here is to a passage from the *Phenomenology of Mind*, where Hegel describes the function of the Epic narrative as the invocation, or call, through the mimesis of the 'voice of the dead' (*mnemosyne*, memory), that cuts a 'ditch' in the earth, a rift or crack in time, through which the dead return to seek revenge on the living. Consequently, it is only in such moments that the gods have 'something to do'—to provide a measure of justice, victory and *kudos*—that there is the chance of sealing or closing up the ditch in memory and restoring order to time.[21]

Jacobs notes of the status of memories in Benjamin's *Berlin Chronicle*, namely that they form "a medium in which debris and buried ruins are reinterred as one probes, a digging in which no thing is brought to the surface. And yet Benjamin hardly bemoans a loss of treasure, but celebrates, rather, the dark good fortune of the digging itself and even the failure to find."[22] Here it is not the end-point but the subjective creative journey and the process of memory that count.

Furthermore, Jacobs underscores why Benjamin failed to receive academic desserts: "Benjamin, like others before him, dissolves an old genre (literary criticism) in order to found a new genre that combines fiction and commentary in one."[23] This is Benjamin's most valuable intellectual contribution and legacy. His paradoxically productive cultic status as a writer of experimental and creative interdisciplinary work legitimates new cultural effects such as the community of disciplines of contemporary literary and cultural theory and inter-cultural studies. The universality of these disciplines when operating at their best, are on the side of that which can contest the abuse of forms of social power that have co-opted critical and needed academic thought.

Consider another critical volume of Benjamin, composed by Pierre Missac across some five decades. Missac was introduced to Benjamin by none other than the writer and medieval librarian Georges Bataille. In Missac's tome, we note Benjamin's enforced peripatetic existence, which fuels his trans-disciplinary and transnational investigations. Neither a department nor any geographical, institutional or ideological school tie down Benjamin's wings,

> material circumstances cannot be ignored [...]. This is particularly true for Benjamin [...] leading him to take refuge in the suspended temporality of travel, forcing him to move ceaselessly from one place to another, or preventing him from doing so—making, in short, a passant, a transient, of this man who was born to be a flâneur, and making of the transient a fugitive.[24]

The brutality visited on Benjamin as so many truncheon blows from the academic community the "the unavowable community" (Blanchot), teaches one to think what underwrites that dominant day-to-day reality under *the universal of bureaucratic capitalism* (and today more than in Benjamin's era digital technology).

Missac writes here with passion: "Benjamin's fate can be defined as extending 'from one suicide to the other,' the phrase 'from one war to another' is just as accurate. [...]. But war would have its revenge,"

> making the machinations of the Little Hunchback, whose worst exploits were no more than adolescent pranks, seem ridiculous. [...]. Benjamin, who would not be its last victim, had foreseen it. His body, which, despite what some have said, did indeed exist, disappeared after his death. We have nothing but one more death without burial among so many others; no name on a common grave, even for someone who, while alive, provided a name for the nameless [...].[25]

That Benjamin endures 'one suicide after another' may also encourage him to commit egoistical and interpretive self-subtraction in his intellectual investigations. This perhaps adds to his depth, insight and, most of all, true authority of what we may call impersonality or Adorno's non-identity. Benjamin had no official long-term post that gave him cultural or academic authority. This historical condition though seems to help Benjamin forge new compositional genres for which there is as yet no name, except perhaps creative and experimental philosophical criticism or creative and experimental cultural studies. In a word, we need new categories to grasp Benjamin's emancipatory work in language and in thought that sought to revolutionize thinking and communities.

To bring into focus Richard Wolin's study, "Benjamin's profound identification with the 'destructive character' who appreciates 'how immensely the world is simplified when tested for its worthiness for destruction.' The destructive character is anything but goal-oriented and devoid of an overarching vision of the way the world should be." Wolin continues by quoting Benjamin: "'He has few needs, and the least of them is to know what will replace what has been destroyed.' It was in the same spirit that he enthusiastically cited a remark of Adolf Loos: 'If human work consists only of destruction, it is truly human, natural, noble work.'"[26] Here what Wolin suggests is a conceptual if not public persona of Benjamin as a saboteur or even Nietzsche-like transformative agent of the false, the negater of canonical truths, in order to create textual and ideological space for establishing new truths. Furthermore, Wolin notes that

the more manifestly historical life appears destitute of salvation, the more inexorably it presents itself as a ruin, the more it refers to that sphere *beyond* historical life where redemption lies in store. This sphere can only be reached through the utter *devaluation and mortification of all worldly values.* Just as the critical mortification of works of art points the way to their ultimate salvation, so, too, the *mortification of historical life serves as the negative indication of the path to redeemed life.*[27]

The same may be said of Benjamin's life narrative and work. This is due to how in ironical-tragical fashion, the genuinely thoughtful subject institutes Benjamin's outside the university status and mode of functioning. Would this therefore be for the production of a more substantial academic-intellectual community? Wolin also delivers a pointed statement about Benjamin and Bertolt Brecht: "both men [...] were inspired by the possibility of transforming art itself from within, and thus preventing it from degenerating to the level of mere consolation. Both men [...] realize[d] the inherent foolhardiness of attempting to reach the masses directly; instead, they sought to influence other left-leaning intellectuals of similar background."[28] So here Benjamin and the subsequent specter of his cultic status may affect the propensities and proclivities of the community of other academic- and thinking-being leftists. To exercise interventionary force on the multitude would be ineffectual for Benjamin and Brecht. This need not mean Benjamin and Brecht throw in the towel with respect to contesting abusive power and injustice. Instead, the exact opposite holds for Benjamin and Brecht's strategic and dialectical vision of possible futures.

What Wolin writes about Adorno on music stimulates our account: "there is the growing cult of musical 'stars,' the beneficiaries of a totally artificial and contrived buildup on the part of the industry."

The result is that the specific quality of this or that individual song ceases to matter [...] and it is purchased merely for the sake of the *name* of the artist. Art thereby regresses to *cult* in the full-fledged totemic sense of the word. It becomes nothing more than a *fetish*, part of the logic of commodification or the 'fetishism of commodities' in Marx's sense.[29]

Here cult status would be a bad, repressive and deceptive thing, a name brand that debases one's taste and not a good or real thing that mediates revolutionary insight and energies that promote refinement. Crucially, for Benjamin, Wolin notes that the preeminent "danger of modernity is that its radical disrespect for tradition runs the grave risk of totally eradicating our links with the past, thus squandering that invaluable 'temporal index of redemption' which tradition contains. An *authentic* sublation of past would necessarily *preserve* the promise of redemption that has been sedimented in the artifacts and ruins of traditional life."[30] This also reveals some cultural and historical effects of Benjamin's insightfulness and cultic status over against the overly trendy figure and deed in a capitalist system that places a premium on consumerism and consumption. By extension, this indexes the need to transform older notions of community and the creative life. With regard to the gift and to the problem of the cultural inheritance of Walter Benjamin, the power of redemption thus lies in wait for the practice and exercise of forms of community and the creative life.

For Leo Bersani, "The disease of modernity (more profoundly, of history) that Benjamin analyzes is [...] the disease of his perception of modernity. [...]"

> it always *has* to be a question of 'truth' breaking in upon, or being made to emerge from, degraded phenomena [...]. It is tempting to see Benjamin's great popularity today as a sign of our complicity in such mystifications. It is perhaps, more pointedly, a sign of the extraordinary hold on our thought of the culture of redemption. For in Benjamin we find the traits most deeply characteristic of this culture: the scrupulous registering of experience in order to annihilate it,

and the magical and nihilistic belief that immersion in the most minute details of a material content will not only reduce that content but simultaneously unveil its hidden redemptive double.[31]

Amidst the chorus of applause that Benjamin's work now receives in certain contexts, this material invites one to think of his writings afresh. Yet the remark—"It is tempting to see Benjamin's great popularity today as a sign of our complicity in such mystifications. It is perhaps, more pointedly, a sign of the extraordinary hold on our thought of the culture of redemption"— misses the point that the sort of redemption Bersani critiques in *The Culture of Redemption* has more to do with US positivity and with the cultural politics of right wing élites such as William J. Bennett (1943–) and cultural conservatives than with Benjamin. In a word, for the sake of his overall argument Bersani tries too hard to pigeonhole Benjamin. A scholar as subtle and forceful as Bersani would not typically do so. Still, some contours of this Bersani criticism of Benjamin remain to be thought of again and again as a safeguarding of Benjamin's legacy, which is on balance, a good form of cult status instead of a retrograde version in which one may find more content to do with the name of the figure being adduced than with the qualities of the work produced.

In spite of the explosion of discourses on Benjamin's (de) creative philosophical criticism within the community of the humanities in the academy across the past few decades, the true social, political, aesthetic, moral/ethical and cultural effects of Benjamin's project have only begun to be felt. This occurs even as the wind in Benjamin's sails continues to gain an ever widening and influential force. Precisely this wind might stand behind a praxis and exercise of creative existence for another commons to come (l'avenir) that combines critical thought with collective action, agency and struggle.

The *munus* (the gift) of Benjamin's example stands in our present history as a form of embodied *now-time* for passionate lives of responsible creative reading, thinking and writing to redeem the failures of the past. For the mobilization and actualization of the power of the impossible would rule the hour, as does retroactively Benjamin's compositional work, however much that (de)creative output was travestied by forms of enclosure and exclusion. Yet the marginalization of Benjamin's iconoclastic work during his writing career has paradoxically helped to insure its staying power. The corpus of texts lives on as a powerful instance of daring and experimental philosophical criticism for real universality and for the impossible/possible creative world spirit.

Chapter 5

Bearing Crosses for Joyce's
Finnegans Wake (1939)[1]

Finnegans Wake constitutes the present textual support to elucidate basic coordinates of the problem of mutual communal reality and the creative life. Within the encompassing design of this text on the paradoxes of the power of the impossible, Chapter 5 will explore relations between reader, text and author as a way to examine, to deepen and to firm up understanding of true creativity (aka decreativity) and forms of togetherness.

When the young Benjamin argues, "Since the Middle Ages, we have lost our insight into the complex layers that compose the world and its best features"[2] we may take one interpretive tack, that this partly concerns the pace of modern life, and its impatiences that impede thoughtfulness. This productively combines with the necessity of the immunizing patiences needed to create something of lasting value: be it a gothic cathedral or a product that would be the fruit of inordinately good and energetically injected work; or, that would tap into the energies of loyalty to a textual project, of which Jacques Rancière writes: "the halo of sainthood would start with the modesty of this labor of attention";[3] so then, it is my contention that the minor and centrifugal concept of infinite patience in one's readerly mode of existence is required to engage one of the more advanced works of literature in English since the dramatist William Shakespeare: "Shikespower!",[4] "Chickspeer" (*FW*, 145), "Shakhisbeard" (*FW*, 177), "Scheekspair" (*FW*, 191), "Great Shapesphere" (*FW*, 245), Joyce's late-style high modernist baroque and post-modernist/neo-baroque masterwork, *Finnegans Wake*.

The subjective practice of patience includes the act of reading for pondering, interpreting, pausing and engaging various sorts of creation, such as cognitive and communal acts that serve as instances of 'now-time'. For Joyce's most masterful masterpiece assuredly needs a reader within the straight and narrow of uncommon resources of an immunizing and monastic patience. Nothing less is required to do the text any measure of experiential or interpretive truth and justice. Umberto Eco's *The Aesthetics of Chaosmos: The Middle Ages of James Joyce*[5] takes a measure of Joyce's medieval sensibility. But here the concern pertains to the notion of an exercise and practice in patience that was so vital a property of one spirit of the Christian tradition of the medieval era via Thomas à Kempis's *The Imitation of Christ* (*De Imitatione Christi*), and in the late twentieth century, in Maurice Blanchot's late-style fragmentary *The Writing of the Disaster* (*L'Écriture du désastre*).

The basic thesis here indicates that Blanchot and Kempis are closer than what orthodox forms of literary/intellectual historiography may teach us to believe, and that with the Joyce of *Finnegans Wake*, these three figures constitute an illuminating trio to tackle the concepts of the strange/the stranger and the patient, and by extension allow us to think about the problematic of forms of existence, creation and community. In so doing, parenthetically, the text enacts Daniel W. Smith's take on Gilles Deleuzian aesthetics, which entails (drawing from Deleuze's own early *The Logic of Sense*) "1. *The Destruction of the World* (Singularities and Events) [,] 2. *The Dissolution of the Subject* (Affects and Percepts) [,] 3. *The Dis-integration of the Body* (Intensities and Becomings) [,] 4. *The 'Minorization' of Politics* (Speech Acts and Fabulation) [,] 5. *The 'Stuttering' of Language* (Syntax and Style)."[6]

Kempis in a fifteenth-century Latin text (c. 1418–1427), *The Imitation of Christ/De Imitatione Christi* records such things that invoke the relation the reader might have to Joyce's neo-baroque perfervid late modernist *Finnegans Wake*. Kempis: "it is only by patience and true humility that we can grow stronger than all our foes."[7] As for *Finnegans Wake*, it is only with critical and attentive patientness that we can truly unfold the multiple folds of meaning and of sound effects of Joyce's text. It may also be a way to 'grow stronger' than the 'foe' of the enemy work, *Finnegans Wake* if not also the 'foe' of the nemesis author, Joyce. A form of immunizing patience and even of 'humility' the text requires, for it needs unstinting, if not courageous persistent energy on the reader's part, to pursue patient textual analysis. Or, as *Finnegans Wake* itself goes, "Now, patience; and remember patience is the great thing, and above all things else we must avoid anything like being or becoming out of patience" (*FW*, 108). This is of paramount importance if, as Edward W. Said says of two more (neo-) baroque authors, "The rare perfected text, however, is like Mallarmé's *Livre* or Joyce's *Finnegans Wake* — a form of perpetual writing, always at the beginning."[8] In *Finnegans Wakean* truth, Joyce's principal output continuously occurs at the emergent center of things; this is why it needs always to be read and reread. For it is precisely that sort of aesthetic object that wants in the Saidian-spirit to get back to one *now-time* example that would be the beginning of things, and in so doing to offer itself up as a new experience of the textual world for new awarenesses and understandings.

The late-style Joyce parallelepiped activates the participative structures of reading and of looking wherein in this book of the night, dawn continuously breaks for a world spirit. A new line of light is on the horizon that might speak to our contemporaneity and to our horizons too for existence and creation, insofar as how we read also informs how we live. Existence comes from existence, creation arises from creation, the commons derives from the commons and practice makes refined if not perfect.

Joyce was exiled both biographically and literarily from his native cultural soil, and so too are his readers driven into exile from canonical or regulatory and instrumental forms of meaning. In this way, the Joyce-text in Deleuzian parlance, "stutters". For like all art, his book in part invokes the communal aspect of a people or a commons as of yet to come in "a minorization of politics" Deleuze-style. As for the perspective the individual with forbearance displays? The awesome force of the patient subject and of the trials and tribulations she must endure inform the counter-spirituality of peculiar patience embedded as minor and centrifugal concept and practice regarding one's engagement as reader agent in the construction of meaning and experience with the textual and ideological space of *Finnegans Wake*.

Joyce enacts the crowning as molar and centripetal authority-figure. Or: as Sheldon Brivic argues of a Derrida-essay, "Joyce plays the role of God powerfully in the language of the *Wake*."[9] Indeed not unlike Yahweh who has an ostensible perverse sense of humor, so too, one might argue, does Joyce. For Joyce has as well other Yahwistic characteristics, such as extreme demands on his readers as subject-agents to exercise their radically (de)creative powers of reading and of thinking: incarnate forms of immunization and community for the world spirit.

As for the classic insomniac Joycean "ideal reader suffering from an ideal insomnia" (*FW*, 120), consider the following from Kempis: "Why do you look for rest, since you are born to work? Dispose yourself to patience rather than comfort, and to the carrying of the cross rather than pleasure" (*IOC*, 81). The wellspring and agent of maturation and justice, the care, attention and recognition of courageous and joyous exercise and praxis of patience allows for something wonderful to happen. Pleasure reductively defined too should be discarded for the power of the cross. Something comparable may be said of Joyce's last novel-testament, in which despite the jouissance effect of *Finnegans Wakean* language, it takes considerable, if not decidedly strange patience, to get to the level where one can experience complex and non-reductive *Finnegans Wakean* aesthetic pleasure and en-joy(ce)-ment. For one must first bear the crosses of the cultural experience and time of reading the individual *Finnegans Wakean* page as an agent within the global community of literature.

That one has crosses to bear, and perhaps even mount the cross as *Finnegans Wakean* reader when necessary as a form of immunization, may herein be gleaned: "Look up or down, without you or within, and everywhere you will find the Cross. And everywhere you must have patience, if you wish to attain inner peace, and win an eternal crown. If you bear the cross willingly, it will bear you and lead you to your desired goal, where pain shall be no more; but it will not be in this life" (*IOC*, 85–86). "Inner peace" then as an aim is exigent, for the long-term victories and gains obtainable by steadfast tranquility will result in "an eternal crown". It is one scourge of the present age of diminished expectations, to eschew engaging such a document as the eminently immunizing *Finnegans Wake* precisely because of its extravagant neo-baroque strangeness and uniqueness. Yet contrariwise, the text asks for a broad-minded, even democratic bow to its wonderful weirdness, which after all is what makes it a conductor of Niklas Luhmannian "variability" (or creativity in more classical humanist parlance). For such textual oddness contributes to how the *Finnegans Wakean* reading subject may in Rancière's words be forced to a state of affairs wherein "making a virtue of usefulness, playing the card of function, is merely to preserve one's dissimilarity".[10] The patient labors *Finnegans Wake* summons enable the reader to transform the ancient Greek and Nietzschean tradition to become who they are; to retain their particularity.

Concerning the task of reading *Finnegans Wake* wall-to-wall––a patient exercise that requires considerable practice? One must say no to the grand temptations of engaging the major strategy of centripetal impatience, and yes to sacral reading time and space with the difficulty if not discomfort of *Finnegans Wake*. The book's 'variability' and difficulty constitute it as a top-level tome and as companion for a strong and creative reader subject and even reader object. As a literary/cultural Everest, *Finnegans*

Wake institutes a powerful reader able to climb to the peaks of imaginative literature.

Also, the 626-page *Finnegans Wake* deconstructs one's interpretive identity, even univocal identity itself, so that a radical exacerbation of multiple readings coexists. Hence Joyce's work undermines the idea of the egoisms of forms of impatience, and also by extension of forms of the world and of society, such as suggested in Kempis. Text/reader or author/reader relationships of authority, domination, power and intimidation too are on some level blown to smithereens. This is so insofar as *Finnegans Wake* constitutes a dissensual, and not a consensual, cultural system, which mediates the minor ("minorization" see Smith above on Deleuze's aesthetics) strategy of the complicated volume. As such Joyce's book awaits its readers and its communal/political subjects yet to arrive.

What is more, the notion of *Finnegans Wake* as a spiritual weapon in a hostile and impatient world is to be incorporated for a reading agent mediated by so many immunizations and forms of updated cultural weaponry. Assuredly the corruptions of the social order will attempt to hijack the good text from its immunitary function: to be read and re-engaged. Anti-progressives with regard to *Finnegans Wake* will be in some publics a dime a dozen. Subversive readers therefore, to echo Marx and Engels, must unify. In an injunction from Kempis that reminds one what *Finnegans Wake* needs for its ongoing reading, "Dispose yourself not to rest, but to patient endurance" (*IOC*, 141). Quiet and patient even minor centrifugal steadfastness with the practice of reading *Finnegans Wake* then is what is exigent, which includes reading the work out loud and even just looking at and observing it. The patient attention required of the reader of *Finnegans Wake* is undoubted and has the last laugh, if not the last word. The common experience of the community of readers of Joyce's *Finnegans Wake* promotes patience.

As to the ideology of productivity for productivity's sake

in intellectual work, Søren Kierkegaard puts paid the truth to that lie: "A real achievement, the fruit perhaps of several years' strenuous work, always enjoins a certain silence—which embarrasses the age, indeed causes offence—it has something of the odour of aristocracy. [...] The whole age is, from one end to the other, a conspiracy against real achievement [...]"[11] (1st ellipsis with brackets in original). That Joyce took seventeen years to compose *Finnegans Wake*, bears the issue out of the patient and immunizing communal-like energies required to produce good writing. Or, as Theodor W. Adorno declares in *Minima Moralia: Reflections from Damaged Life*: "Since there are no longer, for the intellectual, any given categories, even cultural, and bustle endangers concentration with a thousand claims, the effort of producing something in some measure worthwhile is now so great as to be beyond almost everybody."[12] This may seem manifest, including the difficulty of writing something good and of lasting value about *Finnegans Wake* for the community of the work's scholars and general readers.

Let us now enlist Blanchot's major late modern/postmodern neo-baroque late work that telescopes in allegorical fashion the catastrophic losses and outcomes of the twentieth century, *The Writing of the Disaster* (which the present author also engages vis-à-vis *Finnegans Wake* in a different tack in another study on *The Philosophical Baroque: On Autopoietic Modernities*), so as to spotlight the concept of patience that figures so prominently in multiple ways for constructing the communal aspect of a *Finnegans Wake* community subject and object. First, Blanchot mentions: "Patience opens me entirely [...]. Patience can neither be advised nor commanded: it is the passivity of dying whereby an I that is no longer I, answers to the limitlessness of the disaster, to that which no present remembers" (*WD*, 13–14). *Finnegans Wake* enacts this process with a certain exactitude. Patience opens a window onto the minor and centrifugal passivity involved in perishing, including the reader's minute "dying" in spending time reading the compositional work of *Finnegans Wake*.

US scholar Herman Rapaport writes of "the condition of Joyce's *Wake*, the sign of an ancient fear that has swamped Joyce's text in a war in which language becomes what Blanchot calls the *écriture du désastre*."[13] Blanchot adds furthermore on an immunizing procedure that opens the self for another experience of the breakdown of a relational energy of another possible outcome, "Through patience, I take upon myself the relation to the Other of the disaster — the relation which does not allow me to assume it, or even to remain myself in order to undergo it. Through patience, all rapport between myself and a patient self is broken" (*WD*, 14). This disbanding of the self also disarticulates the practical fiction of the egoistic interpretive self that finds itself disorganized in *Finnegans Wake*. In this dynamic multiple meanings and identities coexist given how simultaneously different exegetical selves coexist for the production of another sort of creative/interpretive community that would be part and parcel with immunity for the plural self.

Moreover, we read in Blanchot:

> when the imminent silence of the immemorial disaster caused him, anonymous and bereft of self, to become lost in the other night where, precisely, oppressive night [...] separated him so that the relation with the other night besieged him with its absence [...] from that moment on, the passion of patience, the passivity of a time without present [...], had to be his sole identity, circumscribed by a temporary singularity. (*WD*, 14)

The double coinage, "the passion of patience" "had to be his sole identity" accords to the passion of (de)creative writing that describes the Blanchot or Joyce writing hand. The immunizing passion of reading too must thrive. It takes indefatigable mental work to activate the processes of understanding the communal and world spirit facet of the nighttime text that is *Finnegans*

Wake's dream language.

Now, for patience and its nuances and forms. One must tap into the energies of the neutral for Blanchot, the latter of which takes place "between writing and passivity" (*WD*, 14). As for the undeniable, perhaps even atypical forms of masochistic suffering that one may endure while reading *Finnegans Wake* as a form of immunization as well as a community and a world spirit feeling, these words from Blanchot are relevant for de-creative meditation: "Passivity: we can evoke it only in a language that reverses itself. I have, at other times, referred to suffering: suffering such that I could not suffer it."

> If I had recourse to the thought of such suffering, it was so that in this un-power, the excluded I from mastery and from its status as subject (as first person)—the I destitute even of obligation—could lose itself as a self capable of undergoing suffering. (*WD*, 15)

Something close to this should occur if the reader, while pursuing *Finnegans Wake*, experiences herself as a suffering agent with others. Or, rather in a collective community of suffering beings in which that is what is shared. This would mobilize the emancipatory potentials of *Finnegans Wake* as an agent too for a "General Ascetology" about which Sloterdijk expostulates in *You Must Change Your Life* for the twenty-first century. Such a disposition would be beneficial for a rethinking of such concepts as wealth or property and of true radical agency/ies.

For US literary scholar Kevin Hart: "Reading for Blanchot [...] is part of the work [...]. Every work, regardless of its genre, is at heart a 'dialogue,' [...] he has something more like a fight than a discussion in mind. [...]. To read is [...] to make the work communicate. [...]. For Blanchot, the reader as well as the writer is a *makar* [a poet]."[14]

The work must communicate its Luhmannian-variability for

the reader's amplified sense of an emancipatory critical agency for newfangled critical agencies to create and to give a work meaning and value for the movement and event of community. For 'every work is a dialogue' in the critical sense of a struggle, 'a fight'. This is vital, and gives an enlarged sense of force and import to the reading subject, who also becomes an object in an immunizing procedure against this false dichotomy of reader and text. Enter Blanchot again: "passivity is, perhaps (perhaps), that 'inhuman' part of man which, destitute of power, separated from unity, could never accommodate anything able to appear or show itself." Adds Blanchot, "passivity matters to man without moving him over into the realm of things that matter [...] passivity is posed or deposed as that which would interrupt our reason, our speech, our experience" (WD, 16). These are useful claims, for they show how the inhuman part of humankind precisely constitutes that which awaits and understands the new that would engender the new human and new community through fresh awarenesses, understandings, practices and exercises for a new calculus of reasons. This aids our meditations on strategies for engaging a different *Finnegans Wake* community and world spirit to come. Herein Blanchot aims at a new tone and tonality of passivity.

Not unimportant for Blanchot in a claim about an incapacity for passivity to actually go all the way to the end and to truly identify with itself, "passivity is never passive enough. [...] there is in passivity something like a demand that would require it to fall always short of itself" (WD, 16). That "passivity is never passive enough" highlights the potent force of the minor-centrifugal notion, for passivity could produce-create another experience of subjectivity, creation and the commons. Also passivity unleashes the idea of negativity insofar as negativity is itself the historical process of time's power including the power of death. Blanchot poses the question, "If, in the patience of passivity, my self takes leave of me in such a way that in this outside [...]"

> the time of patience [...] has no more support, no longer finding anyone to sustain it, then by what language other than fragmentary [...] can time be marked [...]? But the fragmentary [...] also escapes us. Silence does not take its place [...]. (*WD*, 18–19)

One must be vigilant in reading this passage and its multiple dimensions. Not even silence occurs. This is a situation with a special semantic and creative value. Even the logic of disintegration, and of the fragment, falls out and does not happen.

Crucially, according to Blanchot at a strategic level of engaging discourse, "I must answer for the persecution that opens me to the longest patience [...]. I must come back to knowledge; I must return [...] to the I that knows [...] to the adverse I, to egotistical"

> Omnipotence, to murderous Will. Naturally, this Will draws me thereby into its game and makes me its accomplice, but that is why there must always be at least two languages, or two requirements: one dialectical, the other not; one where negativity is the task, the other where the neutral remains apart, cut off from being and from not-being. (*WD*, 20)

This complex passage lines up with the cultural experience of encountering *Finnegans Wake*. On the one hand, we need the pole of a classically Hegelian dialectical approach. Yet we also need in polar opposite fashion to understand what escapes the reductively standardized Hegelian dialectic (which commentators such as Žižek underscore, not least in *Less than Nothing: Hegel and the Shadow of Dialectical Materialism*, does not capture the truest essence of Hegel's dialectic). Indeed, as a form of subjectivity, the language in *Finnegans Wake* ostensibly wants to escape this specific dialectic of a posited and standardized Hegel. But the language is constantly running up against its own demarcation within the linguistic horizon, which is of the same order of the Hegelian dialectic, per se. This is illumined in how almost everything is dialecticizable in *Finnegans Wake* (that is, you can find the opposite end for any content, form etcetera dialectical effect). In this way, in *Finnegans Wake*, dynamic movement or the fertilizing power of cross-resonance win out over against the precise linguistical unit.

Vitally for Blanchot, "Passivity is a task—but in a different language: in the language of the nondialectical drive—just as negativity is a task in the language wherein the dialectic proposes to us the realization of all possibilities, provided we know how [...] to let time take all its time" (*WD*, 27). Therefore passivity is also an event, or a movement of community that allows time its true potency. Passivity may also be said to constitute a certain task, if not also a structure. Nondialectically, passivity must be an endless task within the dialectic that is language's fate so far in the human tradition.

In a Blanchot-remark that clarifies the understanding, "Human weakness [...] penetrates us on account of our belonging at every instant to the immemorial past of our death—on account of our being indestructible because always and infinitely destroyed [...] this is the measure of passivity" (*WD*, 30). *Finnegans Wake* razes the egoistic interpretable self to the ground with its invocation, provocation and acceleration of freshly forged feelings, perceptions and concepts for recognition in the community movement that is the individual multiple formed (self-) identity. In a Deleuzoguattarian schematic this comprises centrifugal and minor affects, percepts and concepts. So, if we are infinitely deterritorialized as univocal readers, we shall be to that extent activators "of passivity" toward the dynamics of community movements and events.

Pointedly, we glean from Blanchot's late work, "it could

be that all names [...] are an effect of impatience" (*WD*, 39). Joyce's writing of high attentiveness—witness his 17 years of slow laborious attention to *Finnegans Wake*—reenact this sort of process of compositional patience. Also, that the unit of composition of the Oxford English Dictionary the mot (the word) is impatient, shows why Joyce sought to engender time and again the new word. Thought's justice requires new words to capture new realities.

Curiously, in Blanchot, "If spirit is always active, then patience is already nonspirit: the body in its suffering passivity [...]. Patience is the cry beneath the word: not the spirit; the letter" (*WD*, 40). This makes critical sense, and yet in the ongoing world-historical struggle between power and spirit one wonders if patience is not also on the side of spirit as well as on that of a new form of political power? In this case, would not Blanchot be mistaken? In another instant, from Blanchot's late-style text, "When knowledge is no longer a knowledge of truth, it is then that knowledge starts: a knowledge that burns thought, like knowledge of infinite patience" (*WD*, 43). This is a radical truth for radical creativity, and even for a revolutionary thinking community event of the world spirit. The exercise and practice of reading *Finnegans Wake* evokes this dimension of a transformation. Blanchot's thinking welcomes us to consider and to experience this phenomenon as a reading agent and object.

In more thoughtful claims from Blanchot we read of a crucial difference between "'it is necessary' and not 'you must' — perhaps because the second formula is addressed to a *you* and the first is an affirmation outside law, without legality, an unnecessary necessity. All the same, an affirmation? a manifestation of violence? I seek a passive 'it is necessary,' worn out by patience" (*WD*, 44). The title of the present chapter, with reference to 'bearing crosses', owes something to the foregoing, with respect to the idea of 'it is necessary' to bear crosses. Freedom itself would be grounded by a concept of itself that would incorporate precisely the notion of necessity. What is more, from Blanchot, *"But something binds me to this ancient adventure, infinite and foreign to meaning, though all the while, at the heart of the disaster, I continue to seek it as that which does not come, and to await it, when it is the patience of my waiting"* (*WD*, 44). This articulates the nexus of patience and strangeness for the reader of Joyce's last major work; for it requires patient forms of primal energy, including for the production of forms of community as so many positive entities and movements. Here though there is no easy recuperation for meaning. Meaning must be fought and struggled for with a deep and rebuilt critical agency that would profit from figures and forms of the creative critic, and so by extension of the exercise, force and practice of the (de)creative reading life for a cultural sensibility to come. This would be an index of forms of immunization and of the world spirit commons. Joyce scholar Harry Burrell asks of the dedication that the complex *Finnegans Wake* provokes: "Why do some of us spend a lifetime rereading, puzzling, and writing about it? [...]. The answer has to be that it is esthetically satisfying as no other form of literature has ever been. It is perhaps the epitome of twentieth-century artistic endeavor in all the fields of the arts."[15] Not only this, the community-relations that the book invites and constructs inspire its engagers to ardent work in and devotion to the textual space of Joyce's summa tome.

In addition, for Blanchot, in a gesturing toward a certain power of the drive and of the spirit of asceticism, "to write without desire belongs to patience, the passivity of writing" (*WD*, 44) and the reclusive writer adds the following statement, "In its patientness the body is thought already—still just thought" (*WD*, 45). These two extracts make sense for the construction of another sensibility for community and the creative life or for a finely accomplished balance between these two figures and forms of being: creativity and the commons. Patience emerges here as a major player.

The institution of death? In Blanchot it "is the infinite patience of that which is never accomplished once and for all" (WD, 69). Moving on to the Blanchot-neutral, which is the outside, and the impossible, "We should perhaps, while keeping well outside of mysticism, hear what we hear not: the undemanding, the disastrous demand of the neutral—the effraction of the infinitely passive" (WD, 74). Exactly the impossible we need today for another sociality and community. In such a dynamic move and modality of impossible/possible creativity, we may exist and create in ways commensurate to our potentialities. This idea of "the infinitely passive" also maps onto a threshold experience wherein the reader as agent and object via passivity gets back to a new beginning, so as to begin again with new contingencies on hand that might be played with and engaged to effective ends; this would be like Agamben's notion of decreation.[16]

In a (de)creative mobilization of the force of suggestion, the reader of Joyce's late-style work brings the novelistic or the new into existence. *Finnegans Wake* wants to actualize this power of being at the heart of engenderment, of that which does not yet exist, because patience has not short-circuited a negative telos or goal. Furthermore, Blanchot adduces "Valéry: '*The thinker is locked in a cage and paces indefinitely between four words.*' What is said pejoratively here is not pejorative: repetitive patience, infinite perseverance" (WD, 107). The repetitive and strange sort of patience that spawns a certain steadfastness describes this activity of exercising and creating with the *munus* the gift of *Finnegans Wake* that constructs between the reader and text another sort of community relation if not immunization. Therefore, a strangely cosmic and affective magic-like readerly participation *Finnegans Wake* requires; this would be for a cosmic and magically participative citizen to engage in a democratic salute to the cosmic riches of the contents and formal aspects of *Finnegans Wake* for the general cultural sensibility standing behind one's creative projects and commitments.

In a word, a provocatively weird double dosage of patience may mediate a new verbal and political order, a renewed world to emerge from these mockeries of words from the jazzing of *Finnegans Wakean* ones. For the fundamental point has been glossed over; if *Finnegans Wake* is difficult, it is because we must patiently struggle and suffer for the achievement of our meanings. Patient strangeness or strange patience is where extreme idealism and extreme realism meet for new events, forms and movements of critical and political agency, hope and perseverance. The continuous lost opportunities for meaning in *Finnegans Wake* cast a spotlight instead on those that really matter in ordinary reality for our forms of individual and collective experience and struggle precisely for the individual and for the creative commons of the world spirit.

To move registers, Luhmann argues in a book of essays translated as *Observations on Modernity* "when observing observations, it is interesting that they are formulated at all. And it is possible, reverting to the usual manner of socioscientific explanations, to conclude from this that society develops figures of thought with which it can endure the unobservability of the world and allow intransparency to become [end of book no punctuation mark in text after 'become'][.]"[17] This is true and it is perhaps telling that there is no punctuation after the word, become, in this Luhmann book. The movement of the becoming community continues its growth, task and struggle to come into being. There is also no period on the last page of *Finnegans Wake*.

In another worthy Luhmann point, "The more complex the system becomes and the more it exposes itself to irritations, the more variety the world can permit without relinquishing any reality—and the more the system can afford to work with negations, with fictions, with 'merely analytical' or statistical assumptions which distance it from the world as it is."[18] When Luhmann notes, "What is at stake in art is not a problem to be solved once and for all but a provocation—the provocation of a search for meaning that is constrained by the work of art without necessarily being determined in its results"[19] it teaches us to know that the task of the artwork is to stir us into the dimensions of a struggle and a project. As for being patient for the effects of meaning, we read in Luhmann "the work of art presents itself to observation as a series of intertwined distinctions, whereby the other side of each of these distinctions demands further distinctions."

> The work becomes observable as a series of deferrals (*différance* in Derrida's sense) that objectify the perpetually deferred difference in the 'unmarked space' of the world, thus rendering it unobservable as difference. All of this shows [...] that a work of art emerges only on condition that the world's invisibility is respected.[20]

Without a doubt this is the case. The 'world's invisibility' has some concordance and confluence with the power of the impossible, and of the world spirit, which is everywhere to be found if the right evental energy and disposition are locatable.

This present unorthodox reading of *Finnegans Wake* offers hints for how to resist an impatient world in order to exist and to create/decreate. Also: to be together in heterogeneous, and even peculiar forms and movements of human, posthuman and nonhuman togetherness and inter-cultural agencies and communities as so many exercises and forms of practice for the world spirit as so many indices of a more real and valid universality. In a world of power, the *Finnegans Wake* problem thus might provoke our futurity for the oppositional and counter-creative energy of the life of the spirit of mutuality, cooperative responsibility and our shared universalism.

Chapter 6

Bataille's *The Atheological Summa* (1943–45)

To expand this investigation for a deeper and a more radical understanding of the politics of possibility for thinking communal reality and the (de)creative life, this chapter will elucidate coordinates of a general aesthetics of individual and communal existence from Georges Bataille's trinity of texts entitled *La Somme athéologique/The Atheological Summa*. The present account will also take a backward glance at Bataille's predecessor Thomas Aquinas (circa 1225–74), to contextualize Bataille's emancipatory theory of the general economy that allows us to rethink and to reconceive notions of community and the creative life as so many indices of a more genuine universality concordant with cosmic structures of being, such as a world spirit.

Before Bataille's *The Atheological Summa/La Somme athéologique*, there was in the late thirteenth century Aquinas's *Theological Summa* (*Summa theologiae/Summa Theologica*). Both of these megaworks of roughly 680 years of temporal distance between them may be seen to "borrow" from the vocabulary of Roberto Esposito in another context (that of the law): "to immunize the community from its self-destructive tendencies [...]."[1] In Aquinas's case, this self-immunizing function gives birth to forms of textual creation for Aquinas found the specificity of his drive or passion, or Spinozan immanence. In an account from Davies we read of Aquinas's propensity for

abstraction or concentration. One of the most famous concerns an occasion in 1269 when he was dining with King Louis IX of France. According to his biographer Bernard Gui, Aquinas, who seemed often to be 'rapt out of himself' when thinking, spent most of the meal pondering on the Manichees (a religious sect dating from the third century AD). Suddenly he struck the table and exclaimed, 'That settles the Manichees!', whereupon he called for his secretary to come and take dictation. He explained to the alarmed dinner guests, 'I thought I was at my desk.'[2]

This illuminates how Aquinas's mode of being went hand in hand with his desire for a form of cultural output that proves a major revolution in contemplating on precisely such classic subjects as spiritual adventures of existence, the commons and creation.

After a period of torrential creativity Aquinas died at the age of 49, a reminder of the importance to pursue the creative life and community while one still has (now-) time and agency to do so. In a pre- yet also proto-Leibnizian mode of being, Aquinas's polymathic approach to thought and to culture—he engaged philosophy, science, theology—aids and abets Aquinas's (Doctor Angelicus's) capacity to create influential ideas about existence and community, ancient thematic concerns that have preoccupied the human experiment. In Davies's account the Doctor Communis (Aquinas), "gave his life to God and he did so wholeheartedly in a way which came to inspire others" (*TTA*, 14) and "he was very open-minded. Unlike many of his followers, he was a cautious thinker not given to supposing that any one authority has all the answers" (*TTA*, 16). So, with regard to method, Aquinas would endorse a certain rapprochement or syncretism, as well as a broad-mindedness to contest forms of provincialism and dangerous narrow-mindedness if not ideological fascism (nationalism, disciplinarizing professionalisms, scientism and so forth) for instead forms of community spirit building cosmopolitanism and universality. Wide mindedness is precisely what we need today in an era of soft authoritarianisms mediated in many contexts by what Dupuy articulates:

> The debilitating character of specialization is largely responsible for this alarming state of affairs. [...]. Hypercompetitive—which is to say hyperspecialized—science can hardly contribute anything of value to a generally shared sensibility that might, in its turn, shape society's capacity to act upon itself for the good.[3]

Aquinas's ecumenical mode of intellectual production militates against this, which is one reason why this friar is more influential and important than the more publicly recognized intellectuals of his own epoch. On this, there is an affinity between Aquinas and another protagonist in our study, Benjamin, who also sought to immunize himself against an overdone specialization. The gift the *munus* of their example is to actualize a polymathic creative life. And to say no to money, power and titles.

Furthermore, in his questing for truth the eclectic Aquinas believed multiple sources may aid real knowledge. This syncretic belief and practice would also prove of help today as a general exercise and practice in comparative cultural work. Crucially, Aquinas made his basic subject area problems of existence, creation, community, destiny and God. These topics are of lasting fascination in the human experiment and inform the current textual exploration. Faith, hope and charity are the key theological virtues for Aquinas, which permit access to God, not through nature but via grace. The classic trinity of Christian virtues that accord to powerful spirits of grace, namely faith, hope and charity inform the logic of development of community relations and of the creative life. This is so, even as we try to imagine forms of political, (de)creative, and educational hope for the individual and for the collective symbolic substance.[4]

To move to Bataille's Aquinas-inspired title *The Atheological Summa*, we read of several lines of approach to the question of what constitutes the sacral aspects and spaces of experience; also, of what various avenues of inquiry may say to the contemporary situation in the mid-twentieth century, just as it requires a considerable overhaul of its own sort of theological rationality or sacral return, which itself might be called an (in)authentic (so a true authentic) non-sacred. First, for Bataille, "Time is freedom"[5] and richly, "There is no wall between eroticism and mysticism! It's really quite funny—since they use the same words, deal in identical images, and they refuse to recognize it!" (*ON*, 131). Indeed we may say that today it is for those who have time on their side to say, *they are truly free, rich or wealthy.* The importance of freedom we herein discern: "In the essence of humanness a fierce impulse seeks autonomy, the freedom to be. [...] is it any wonder that people today are dying for it?" (*ON*, xxi). Freedom as autonomy as a new sacred we may thus infer. Bataille frames this point earlier in a cry for immunization and community in *Guilty*:

> Your business in this world isn't to assure the salvation of a soul anxious for peace. Nor is it to provide your body with the advantages money brings. Your business is questing for an unknowable destiny. Because of this you'll have to struggle by hating limits [...] which the system of respectability sets up against freedom. [...] you'll need to arm yourself with secret pride and indomitable willpower.[6]

The challenge here is to burst the bounds of limits, and to say no to money, power and titles, to exist and create, for another commons and by extension too for another figuration and form of freedom and destiny. Also to be a contrarian spirit, and to overcome limitations set by the superegos (the consciences and value-ideals) of others and walls that have been erected to thwart radical creativity/decreativity remains a goal for an effective and potent decreative/creative life. A strategic vision for destiny is crucial for Jean Baudrillard and for this work. Therefore, it is impossible to overestimate this point here from Bataille. Time and again "secret pride and indomitable power" are both something that our figures and laborers in the present study illustrate in their work; for without such qualities they would not have been capable of their contributions and deeds.

Baudrillard maintains a need to think in bigger terms: "It's the destiny of the species that's in play. Now, it's much more difficult to believe in a project of the species."

> Even in our own day, nine-tenths of humanity is outside [...] a system of interpretation and recording which was born with modern times and will disappear. History is a kind of luxury Western societies have afforded themselves. [...] that it seems to be disappearing is unfortunate for us, but it allows destiny [...] to take over.[7]

In this model of thinking, destiny should concern us at the level of the individual and also of the species: also the curves of destinies, and of the need responsibly to take care of the future of the race, of the planet and of much else besides. Critical caretaking for systems of care should be paramount. In a related key, Baudrillard laments "the absence of destiny. We no longer live against the horizon of death—that is to say, the horizon of the symbolic murder, which would give a fantastic energy."[8] And because community can exist concomitantly with death it further diminishes our access to community in the contemporary material and spiritual situation of advanced capitalism and digital technology. Again Baudrillard, "The weakening of destiny, the lack of destiny, is our big issue."[9] It is imperative that we think of the end of what we are doing in regard to proper care and attention as forms of recognition that would be of service to the truth and to a laudable destiny. The limitations of a corporate modeling of life and so too of conquering individuality therefore need a reassessment for their recomposition, reconstitution and restructuring. The festival of capital requires this sort of attention for the life process, otherwise the toxic and dangerous aspects of the current system will get the upper hand to the detriment of forms of creativity, community and universality.

Conversely, in a lighter note Bataille contends, "The universe is FREE: it doesn't have anything to do" (G, 96) and argues: "I'm teaching the most cheerful and most difficult of moralities [...] since the difficulties in it aren't overcome with effort [...]" (G, 96). So although we endorse the idea of the (de)creativity of noble effortfulness to achieve our aims of realizing forms of the creative life, with Bataille we are given a crucial nuance that a certain intentionality and voluntarism is inadequate. Namely, there is also a levity or lightness of touch or creative indirectedness necessary to evacuate the makeshift entity of self-identity. The immunizations of creative work, community, discipline and play require here another rhythm and so too another exercise, practice and structure. The necessity of alienation to attain freedom Bataille evokes when he indicates how every individual "learns with bitterness that to struggle for a freedom is first of all to alienate ourselves. [...]. I can't acquire anything at all: I can only give and give unstintingly without the gift ever having as its object anyone's interest" (ON, xxvii). This effervescent stance reveals a desire to resist the reification of one's consciousness, for a self-identity in the service instead of a certain cosmosization or universalization of community relations. For one should self-give on behalf of the general and universalist community spirit. This is key as an existential device and drive of power and agency in a world preoccupied with constrained, destructive and reductive understandings of power. Notions of self-loss or self-surrender (with a nod of solidarity here to Mari Ruti's beautiful work on The Call of Character, 2014) combined with loyalty or persistence are relevant as a way to actualize self-finding. So what we need is a little more alienation, in order to find and to jump-start our projects as so many forms of self-overcoming and self-excellence.

As for the creation, exercise and practice of existence, Bataille reflects, "An entire human being is partly a clown, partly a God, partly crazy… and is transparence" (*ON*, xxix). This has congruence with the idea that the more reality a being has, the more that being contains truth aspects. In Bataille it is a non-instrumentalized mode of being that may attain true heights, "The only possible way for dissipation to reach the summit is by not intending it. The ultimate moment of the senses requires real innocence and absence of moral pretensions and, as a result, even a feeling of evil" (*ON*, 38). So Bataillean heroism has something unselfconscious, and a subtending sensation to it of nonorthodox subversiveness, insofar as such conduct will not have been precisely calculated in an era dominated by calculative thinking.

In another claim: "I regard the summit about which I've spoken as freedom" (*ON*, 46), which underlines the concept of liberty in *On Nietzsche* a tome that employs Nietzsche as an occasion and a point of departure to discuss the textual and ideological space of Bataille's own philosophy and thoughts (more than those of Nietzsche himself). Indeed, in Bataille's earlier *Inner Experience/L'expérience intérieure*, "The idea of being the dream of the unknown (of God, of the universe) is, it seems, the extreme point which Nietzsche attained."[10] This accords as much to Bataille himself, as it does to Nietzsche. Here the idea of (de)creativity would be key: to live at one with it and to base one's existence on (de)creativity. Use of the "de" in front here of the word creativity designates a more refined analysis or notion of a positive creation in a destructive world of overproduction and overkill structures, and etcetera, which often misapprehends true creativity.

Consider now Bataille's investment in combating against things as they are: "All profound life is heavy with the impossible"

(*IE*, 58). Our age also requires the idea of the impossible. Only thus can we begin to seek concordantly and concomitantly the advent of some different more worthy existence and community. The rendering possible of the impossible needs to apply to social and economic dimensions of existence in our contemporary situation in the same fashion as it does in other fields of attention, such as those of genetic engineering or of the capacities of the digital and the technological per se in its various most widely avowed manifestations. There is no reason for why positivistic areas of concern should have a monopoly on the social use of the categories of the possible and of the impossible. That is a sign of an authoritarian epistemological tyranny at work in the context of the larger vision about what is impossible and possible in our ideological and practical universe/multiverse. We do well to heed these lessons as we move forward into the third millennium.

Bataille makes the acute point: "knowledge is in no way distinct from me: *I am it*" (*IE*, 110). The idea that we can only create that which is part of how we live, teaches us to know about this concern for community. This holy grail quest to express the negative that drips from the Nietzschean page Bataille invokes, "Non-knowledge communicates ecstasy" and: "I have from the start wanted the extreme limit of what is possible" (*IE*, 123). This resonates with the title of the present study. The import of ecstasy may also be discerned in a key way: "The idea that there's no necessity in the world of objects, that ecstasy might be adequate to the world (and not God or objects to a mathematical necessity) appeared to me for the first time. Lifting me off the ground" (*ON*, 166). "Lifting me off the ground" holds a miraculous aspect. A miracle Bataille would want for the modalities of individual creation, existence and community to come. Maybe that would be the secret miracle of the achievement of meaning within the cultural medium of history for radical community and the creative life.

To return to Bataille's affecting and provocative *Guilty* (*Le coupable*), one of three works that form *The Atheological Summa/ La Somme athéologique*: "True desire is a desire for desire, not satisfaction" (*G*, xii). This has some correspondence with the ontological concept of drive that may be found in theoretical psychoanalysis. From the same volume, "more than truth, it's fear I'm after" (*G*, 6). This illumines how Bataille retains a (neo) baroque vision of fear of the beyond precisely because there is nothing beyond. Bataille writes in a turbocharged big finance neo-baroque world dominated by the universalism of a profit economy, "From now on I have to respond to impulses of freedom and whims" (*G*, 11). This retains a child-like exuberance, a counterblast to that of the world of the hegemony of the seriousness of financial capitalism and technology. Even sexual pleasure taps into this effervescence: "When I'm feeling such pangs of lust, I know best what I am" (*G*, 12). The question here though would be one of how to translate and to transpose (to sublimate in a word on some level) those intensities toward positive and productive ends and experiences for a love of existence, creation and the commons. For is not Bataille in fact part and parcel of a certain fashion of his time in making such critical observations? Would not the act of sublimation of such bodily intensities entail an activity that would constitute the ideal conditions for the production of creative knowledge work?

Further, Bataille elicits a combative tonality as a site for struggle when he writes that he is "determined to become a war-zone myself" (*G*, 15). Here Bataille as conceptual persona and as author transmute into a creative and ideological space for the production of something other. The librarian also seeks different registers from the conventional ones for cognizing phenomena when he speculates, "Laughter, lovemaking, even tears of rage and of my own impotence in knowing, these are means of knowing that can't be located on a plane of intelligence" (*G*, 16). A many-faceted non-knowing way of knowing might thus here be hypothesized. This is so even if the current study espouses the life of intelligent existence, for that too incorporates this disavowed or unconscious way of cognizing.

The absolute importance of the Nietzschean power of the false, the falsification of established doxa and values in order to create ideological space for the creation of new ones, Bataille articulates, "the value of knowledge, it seems, depends on its ability to make any conclusive image of the universe impossible. Knowledge destroys fixed notions and this continuing destruction is its greatness, or more precisely, its truth" (G, 25). Therewith we need an art of knowing how to stay in nonknowledge. Similarly, for Bataille's valuation of existence: "Isn't the whole secret of life the innocent destruction of whatever threatens to destroy enjoyment of life [...]" (G, 149). The notion of "the possibilization of the impossible" that Derrida champions in *Politiques de l'amitié* (1994)/*The Politics of Friendship* (1997), others share too from Jacques Rancière to Slavoj Žižek to Alain Badiou's notion of "laicized grace" (see Chapter 10). With Bataille this might herein be scanned, "the wild *impossibility* that I am, an impossibility that can't avoid limits but can't stay inside them either" (G, 25). The post-Hegelian notion that individuals might effectuate real social transformation Bataille also heralds.

The neo-baroque, polymathic and post-William Blake, Bataille argues of the need to "express life's exuberance by shouting at the top of my lungs" (G, 33). Here the potential energy of something like a God agent, or of a supreme being, needs reaffirmation and remediation. For those who complain that the cult of energy only adds to capitalist aggressivity, a certain energy must subtend even injunctions to be lazy, to not work, to embrace slowness, laxness and so forth in our projects, be they existential, intellectual, moral-ethical or political. In a statement that points toward Bataille's own later writings on the concept of the surplus economy, "useful objects have been responsible for our circumscribed individuality (short-sighted egotism) and the general banality of all our life" (G, 36). The forces of creativity would ask for a de-banalization of our life narratives by discarding the object and embracing the void that is always there for the sake of our life projects. The concept of life Bataille proceeds to celebrate in eroticized fashion: "Now all I want is to live—intoxication, ecstasy, my existence as naked as a woman's when wracked with desire" (G, 40). In regard to the limited linguistic power of words to represent what they purport to stand in for, Bataille considers, "The world of words is laughable. Threats, violence, and the blandishments of power are part of *silence*" (G, 40). That literature and silence comprise a fulcrum around which one may turn to excellent effect constitutes a form of communication and experience.

Thus, Bataille submits in a remark of coruscating intelligence about the meaning of silence, "Sovereignty isn't speaking—or it's deposed [...]" (G, 41). This strikes one as true. Sovereignty opens onto Nietzschean-like limits for Bataille when he ruminates that, "humanity's limit-point is divine. Or [...] humanity is divine when experiencing limits" (G, 105). This traverses the potent idea of existence, creation and the commons that occurs precisely because it would experience limits as limit experiences to be surmounted and travelled beyond, even further than a classically conceived God agent.

Consider one of the most enigmatic statements in all of Bataille, and one that is a radical inversion of Leibniz's philosophy: "Future holiness will long for evil" (G, 41). This may discomfit us in the wake of World War Two, the death camps and so on, as something unconscionable to speak about, and yet it is a question not of evil, but of the need to break some materials (metaphorically) on certain occasions to make one's point. Also it was of course for many communities, let us not forget, that surely leading religious figures were radical evil par excellence. This stance from Bataille is also a commentary about the necessity of a culture of rebellion on behalf of meritorious historical aspirations and struggles. Additionally, in a claim that valorizes ecstasy as an access to a space and place of transcendence, "Only 'sovereign' being knows ecstasy, if ecstasy isn't accorded by God!" (*G*, 41). Further, from the same text in another clarification, "sacrifice is on the side of evil, evil that is necessary for good" (*G*, 20) and in another tome that engages Nietzsche: "I think the basic aspect of the *will to power* is overlooked if it is not seen as the *love of evil*: not as usefulness, but as a value signifying the summit" (*ON*, 148). These remarks from Bataille may be seen in a post-Nietzschean light. Capitalist insubordination Bataille here aims at, not "evil" per se, but instead the wherewithal to combat the world of finance that would with a corrosive power over-standardize and regularize one's life substance and mode of reality. That is the real evil that must be toppled by Bataille's sovereign evil that allows for more moral-ethical modalities of being for radical creativity and communal forms alike.

In a crucial point from *Guilty*: "Constant human errors would express the incomplete character of reality—and so of truth. Knowledge proportionate to its object—if that object is incomplete in its very being—would develop in every way" (*G*, 42). This rings true with respect to the basic unfinished nature of reality and of knowledge in the field of quantum physics. This also informs our overall sense of the nature of things and to the rightness of our claims for the invention and renewal of the processes of the creative joys and activities of life to intersect with and to conduct cultural communities.

With Bataille an experience of the relaxational as a way to depart the fictive self he aims at as something that has emancipatory potential, for the authority of a fictive self mediated by the symbolic order is problematic. The concept of transindividuality Bataille asks for when he suggests, "Truth starts with conversations, shared laughter, friendship and sex, and it only happens *going from one person to another*." More Bataille, "How little *self* matters then! [...]? I don't believe in God—from inability to believe in self. [...]. If we didn't project the *self* on the absolute we'd be convulsed with laughter" (*G*, 44–45). These important statements hold value; certainly many are as against the claims of capital, such as that of the discrete and consuming self. But if, "Truth has the structure of a fiction" as Jacques Lacan famously claims, then it is still possible and desirable, we may contend, to retain the idea of a God and of a self in the practical world and for practical reality. Only in this case the identity of each, a God and a self, should be subverted from within so that a Godless God or a 'selfless self' (Lacan) would be a proper state of affairs. Also, for Bataille in another form of universality: "The bottom line is: Anyone and everyone is part of me. Fortunately we usually don't notice this. But lovemaking brings out this truth" (*ON*, 93). This has implications for modes of community, existence, and creation in a way that require us to take social agency in a broader fashion, and so in a wider critical account that include the notion of transindividuality that many including Étienne Balibar, Bernard Stiegler and the present author try to bring out.

When Philippe Lacoue-Labarthe, among others, write of ecstasy as perhaps the key agency of transcendence of the later twentieth century if not beyond, one might be forgiven to imagine that this mentality may have in mind consciously or not Bataille's point, "If people never had the urge to look for pleasure (or joy) [Spinoza's key term, *laetitia* in Latin] and if the only thing that mattered was repose (satisfaction) and equilibrium, then the gift I'm contributing would be without meaning. This gift is ecstasy, it's a fitful play of lightning..." (*G*, 47). This could serve as a test case for thinking a new source of freedom, to wit, radical ecstasy and even joy for our political, social and cultural enterprises.

Bataille's self-confidence, icy resolve and courage are patent, "I'm hard and lucid in my mastery and decisiveness. Too sure of myself to stop where others can see only failure" (*G*, 62). Thus, both general and intellectual courage and a quality of will are necessary here for existence and creation. Moreover, for Bataillean fortitude: "Kindness, independence, contempt for conventionality gave me the self-confidence of a gambler" (G, 106). Existential and intellectual bravery shine out. Bataille's erotic aesthetics may be seen in these two provocative, if not for some problematic extracts for their morality, even though I believe that Bataille was always after a superpower morality: "Thought and morality can only be impoverishment if there's no glorification of the nakedness of an attractive whore intoxicated from having a male organ in her. Turning away from her glory is averting your eyes from the sun" (G, 68) and: "(You can't separate the body from the head either)" (G, 69), which nicely and paradoxically encapsulates a post-Spinozan erotically charged moment that may also be read in a rather more metaphorical way as about affirming the revolutionary energy of the power of the creative life and of forms of mutuality as community. In this context, the medieval librarian also writes, "With women, chance can be seen in signs readable on the lips, kisses that recall moments of deadly tumultuousness" (G, 77). This is an aesthetic moment of pure Bataille for its estimation of the sovereignty of chance, ecstasy and energy. As far as being a key site of struggle for the present effort to elucidate the construction of conditions for forms of community and the creative life, this foregoing passage may discomfit readers for its indulgence in commodified pleasures that are more a part of the problem than of the solution.

The charged and important concept of chance here also crops up: "reflection on chance strips the world bare of the entirety of predictions in which reason encloses it. Like human nakedness, the nakedness of chance [...] is obscene and disgusting: in short, *divine*. Since the course of the things of the world hangs on chance, this course is as depressing for us as a king's absolute power" (G, 71). Radical contingency then emerges paramount. In one reading therefore, the contingent character of reality is superordinate, which is discomfiting, for it evades the effectivity of all forms of conscientiousness and care, and yet this reality must be embraced and overcome with radical courage and with risk-taking. Additionally with regard to the same notion of chance, Bataille claims: "To want chance is *amor fati* (love of fate) [...]" (*ON*, 120). To test fate is perhaps the big thing; to create to surpass the limits of what is thought possible; that is, to bypass and transcend the discrepancies between ideals and reality to find new and efficient structures for the greater society would be the great thing including for the universality that we all innately share with one another. For we require these better and even bigger structures today for the aspiration and construction of a more truly world society.

As for Bataille's continuous concern with stretching out the possibilities of what is possible consider this remark, "A human being is also the opposite of a human being—the endless questioning of what his name designates!" (*G*, 77). Bataillean (and even thus arguably Galilean) morality points toward "it's not easy to maintain my childish 'take' on things (a laughing playfulness). Innocence and confidence are cruel [...]" (*G*, 99). The severity of the essence of "innocence and confidence" finds a place. In a claim that shows influence from his philosophical master, Nietzsche, Bataille also writes with provocativeness, "I'd belong to a somewhat changed species of humanity, one that has to overcome itself. This species would combine action and questioning (work and laughter)" (*G*, 110). This also sounds like what Negri-Hardt argue for, as far as engendering the mode of a new community of humanity with 'a new anthropology of the human' that we discussed in Chapter 2. Also, it accords to our sense of things that something absolutely if not intolerably radical would be necessary for the construction of a true world society community in which human intentions could exist and create for a creative commons. This would also be where a world spirit would be found. In multiple regards here a certain self-overcoming is paramount.

Bataille also pens for an enlarged picture: "I write for a different world—one that's indifferent to anything, anybody" (*G*, 113) and, "What am I if not a ray from some long-dead star [...]" (*G*, 113). What figure or temporality would embrace these two statements? Benjamin inspired messianic time of messianic instants? And what conception of space or territory? For both of these statements are notable for the decreative space they invite the reader to enter into for forms of critical and imaginative transformation. Would one response not be something as I have already suggested? Namely, Benjamin's 'now-time' of transtemporal possibility and forms of agency? Would not another response be something like a project of self and so by extension of other (communal) redemption? This is an instance of 'now-time' possibilities and of the valid power of the impossible. In other words, who will enact individual cultural memory for Bataille after his death, so that a revolutionary 'now-time' may see his cultural material and example as a lodestar to detonate at another period of time for a revolutionizing of the revolution? This is a challenge to take up, and to confront, for the twenty-first century of digital technology and of advanced capitalism toward another discernment of what constitutes true meaning, value and wealth for contemporary agency and universality.

For an anti-systematic thinker (like Benjamin and Blanchot), it is striking that Bataille makes this formulation: "A *system* precise as clockwork governs my thoughts (but I escape endlessly in this incompleteable work)" (*G*, 110). The structure remains open for conceptual cartographers of Bataille's edifice, and of the other temporality it mobilizes and activates. For Bataille too, "Time is the desire for time not to exist" (*ON*, 120). So another temporality is needed to revolutionize the time concept; one that resists reification so that time would cease to be subject to the law of the temporality that creates the interest that gets deposited into bank accounts. For Agamben, as we discussed in tandem with de la Durantaye's work in the Introduction, we need an idea of *kairology* to take the place of *chronology* in order to incorporate the revolutionary rhythms of a Benjaminean temporality of 'now-time'. This proves conceptually helpful for reassessing the problem of temporality in our present encounter with Bataille in thinking possibilities for the impossible: modes of community and the creative life in an era in which the kairological has become pronounced.

As for the concept that the self serves the interests of capital consider that for Bataille in truth, "We want [...] to be freed of ourselves. That's why there is such a feeling of intoxication when we find love [...]" (*G*, 110). This would be so because the self is a pragmatic fiction for the capitalist world. The special concern for revolutionizing the atomized and monadized subjectivity continues in this statement for philosophical criticism: "Essentially all beings are only one" (*ON*, 72), which articulates an idea of the universality that we all jointly experience one with another. In another mention of note, "Christian humility is disastrous, above all contradictory, related to an inevitable obsession with a *self*! Think of the monstrous immortality of the *egos* that are heaven and hell! Think of the God of *self* and the demented way he has ordered self's replication!" (*G*, 115). Ostensibly this is far from Aquinas's cultural work, and yet I submit not, for the basic energies of the power of the universe are being reaffirmed and remediated: existence, creation, and the commons, however differently defined under Bataille in the twentieth century as against under Aquinas in the European Middle Ages.

Bataille clearly wants the following basic coordinates to serve new forms of existential and geopolitical identification, "I'd like from now on to see the *self* in relation to something else" (*G*, 115). The autonomous and relational self should be in relation to something other than the conventional identity of a self classically conceived as well as normative forms of capital, ownership and property, not least because, "At the summit man is staggered. He is, at the summit, God himself. He's absence and sleep" (*G*, 116). In another word, the messiah has already come, or more exactly "we are ourselves the Messiah" (Löwy). We are thus too on some level absent. It is here that the Bataille concept of immanence imposes itself: "the return to immanence takes place at the elevation at which humanity exists. It raises humanity to where God was, bringing back to a human level the existence that seemed to overwhelm us" (*ON*, 145). In so doing, humanity discards the 'big Other' function in order to take infinite responsibility for itself and for a God who desperately needs aid on its behalf. Contrariwise, for Bataille as for realizing the keynote of a level of immanence in one's life work and narrative, sovereignty shines out in another divine law from that to which many human subjects have hitherto subjected themselves. The arguable intention of this Bataillean gesture is to attain through the grace of immanence one's creative modus vivendi.

In a strategical vision, for Bataille's system the gift or *munus* of "—immanence is received and is not the result of searching for it; it is wholly and entirely governed by chance [...]. **—immanence** exists simultaneously and in an indissoluble movement as both an immediate summit (which, from all standpoints, is the same as the individual's destruction) and a spiritual summit" (*ON*, 149). With Bataille, as with Spinoza (see Chapter 1), immanence is a mountain range from where one can recognize within one's self new chances for existence and creation, and so by extension too for the commons. Immanence again is another word for the unconscious and even a certain grace. What is more, creative, general and intellectual courage, discipline, humor and steadfastness are all needed to attain its high status. Intriguingly and importantly for Bataille, "although the summit escapes me when I search for it [...] I can make my life an ongoing evocation of possibilities" (*ON*, 149). What could be of more importance for thinking about existence, creation and community than opening up a prospect to an entirely different set of adventures, (im)possibilities, and procedures for new enterprises? These thoughts from Bataille are worth pondering for current and future generations trying to bring into existence the impossible summits, the highest aspirations, of models and modes of community and the creative life.

Accurately, for the Bataillean version of Nietzsche, "The state of immanence signifies *beyond good and evil*. And is related to nonascesis and to the freedom of the senses. This applies also to the innocence of risk. Upon reaching immanence, our life has finally left the stage of the masters behind [...]" (*ON*, 153). However, on the contrary a spirit of asceticism is necessary, however creatively and imaginatively defined and remediated. Therefore, exigent and helpful is a radical ascesis without fundamentalism; we must build on, extend and transform this tradition. Crucial here too with respect to the Bataille passage is that we have left behind the authority of the 'big Other', so that creative and community building agencies are upon us. We will have thus attained a sovereign immanence, an existence, creation and community of self and of other predicated on intersubjectivization for our ethical-moral, intellectual and political projects. A Nietzschean energy dynamics may be seen in the foregoing. This is when things are happening in an efficacious way: when we cannot define matters in a precise and overdetermined structuring sense that would over-instrumentalize our efforts.

In Bataille, "Only transcendence (discontinuity) is understood. Continuity is not understood except as related to the opposite. Pure immanence and the nothingness of immanence equate and signify *nothing* [...]" (*ON*, 160). The idea that nothing constitutes the true definition of sovereignty is a central motif in Bataille's corpus of texts. Crucially, Bataille exclaims, "insanely dedicating ourselves to the lie of transcendence! But in its dementia this lie lights up immanent immensity. [...] a true foundation before which the vanity of transcendence dissipates. [...]. And truly, we're guided to that point by a commonly noted light proclaimed by the word FREEDOM" (*ON*, 165–66). The empty space of freedom here would communicate the ideas of existence, creation and community locatable in our limitless immanence before our very eyes that we nonetheless are unable to access.

With respect to the concept of joy as against that of happiness as the highest value may be discerned in the following lines of Bataille: "Only a choice for celebration allows life to be lived [...]? Redemptive strength can be found only in explosive (and eternal?) joyousness. [...] Moralities, religions of compromise, hypertrophies of intelligence, all arise from the sadness that follows the time of celebration" (*ON*, 137–38). This may seem a harsh indictment of "moralities", but dialectically for Bataille we should enact "a choice of celebration" if we are to exist, create and live in meritorious communities. Also I incline to say that it is valid to argue as others already have that Bataille aims at a hypermorality. This view has detractors; Sloterdijk argues without noting Bataille's name, "Hypermorality plays into the hands of defiance and moral entropy."[11] This is a problem to reflect on for the Bataille apologist. In addition, what happens after revolutionary overthrow occurs is the crucial issue for making community relations work in equal-minded, free and just ways.

As for the politics of writing and of the reader for Bataille: "I'm so lacking any inclination to write for the unfriendly that, from the rest, the others, I ask *intuitive* understanding. Only friendly eyes can see far enough" (*ON*, 144). The cultural practices of friendship then if not also of kindness (Spinozan *modestia*) pave the way for liberatory becomings for existence, creation and community. This cannot be underestimated in a bourgeois cultural era preoccupied with commodities, power and status. Yet is this form of friendship not also a hypermorality and a form of community of the *munus* of *cum*? And is not Bataille's philosophy in its basic structure an extreme supermorality?

For literary scholar Leo Bersani, Bataille is "one of the first writers to reject the great modernist project of a domination of life through art."

> [...] the culture of redemption dreams of the erasure of history in art through a massive, encyclopedic, and transfiguring absorption of history into the artist's work. [...] but on the whole *Ulysses* and *A la recherche du temps perdu* have little patience for structurally unassimilated material or false starts. They seek to exclude the kind of repetition that makes visible within the work itself the actual process of working, the discovery of sense as a succession of always threatened, always local achievements. In this respect, Bataille's predecessor is D.H. Lawrence, for whom art was also a tormented encounter with sense rather than the occasion for repudiating experience by monumentalizing its meanings.[12]

Yet, as against Bersani, the idea of redemption is one to which Bataille himself too may subscribe, concerning the idea of redeeming one's existence and creative acts for another community to come. Additionally, Bataille's participatory and self-dialecticizing remarks are spoken to by Bersani who says that Bataille's (and Lawrence's) "fiction is compelled to abdicate any authority for resolving the dilemmas it poses, any superior point of view that could justify a broader cultural claim for art as a vehicle of truth."[13] This is true. Still the strong provocations remain from Georges Bataille to stir us to create and to exist with, for only then will our lives not be lived in vain, as he feared his was.

Volume one of Bataille's *The Accursed Share/La Part maudite*—the share of that which is in surplus in a society in regard to energy for expenditure that we are condemned to share as opposed to rejoice in—argues for a more capacious general economy that reveals how "present forms of wealth make a shambles and a human mockery of those who think they own it [...] genuine luxury requires the complete contempt for riches [...]. Beyond a military exploitation, a religious mystification and a capitalist misappropriation [...] the lie destines life's exuberance to revolt."[14] This asks us to rethink how we define wealth and our relation to it. The culture of revolt that Julia Kristeva writes of eloquently in two volumes would aid and abet this project, and yet what Bataille's theory in the twenty-first century also needs is a productive concept of work and discipline for his community that would eschew the expropriations of financial capitalism and technology. What prevails though in the present history is an increasingly militarized society that is hoodwinked by the bogus religion of commodity fetishism and the capitalist power of exploitation.

In Michael Richardson's incisive account: "Bataille therefore never wrote to convince but to provoke the reader into his world and make him complicitous with his thought."[15] This is true, for the Bataillean book is above all a question or an exclamation mark, and an inspiring invitation, for further thinking in its textual space. Also Richardson submits that "Bataille's concept of knowledge was always moral in nature. [...]. It is first of all essential to realize when approaching Bataille's work that before we can contemplate non-knowledge we must first pass through knowledge" (GB, viii–ix). This would be a trajectory and a dialectical movement of the first importance for one's cognitive work about the paradoxical moral quality of Bataille's work. Richardson ponders Bataille's newfound stardom from the advent of populist late capitalism in the 1980s to 1994 when his own critical work was published, that perhaps the general cultural sensibility was prepared "to appreciate a thinker who had long scorned the whole principle of an economics of accumulation and utility to assert that the basis of economic health was a principle of pure exuberance" (GB, 3). No doubt it is true that under post-industrial capitalism, and before the onslaught of the coup d'état of corporate late capitalism, there was a greater hearing for Bataille's intellectual proposals. Bataille's kinship with all the nonconformists out there remains a para-baroque Leibnizian phenomenon, because it asks for the prevention of any reduction or instrumentalization to a destructive degree of our intellectual lives.

Here is Richardson on Bataille's relation to specializational knowledge and power, and to the wide-ranging nature of the latter's expansive intellectual outlook that academic orthodoxy condemns: "he felt it was not possible to contemplate philosophy without taking economic factors into account, nor the economy without considering the effusion of poetry. Such a project of totality is clearly unrealizable within the span of one person's life experience, and this is one of the 'impossible' paradoxes Bataille never flinches from in the way he approaches his material" (GB, 9). So, to understand the totality of matters by demolishing traditional dogmas about intellectual work was Bataille's cardinal and paradoxical cultural aim; Bataille's own model for how to pursue an intellectual career had dignity in its train; this modality of being forces us to rethink the whole organization of the academy and of knowledge for a more true and real academy of intellectual culture to reach fruition. This extract also highlights strategies for the revolutionary scholar of whom Bataille would be one signal and paradoxical example for how to exist and to create new theories of community. This is all the more important for our present situation in which the university embodies a factory of experts often averse to asking the big picture questions. Three contemporary thinkers who evade the factory effect to some degree are Agamben, Sloterdijk and Žižek who with their courageous, unorthodox and wide-ranging investigations bring fresh grist to the mill. More distantly, we may add Deleuze, Benjamin, inter alia.

Bataille for Richardson in another claim "believed that the basis of thought particularly lay in analogy" (GB, 9). So the folds of so many analogies would be a creative act for imaginative work. Furthermore, Richardson reminds us that, "If the essential element in Bataille's thinking is the social, it may be said that the recreation of communal being is his most immediate concern" and for Bataille, "The fundamental element that makes possible the unity and continuance of society is the *sacred*" (*GB*, 34). Community being and the sacred then are for Bataille's work nodal points of contact, which help to establish a convincing connection between the two for the construction of a collectivity that allows for creation/decreation and redemption as so many enterprises and forms of immunization.

Concerning Bataille's engagement with social reality in the financial sphere, Richardson teaches us that capitalist standardization operates in such a way that our social order

> becomes uniquely homogeneous in a way that causes all aspects of its fabric and its very nature to reduce people to their social roles, so denying them the communal effusion to be discovered in the heterogeneous activity that is essential to true communication, thereby tending to destroy any creativity and collective effervescence that does not serve a useful purpose. (*GB*, 35)

Capitalism homogenizes, standardizes and evacuates the particularity and creativity of the independent individual. To rearticulate the connection between human agency and community being remains a paramount and a difficult task in an instrumentalized world; this must be incessantly exercised and practiced to institute radical creativeness and effusiveness.

Additionally, Richardson writes on the problem of standardizing functionalism in Bataille's theoretical edifice: "a homogeneous society leads to the destruction of the idea of religion and so denies the sacred [...]. By so doing, it denies itself, since the sacred lies at the heart of social being. [...] the sacred is revealed in bodily exhalations [...] extreme emotions [...] socially useless activity [...] which take the form of a heterology [...]" (GB, 36). This is fascinating when one thinks of forms of popular and mass culture as active engagement and solidarity with the sacred that explode the social body. Popular and mass culture can often be just as interesting and even more so than so-called high or refined culture. One must take a closer look for one's self at this paradoxical truth. Also for Bataille, "sovereignty may be said to be the determination to have done with ends and live entirely in the instant. It represents an existence freed from worry, in which utilitarian principles are considered to be of no account. It also implies being able to recognise one's own insignificance and laugh at the fact" (GB, 39). This model of existence and creation also requires another temporality, that of the Benjaminian "dynamic *instant* [...]. Such a conception would grasp the present moment in and for all its revolutionary potential" (GA, 102). The confluence here between Bataille and Benjamin would mobilize another relation to temporality in the service of impossible/possible forms of community and the creative life.

According to Richardson's take on Bataille, "Our existence itself is impossible. We should [...] not be able to exist at all, and yet [...] we do so in an equilibrium that [...] has something of a miraculous quality. This paradox is the true 'impossibility' of the universe" (GB, 39). The foregoing proposal is both paradoxically reasonable and realistic. Existence, creation, and the commons then are as apt and even *miraculous* paradoxes of being and becoming. Paradox too is a wellspring of value. Also, paradox is a key to being in the true, which in the end should evoke the scope and tension that laughter can so powerfully release for thinking and being for forms of community and the creative life in Bataille's star general economy.

The incomplete nature of reality and of knowledge is another key Bataille point. This is likewise for quantum physics for understanding both quantum and ontological reality. Vocationally speaking, we read in one claim that Bataille questioned, "How was it possible to retain the sense of vitality and necessity that was the hallmark of true scholarship if one needed to earn one's bread by such activity? Bataille worked as a librarian for most of his life [...] as a means to make a living while pursuing his committed research in other areas" (GB, 41). This is true in many regards. Yet whether this would be at all possible on a large-scale in the hyper-corporatized and specialized twenty-first century academy is doubtful. There certainly are isolated cases, but generally no considerable movement or school exists for the exercise, practice and production of such forms of creative work on a large level. However, some places such as the New School for Social Research in New York City, or the EHESS in Paris, assuredly exist. Be that as it may, this offers the ultimate paradigm for how a true scholar should exist and create. Richardson goes on to argue for a Leibnizian or Spinozan extra-academical activity amenable to the mode of intellectual production of a Bataille, among others, when he pens that during Bataille's cultural era "it was not expected that [intellectual work] should be confined to the context of academia. The inter-war years [...] in France, offered to writers and artists a context in which they felt that their work was of vital importance [... and] had a real consequence for human destiny" (GB, 41). An era of 'maverick intellectuals' sounds provocative for new forms and figures of existence, creation and the commons. Wide-ranging analyses, compassion, criticality, humility, solidarity: these are the values and forms of praxis a framework would prize for cultural work that might have "a real consequence for human destiny". This we need in our present age that marginalizes, if not disenfranchises, such intellectual work. A violently conservative neoliberal age requires non-commodifiable values to instance themselves in cultural work for forms of radical democracy and of the cultural commons.

Bataille views the communal as constitutive for the individual, and her chances for existence and creation. This is disjunctive from where we are now at in twenty-first century consumer capitalism and digital technology. Richardson gives an account of the institution to which Bataille was attached and a founding member during its tenure from 1937–39, "the College of Sociology required that those who participated within it should feel under a moral obligation to act upon the results of their research. This was seen as a form of activism that would be defined as a 'sacred sociology'" (GB, 55). In Bataille's own life-narrative, we may see how he himself took into account the notion of interested knowledge and of testing his ideas with experiential data in the spirit of existence and creation. That the idea of a 'sacred sociology' was the aim, shows the seriousness with which the College of Sociology conceived their task. For Richardson's version of the on some level proto-Aquinas and Nietzsche figure of the twentieth-century Bataille: "the sovereign operation requires placing one's being in question [...]. Unlike Sade or Nietzsche, unlike Bataille himself, Heidegger was unwilling to place his life in stake through his research. This devalued his claims towards sovereignty. Bataille made the same reproach against Hegel" (GB, 59). Thus, Bataille esteems sacral experience of an independent thinker over against that of the profane work of being a university scholar; courageous risk-taking is necessary in this model for a better form of existence and creation for the community of thinkers and of the world at large. Richardson quotes Bataille on Hegel, "By taking work (discursive thought, project) for existence, he reduces the world to the profane world; he negates the sacred world (communication)" (GB, 59). In Bataille's reading of Hegel, an investment in communication and community is lacking. On the other hand, in Hegel's thought, it is the case that community is a manifestation of Hegelian spirit.

Richardson argues in an important claim for Bataille's general economy, "life is essentially energy that strives to expend itself uselessly. As it founded itself in work, so humanity has needed to control this basic principle [...]."

> Bataille questions this assumption [of scarcity] by emphasizing the importance of useless consumption and [how] perhaps even in all societies prior to capitalism, it was the needs of consumption that were considered primary, not those of accumulation. (*GB*, 69–70)

This offers up a new spirit and definition of economic wealth on which to reflect. It would be our needs for "useless consumption" that would matter, and not for what prevails today, "accumulation". Added to this, it is energy that is more important than matter or mass. This also informs cutting-edge work in the natural sciences, such as Einstein's theoretical physics and quantum mechanics. It is also at the heart of work on the philosopher Martin Heidegger by such scholars as Kenneth Maly in *Heidegger's Possibility: Language, Emergence—Saying Being* (2008). With Bataille it is not safety and security that are the main preoccupations, but rather tapping into the potentials of immanence and of its concomitant joys that open out onto forms of a general and universal economy and heterology.

From a wide angle of vision on this complex topic of *homo economicus* and of Economics with a capital E, Richardson argues that the concept of generosity, or of self-giving, is primal: "A society that loses some of this prodigality [...] has in effect established constipation as a principle [...]" (*GB*, 71). To exist, to create and to construct a commons thus requires something other than 'a principle of constipation' for instead a general economy of self-expenditure. Courage and hope should replace fear and constipation. A universal generosity would create another relation of companionship for a more egalitarian and liberal society in which to exist and to create new articulations and effects of human possibility. Here the donation or the gift of *munus* shines out for the making possible of the impossible.

Even more, in Richardson's account, "economic needs from expenditure to accumulation serves to unbalance mankind's inner sensibility. It means that we become shackled to possessions [...] something which also serves to alienate us from our own inner needs" (*GB*, 72–73). Crucially we need therefore more mutual, responsible, spiritual and thinking ways of living and being. For Bataille our relation to objects must be transformed. Such a newfangled attitude or disposition taps into the spiritual and thought structure of things to negate their luster as commodities on display passively to consume and to over identify with as the false core of our being in a society of advertising, big finance and consumerism. Instead, we should identify with our true forms of alienation and push them to the limit of our courage and capacity, so as to make something good out of such alienations, be they a cultural figure, or idea, or form of being. Also, we should consider the notion of good forms of de-growth to contest the current religion of growth. For this again we have to pose the question: what is truly valuable?

Moreover, in Richardson, Bataille's dialectical and total way of thinking means that as is the case with persons "society too suffers from depression and light-headedness, knows fear and despair, exuberance and hope and is subject to the need for laziness, anger and general effusion. It has as much need of non-productive expenditure as individuals themselves" (*GB*, 73). This explains the importance of various forms of pop culture energies: sports, music, games, etcetera. For such activities discharge energies that otherwise may be bottled up and lead to physical warfare. Also, Richardson notes, "It is the whole ideology of the Reformation that provided the moral rationalization necessary to give accumulation its legitimation. Previously, society was actively structured against individuals assuming power over others or retaining wealth for their own benefit" (*GB*, 75). This makes the Reformation a subtending force for the capitalist project and capitalist rationality, something Max Weber elaborates upon in a 1905 *Die protestantische Ethik und der Geist des Kapitalismus/ The Protestant Ethic and the Spirit of Capitalism*. This is not merely a paradox, but also an explosive contradiction, given that the basic message of the Christian heritage from its founding sage figure, Jesus, is precisely to disenfranchise oneself from material possessions and from a delusional notion of materialism. In addition, Richardson avers that in a post-1962 Bataille world "in which [...] the market [...] determine[s] its own course independently of human needs [...] Bataille's thinking reads as a negation of monetarism" (*GB*, 96). These are accurate claims about the rôle of the market today in relation to the crucially important needs of (post-) human communities and cultures. A negation of a totalitarian money economy or monetarism, in our capitalist globalization, and hyper-consumerism, would satisfy the special Bataillean injunction and summons for a general economy to come into circulation. By extension in thinking what Bataille terms a "General Economy", a "General Immunology" and a "General Ascetology" are as abovenoted what Sloterdijk argues for, and the present author too takes these ideas on board. In a culture preoccupied with wealth and power, these three general notions contain an emancipatory and immunizing potential to move us on to a revolutionary notion of subjectivity and time for a more democratic world society that takes the wellspring of value as one of radical human agency and immanence. Such agency would pursue its power to exist and to create for another commons on the basis of a different definition of wealth and so too a revalorization of new forms of duration and capital. Thus a "general economy" may emerge that would also conduct a more collective sense of agency than that instituted by our current neoliberal age.

As for Bataille's relation to the Christian tradition, consider Richardson's claim that the problem is one "of going beyond it, creating what he called a 'hyper-Christianity' which would give meaning to the experience of life as it was really lived. It was this that Bataille described as an 'atheology' [...]" (GB, 115). This 'atheology' would be a baroque salvaging of theological reason and radicalization of the basic lessons of Christianity. This is something that Žižek in other contexts has espoused, the saving force that is that in a precise sense of the Christian heritage. We need to out-Christianize Christianity so to say. We need to think, and passionately at that too, in order to accomplish this. As Heidegger famously writes, "*Most thought-provoking is that we are still not thinking*—not even yet, although the state of the world is becoming constantly more thought-provoking."[16] This would mediate a valuable general cultural sensibility.

In an illuminating conjunction of Bataille with the Marquis de Sade, Richardson makes the following claim about the element of sociality, "In essence Sade recognised only personal interests; Bataille was concerned on the other hand with the dissolving of personal interest in a universal generosity" (GB, 120). The *munus* then, the gift of a "universal generosity" would be one Bataillean principle for existence, creation and community for a transformation from within of the cultural reality and of the material relations of power in a world society. Such generosity as a form of liberality would also allow for spirits of the sacred and of sovereignty to emerge in a society whose deepest homogenizing impulses evacuate or negate such phenomena as the sovereign mode of being and the sacral dimension of experience. Universalism then would also be given a chance for a more developed and ripe figuration.

With Richardson's edition of Bataille, "our primary need is to re-invent a sense of community embodied in a new conception of the sacred that responds to our contemporary needs. [...]. We need therefore to re-invent myth" (GB, 129). A new conception of the sacred that grounds our societies would mediate a new conception of subjectivity, time and community based on courage and on hope for a reinvention of the mythic and of

Economy as a more universalist general economy. Finally, Richardson asks vis-à-vis the concept of guilt in Bataille, "can a joyful embrace of guilt—such as Bataille experienced through his inner experience—provide the possibility for a re-invigoration of society? How can individualism be transformed back into social belonging?" (*GB*, 130). This is precisely one potential cultural and communal point: to embrace our primal guilt to spawn another conception of time, community and subjectivity in order to coexist and to co-create more potently and harmoniously. If this force of guilt could be transformed, then so could our human and post-human institutions.

This closes our specific engagement with the big and inspiring "Bataille problem" in our attempt to construct possible spirits of community and the creative life. All this takes place under a vast canopy of individual stars that bedazzle in the current theory of community and the creative life. In the next Chapter 7, this point will be further illustrated.

Chapter 7

Existence, Creation and the Inoperative/ Operative Commons in *Invisible Man* (1952) and in *La Divina Commedia* (1308–21)[1]

The present purpose is to rework and refocus the problem of individual existence vis-à-vis community relations and the impossible/possible inoperative/operative commons of social reality in two compositions: the US novelist Ralph Ellison's (1914– 94) *Invisible Man* and Dante Alighieri's (1265–1321) magnum opus for not only medievality, but also for our contemporaneity and after, *La Divina Commedia/The Divine Comedy*. Michel Serres enriches our discussion, "you must search passionately for what you are and not for what they say you are. Don't listen to anyone. Resist the torrent of influence, the medals." Serres again, "To find the contemporary, a difficult thing. To discover what one is, a much rarer invention still."[2]

This chapter then aims to map out new theoretical paradigms and reading strategies for thinking the dialectic of the landscape of the real of existence, or of life as it functions, in tandem with notions of creation within the real of community. This would be however positively or negatively community may be defined (operative or inoperative), in order to think these categories in the imaginary that is the heritage of a US American as well as a more international literary and cultural history. Analytical instruments used will activate a reading of Ralph Waldo Ellison's novel through a multiplicity of theoretical modelings, scaffoldings, inspirations or agents provocateurs for further critical-creative thought on the Real for theoretical psychoanalysis of *Invisible Man* and also of Dante's *La Divina Commedia*.

To expand on the idea of the inoperative, for Giorgio

Agamben, "The condition of the Jews during the celebration of the Sabbath is thus called *menuchah* [...] inoperativity. [...] it is a joyous and perfect reality that defines the very essence of God ('Only God,' Philo writes, 'is truly an inoperative being.... [...]')" (*N*, 104). Also from the same critical-theoretical text, "Even inoperativity belongs to creation; it is a work of God. But it is a very special work [...] which consists in rendering inoperative, in putting to rest all the other works" (*N*, 110). Adds Agamben: "in the Sabbath we celebrate a creation that was destined for redemption (that is, for inoperativity) from the very beginning" (*N*, 110). These citations toss suggestive light onto the present chapter, and onto the concern for the redemptive 'inoperative community' that was also broached in Chapter 2 and that remains operative throughout the present work. The above-indicated mentions from Agamben also tap into the potent notion of self- and collective-redemption as something predestined to happen.

To move from the inoperative to the idea of the 'Real', I assimilate some insights from Alexandre Leupin in his *Lacan Today: Psychoanalysis, Science, Religion*; Leupin argues:

> The Real is not an agency or an order; it is a set whose contents are unknown. That is why it cannot be defined otherwise than by an affirmation of existence ('There is ...') [...] because it remains hidden from us in the unconscious. There are meaning and truth in the unconscious [...] but they are out of the reach of our consciousness. The Real is therefore what escapes any formalization and any representation [...]. It is only through lapsi, evocations, silences, dreams, that we may have an inkling of the Real.[3]

Existence here is crucial for the Lacanian Real. This accords to our understanding, and to the powers of evocation and of suggestion that would be one function of the fictional or poetic work. Furthermore, Leupin also adds, "As opposed to the generalities grounded in the Symbolic order, it is in the Real where we find singularities. The psychoanalytic Real is shared by none, it is unique in each individual (no one can dream the same dream someone else does)."[4] To think the anti-hero (heroic undertakings are not allowed in this book) or if you prefer the protagonist of this novel, the Invisible Man, in light of the foregoing, we might bear in mind that for William Shakespeare (1564–1616), for Pedro Calderón de la Barca (1600–81) and for Freud (1856–1939), the whole of the world is in a manner a dream.

Additionally, Invisible Man may have been taught the basic Freudian theory about actuality; namely, that the underlying drives or impulses in the social order for human being are cannibalism, incest and homicide. Time and again Invisible Man finds these notions stage center in his existence and in his concrete experience in the commons of his world. This is what constitutes the negative commons (Blanchot's 'negative community') or inoperative commons (Agamben's or also Nancy's 'inoperative community') in *Invisible Man*.

Secondly, the Invisible Man is given to think time and again of how to compose an efficacious existence in a world of power. Also he is instead provoked into seeing an effective life, one where life is locatable as the possibility to produce singularity and radicalness; or to tap into the value of what Martin Heidegger calls an "owned existence"; or even to rethink ownership and ownhood as "enowning" in Heidegger's 1936–38 study translated by Parvis Emad and Kenneth Maly as *Contributions to Philosophy (From Enowning)* (1999). Instead Invisible Man rather goes over to the evil Heideggerian "they" or to the Guy Debordian and now proverbial society of the spectacle. Yet, little by little in Ellison's novel piece, we see a figure not too far (however surprising it may seem) from the Dante personage who populates *La Divina Commedia*; to wit, the Dante who is shown the way by his guide the Roman poet

Virgil through both Hell and Purgatory and his great love and female exemplar Beatrice who guides him through Heaven or Paradise. This exquisite image aptly captures the trail that Virgil helps to break open for Dante. This is not unlike what happens between other cultural pair relations, such as that between Spinoza and Deleuze, Derrida and Nancy, Benjamin and Adorno, Balzac and James, Lacan and Žižek, Nietzsche and Bataille, Shakespeare and Welles, Althusser and Rancière, Lendl and Murray and one could continue; the transmission of energy and creative inspiration that passes transindividually from one figure to the other so that the two become permeable with porous boundaries, such is the logic of genuine community and creativity.

Dante and Virgil enter a fortress surmounted by owls. From Dante's *Divina Commedia*, Cantica del Inferno. Ms. 597/1424, folio 48. Italian, 14th century. (Photograph: ©Erich Lessing / Art Resource, NY)

In truth, what the twentieth-century Italian poet Eugenio Montale (1896–1981) writes of Dante throws light on our text by that American specter, Ralph Ellison and of his fictional creation if not alter ego, Invisible Man: "Dante cannot be repeated. He was considered practically incomprehensible and semi-barbarous a few decades after his death, when the historical and religious inventions of poetry dictated by love had been forgotten."

The greatest exemplar of poetic objectivism and rationalism, he remains foreign to our times, to a subjective and fundamentally irrational culture, which bases its meanings on fact and not on ideas. And it is precisely the reason for facts which eludes us today. A concentric poet, Dante cannot furnish models for a world, which is progressively distancing itself from the center, and declares itself in perpetual expansion. For this reason the *Commedia* is and will remain the last miracle of world poetry.[5]

Let us pause here and consider the critical implications. Certainly this valorization of Dante goes hand in hand with a certain estimation of the notion that we have lost the center, but perhaps what we have really lost is the periphery? And this precisely constitutes the problem confronted by Invisible Man who finds himself exiled to the margins of society, edge structures that are devoid of widely recognized forms of meaning and value. Still, the point above is well made from Montale, and instructs us to know that the ideological universe of Dante's time was unusually fertile of creative inspiration for a writer of Dante's giftedness, predilections and sensibility. As a piece of language, *La Divina Commedia* instances a powerful example of the power of the impossible for it continues to exist as a linguistic miracle. The image in Picture 2 captures one true essence of the community element of the poem in its portrayal of the Dante and Virgil transindividual relation.

In the wake of our endorsements of Leupin's understandings of Lacan the actual or the Real of *Invisible Man* accords to the notions of truth, existence, life, meaning and creation, and these radically overlapping and concatenated concerns accord to the ideological attitudes and value ideals that similarly invest the Dantean text in an age, not unlike our own, of a certain middle-ages aspect. For as Montale also notes, perhaps controversially but certainly provocatively: "we no longer live in a modern era, but in a new Middle Ages whose characteristics we cannot yet make out [...]"

If the future sees the ultimate triumph of technoscientific reason, even accompanied by the weak correctives which sociology can devise, the new Middle Ages will be nothing but a new barbarousness. But in such a case it would be wrong to speak of them as 'medieval,' for the Middle Ages were not merely barbarous, nor were they bereft of science or devoid of art. To speak of a new Middle Ages, then, could seem a far from pessimistic hypothesis to the man who does not believe that the thread of reason can unwind *ad infinitum*; and yet an entirely new barbarousness is possible, a stifling and distortion of the very idea of civilization and culture.[6]

Dante was the author to close the Middle Ages. What has not been so noted is the idea that Ellison's book focuses the problem of the new Middle Ages or at least a novel barbarousness and a human subjectivity evacuated of truth content. What we indicate is a doubling in the imaginary of literary culture of an external actual world atrophied of meaning and of value, a nihilistic age given over to the drug spectacle, of the winner of worldly power, and to the excessively artificial that would somehow service the capitalist body. However, this often results in a mutilated body and mind in combat precisely against the untruth of the posited facts stripped of any ideas of deep meaning or of profound value. We could also though give as Hans-Georg Moeller would teach us to think in his text *The Radical Luhmann* (2011) a more ironical, modest and equanimous Niklas Luhmann's systems theory understanding of the current state of affairs that would not be so irked, as it would be released from the pressure to change the order of things in order firstly to understand matters a bit better.[7]

If the biographical Dante has come to a certain big crossroads at the halfway mark in his existence at the beginning in his poem, and hence must engage in that spiritual moment which is as Deleuze and others have already suggested, the moment of the power of decision or what I would like to call the inauguratory problem of decision, then the Invisible Man does as well. Invisible Man comes to realize that the self must inhabit an absence that will one day become a presence. Also that as Immanuel Kant has taught us to think, all knowledge comes from our power of imagination, and that to be one with our imagination is to find the true source for the meaning of being. Instead, Invisible Man finds himself in an environment, though not in a society from a systems theory perspective, of technology and of self-serving, self-interested, toxic and dangerous petty egos out to fix and to control reality, instead of a world that takes meaning of life issues seriously. This is one that would therefore be given to appreciate and to understand the nature of things; for such a lattermost culture is one that would prove not so much sadistic as therapeutic and empathic.

Invisible Man shows the commodification of experience (all the social powers that be reify and commodify Invisible Man) and the spectacularization of reality, and so by extension also of individual identity. What Invisible Man must come to realize by book's end is that the only way to resist hegemonic nihilism in a world of real barbarism, and both material and symbolic cruelty in its train, is to make one's substantive identity one's own project in order to release perhaps disappointed feelings of how one is constricted by restricted opportunities from one's 'big Other' authority figures. The mass of social power against Invisible Man gives the reader to think the following: to change objective conditions may prove one practical aim if not an outcome of the bitter experiences of the multitude of which Invisible Man would be a totemic human animal (a median sample example) and symptom.

It may well be the American axe that fells Invisible Man

spawns the possible future being (would it even be a global being?) at this stage in the reception of Ellison's novel. Is there not a sense in which by annihilating the American social reality, the social commons even, Ellison as author thereby rescues it? The dramatic and novelistic facts of *Invisible Man* teach that the volatilization of American culture is a way of shaking up the classic American experience of the US dream, so that it might return in a new guise, one that would engage the problems of tradition and innovation. Hence the real angle and the real problem for the character Invisible Man is whether he wishes his identity to fall between the cracks in the US reality as a reified self, or mount the cross as a self-owned example in himself to contest how prestige, money and power are rather uselessly holy to most human beings in his fictionalized American society.

Further, relative inattention to notions of humanitarian thinking and acting that would come from a future-oriented world society that takes questions of meaning and value seriously might mean concomitantly an empathic world that would display what Jason Powell writes in *Jacques Derrida: A Biography*, "a desire for purity in the appreciation of life and existence which is the hallmark of high culture".[8] The idea that suffering is a good teacher and that it may transform us and have creative consequences reaches back far into the cultural heritage. For in such encounters one is forced into a broad-minded resolute confronting of nothing that needs redressing. This is the opportunity this comedic novel text gives Invisible Man. And truth to say it would not be far from the suffering Jacques Derrida in his experience of expulsion as a 12 year old in North Africa who according to Jason Powell: "Posited a deeper, purer, more just, promised culture beyond the given one based on the mundane grasp of what genuinely is the case, and the ordinary acceptance of what is just and true."[9] If Derrida's early invisibility caused him to think hard about certain core things to do with all existents as essentially ghosts ("all writing is a trace [*trait*], each public person a ghost, and each tradition a history of specters"[10]) it has something to do with the ontological fact that Invisible Man too might be said a ghost in *Invisible Man*; and it is his ghostly form of being that precisely as in the Derridean ontology the case "that for each ghost there is a promise of something truly real."[11]

That the I does not fit knowledge in practical reality (as many theories tell us to realize not least deconstruction, psychoanalysis and systems theory) proves Invisible Man's Achilles' heel; rather, he might consider his identity irreducible to any I-hood or selfhood, take on an axial attitude (life is a journey) to the meaning of existence and creation, and hence come to realize the highest of human possibilities by tapping into the primal powers and plenitudes of the basic pregiven bounteous things of existence, creation and the commons be it depending on the context a negative or a positive one. For Invisible Man the great concern (amidst all the high comedy and Jazz-like Ellison prose) is the becoming of Invisible Man's identity, and for him to find the specific identity that he is. The cynical reason that surrounds him occludes the nature of his task; or, as Peter Sloterdijk writes more generally, "On earth, existence has 'nothing to search for' except itself, but where cynicism rules, we search for everything, but not for existence (*Dasein*)."[12] This is of course a very Heideggerian point, that we should reinvigorate the question of the meaning of Being and how such meaning may be found not in worldly objects but instead in subjects and in persons. Even more, cultural theorist Simon Critchley serves our conceptual framework well here by reminding us in his classic 1999-essay, "Post-Deconstructive Subjectivity?" of how,

> As Heidegger points out, during the Middle Ages the meaning of the words *subjectum* and *objectum* was precisely the reverse of their modern signification. In the context of the English language, lexicographic evidence suggests

that from the Middle Ages until the eighteenth century the word *subject* was used to name independently existing entities: the subject was that which was acted or operated upon, the 'object' upon which one exercised one's craft. [...]. The modern philosophical use of the word *subject* was the conscious or thinking subject, as self or ego, as that to which representations are attributed or predicated [...] first appears in the English language as late as 1796.[13]

This gives some historical perspective on notions of subject and object. Luhmann's systems theory replaces this duality with system and environment.

Furthermore, Sloterdijk writes in his 1983 classic, translated as *Critique of Cynical Reason,* of the sort of capitalist world to which Invisible Man finds himself submitted in the *Invisible Man*: "So, seduction and rape are supposed to be the two modi of capitalist cynicism? Circulation cynicism here, production cynicism there? Here the selling out of values; there the arbitrary pulping of the living time and labor power of the [individual] for the sake of blind accumulations?"[14] In this ideological world (be it the actual or the reflection of reality in the aesthetic sphere) money and prestige are not power, but their downfall or mirage. For in this modeling of the actual existent, what really matters are not ideas but facts. Yet what of the primal facts of existence, creation and the commons precisely this triple thematic that Ellison's *Invisible Man* forces us to traverse as so many multiple moments and sendings from under a half present writing hand, Ellison's own; or in a word, to try to think about those things that really concern us; or at least for some ideological attitudes we should do so.

For the sake of economy, here are some textual supports for the foregoing observations on Invisible Man; we read as he communes with himself in the Prologue, "I myself, after existing some twenty years, did not become alive until I discovered my invisibility";[15] that is Invisible Man needed to discover that the self has been liquidated in our age of "absent meaning", which has become the central concern (Maurice Blanchot) and of nihilism; and, "I am nobody but myself. But first I had to discover that I am an invisible man" (*IM*, 15). That is, Invisible Man has to discover more about that which is insubstantial about his self-identity in order truly to become who he is. Also, "When I discover who I am, I'll be free" (*IM*, 243); here Invisible Man needs to find the wellspring of knowledge about his subject irreducible to a self in order to become the specific self as subject that he is. Also, we read, "Until some gang succeeds in putting the world in a strait jacket, its definition is possibility" (*IM*, 576); this idea of possibility underwrites chances for radical creativity and the power of the possible/impossible community. More, "Life is to be lived, not controlled" (*IM*, 577). Here it is, in a general economy understanding of things Bataille-style, the power of life as opposed to the power over life that requires affirmation.

In the domain of the theoretical (the contemplative) once again, one cultural pair relation of quotes including one from Stéphane Mallarmé throws valuable light on our continuous problematic; namely, the poet's idea that "the only bombs I know are books"[16] and another from Guy Debord's situationist colleague Mustapha Khayati that "power is ceaseless falsification and social truth"[17] might give us to think that not only is the book *Invisible Man* an explosion of a being of intelligence, but that the individual character Invisible Man should become one as a potent nobody in a topsy-turvy reified and prostituted world wherein Invisible Man is treated as a worldly object. Additional to this, that one 'big Other' authority figure after another in the prose book hijacks what is nonesuch about the singularity of Invisible Man, from Bledsoe to Mr. Norton to Brother Jack to the ontological terrorism executed by the Brotherhood, inter alia, may fairly be said to underline the notion of the horrifying power of primary, of secondary and beyond socialization in a catastrophic social situation that constitutes a sort of 'kairology'. Truth to say, as Heidegger once wrote in his early style magnum opus, *Being and Time*, "Everyone is the other, and no one is himself";[18] that in a nutshell is the Invisible Man's problematic and symptom. Lacan's well-known maxim too that "desire is for the desire of the Other" also percusses our current situation in Ellison's fiction, for time and again the Invisible Man adopts the desires of others around him (symbolic fathers and other authority figures in particular).

Our basic argument here is that the mystery and complexity that enfolds the artistic world of *Invisible Man* moves out onto the plane of a deconstructive attitude that disarticulates mimetic beginnings, origins or centers as to the meaning of Being. In so doing the novel *Invisible Man* instructs us to believe that in an improvisational move, much like the nature of jazz music, the character Invisible Man may not only dramatize chances for a more true, beautiful and cosmic being spirit (in the spirit of a general economy of Bataille), but also for a more originary, pure and innocent composition of a global identity irreducible to a "serial number" (Fredric Jameson) that the individual person instances. Such an operation even within the spectres of the writers and their characters that comprise the aesthetic heritage would make good on the development of Ellison's anti-hero, the Invisible Man, beyond the final page of that novel work. This is what the ghost of Invisible Man offers up to us: the symptom that a more real self may yet emerge, one sensitively attuned to the prime facts and ideas of existence, creation and the commons (both operative and inoperative). In this way, for David Kishik, "the 'new,' that watchword of modernity, does not simply denote new ideas of new things but, above all, Dante's promise of a *new life* (in opposition to the medieval promise of an afterlife)."[19] This point is worthy as a force for the engenderment of radical community and the creative life.

Not only this, for Kishik, "Forms of life cannot be preserved through isolation—they can be challenged only by interaction, which is what a pluralistic, globalized, postcolonial public stage sometimes facilitates."

> Trying today to speak or listen while a million different voices call out at once is quite enervating, but this cacophony is still overcome whenever a single person attends to another and understands what he or she has to say. Every such communication or conversation, as fleeting or insubstantial as it may be, is a generator of the power and form of life.[20]

In addition, for Kishik "buying a form of life is as hopeless as buying love. Forms of life [...] can be paid for only through diligence and perseverance (but also passion and joy), which must be invested in everything we do and say (but also in what we do not do and do not say),"

> in every behavior and every gesture, in every wish and every thought, in every chore and every errand. If people were once able to pursue their mode of living in an organic and unselfconscious manner, in today's cultural hegemony it takes a lot of persistence and resistance to hold one's ground. If for the frivolous life in postmodernity nothing really matters, for the form of life in the coming community everything always matters.[21]

To play also on a title authored by Agamben, this cuts to the heart of the matter of 'the coming community'. *Invisible Man*, therefore by extension and allegorically, may be seen as an index as part of a symptomatology for a society still in incubation 65 years after its publication. Steadfastness, 'perseverance', 'joy', 'passion' are indeed keywords for the form of existence that might conduct creativity in and for the *dynamic instant* of the construction of the commons.

In the dance to come in the exercise and practice between existence, creation and the commons, assiduousness and joyousness will be necessary for unbuilding our complexity-reducing egos for an ever self-generative and self-processing individual and collective life narrative. For those who may pause here as to the relevance of the dancing body for the coming community, one of Lacan's heroes, Spinoza once composed, "We still do not know what a body can do." Finally *Invisible Man* is a charter for the idea that reality so called is a construction. So, constructive self-conception is what is necessary with respect to the symptomatic rôle of how to read the contents of the document of *Invisible Man*. Or: as axiom two from part one of Spinoza's *Ethics* recalls: "that which cannot be conceived through something else must be conceived through itself." Similarly philosopher Hans-Georg Moeller writes that for Luhmann, "Social reality is an effect of contingent autopoietic or self-regenerative processes"[22] for self-steering, free will and human rationality are an immanent effect of contingent social construction.

Such ideas as the foregoing apply to the singular trajectory and spiritual adventure of the Dante personage in *La Divina Commedia* as well as to the eponymous character of *Invisible Man*. The tutelage of a society and of a fiction in both cases proves it so. For these autonomies to develop, there needs to be some self-steering for the radical agency and conative force of the quiet power of independent and virtuous existence and creation. This is also how we might overturn material relations of power and found a society on something other than one structured by the negativities of tension, antagonism and the basic contradictions of class-structure and class-culture and the age-old problem of racism.

Forms and figures of moral-ethical, creative, intellectual and spiritual growth and development would thus enter center stage. They do for Dante in his astonishing poem, as they also do for the Invisible Man in Ellison's masterful text. The power of the impossible thus lives on, including through the very unlikely emergence of these literary documents and the common bond that they form with their readers as themselves models of the relational community and of forms of cultural belonging in the midst of the stars of an immunizing Bataille-style general economy.

Part III

Toward Community with Popular Culture Energies

Chapter 8

The Standstill of a Fully Fledged Reality: Jimmy Connors versus Ivan Lendl at the 1982 and 1983 US Open[1]

Tennis, traditionally regarded as a gentlemanly sport, fractured the community/all sense of community when it allowed Jimmy Connors (1952–) and John McEnroe (1959–) during their playing days to behave as spoiled children, and to denigrate Ivan Lendl (1960–). Community, particularly in the tennis world, requires different attitudes and selection procedures from its participants, including its superstars. The next two chapters will explore this whole dynamic that occurred in a Cold War era of time and that continues to affect the dominant perception and public interpretation of tennis history. Tennis tradition needs to be modified and transposed to contemporary terms and yet retain a deep relation with tradition. The game of tennis thus offers a simplified model of the challenges involved in creating a more equal, just and free society. This chapter as well as the next one then engage what I am inclined to call "the Ivan Lendl problem" or if you prefer "the Ivan Lendl challenge" for it gives us much to think about our contemporaneity, and about such longstanding issues as community and the creative life, not only during the battle days of the Cold War period in which these selected matches took place, but also after including our present history and beyond into a futuristic globalized world.

Bill Dwyre writes in a 2007-article "Lendl lets everyone in on jokes": "A funny thing has happened to Ivan Lendl. He got funny. Actually, he always was. It was the rest of us—the public led astray by the media, led astray by a sense of humor a bit beyond us—that didn't get it."[2] This is true, for the counterpart later picture against received doxa. The oversimplifying and violent power of the media defrauded us of a more valid community relation with the iconographical athlete, and global character, Ivan Lendl. Or a more basic worry: were the media completely devoid of critical sense and of discriminating taste due to how ideologically socialized obtuseness makes otherwise clever people mistaken if not foolish? For the scarecrow image of Lendl as a robot or ideological monstrosity figure prevailed in some quarters. Lendl did not fit their categories and mental grid. On court Lendl refused the surface appearance aspect of the happy positivity ideology, even if his press conferences in the 1980s and early 1990s were always considered among the funniest and most interesting by many a journalist. As cited below, Lendl declared himself in the mid to the late 1980s as one of the happiest of persons imaginable. The pigeonholes offered to us are thus unacceptable as ideological values in the present *kairology*. A more complex and fuller account of Lendl and of 1980s men's professional tennis is therefore needed.

One aim of the present chapter will be to reveal the ideological and representational violence operative in the paranoia of the Cold War atmosphere and in the US media coverage of the men's singles final at the United States Tennis Open in 1982 and in 1983 at Flushing Meadows, New York City, USA, between two of the more successful players in tennis history. This would be from the perspective of matches and of tournaments won and even beyond: Connors and Lendl who won 109 and 94 ATP tournaments in singles respectively during their careers, numbers one and three in the history of the post-1968 Open era of the sport; at this writing the Swiss Roger Federer has 97 and counting. So: we shall also purvey the historical progression of representations of the communist East in origin Lendl's reception in the capitalist West down to the present day. Notably Connors was number one for 268 weeks and Lendl 270 weeks both number one at the time respectively and now each trail only

Roger Federer (310 weeks) and Pete Sampras (286 weeks) during the Open era.[3] However, if one goes further back then we note that big Bill Tilden (USA), "Rocket" Rod Laver (Australia) and Tony Wilding (New Zealand) all held the number one ranking for longer than anyone during the Open era.

In so doing, we shall explore the intersection between tennis and critical theory for a novel theoretical territory and cultural space. More exactly, the present section will highlight the invisible and unacknowledged rhetorical ideology, the reductive violence, the politics, the field of historical tensions and the power of grand slam tennis representation from the viewpoint of the US media during the broadcast of these legendary if not mythic-like tennis matches in modern tennis history on CBS Sports. The palpable background and historical element of the Cold War in these years made possible a number of violent aspects, elements, and functionings to these sporting clashes. In both contests, Lendl was the favorite on paper, if not in the jaws of the New York spirit and home court advantage for the native-born US-American, Connors. Chapter 8 will also point up other facets of these two leading persons in their sport that throw a new light on their antagonistic clashes in these two matches and beyond for our contextualized cultural studies critical-analysis of the immunizing power of community and of the creative life, including of their athleticization.

Theoretical analysis will combine with careful close reading of these two media and sporting events in the USA and indeed in the emerging world society as exemplary for a critical discussion of the twin themes of representation and violence and of how this dynamic intersects with notions of community. For reasons of context, we shall also discuss these athletic figures in the history of their sport. As to the world society notion, even if class struggle makes this an unattained idea, our reading of world tennis stands on the side of the ledger of Žižek, when he writes:

Along the lines of this constitutive 'homelessness' of philosophy, one should rehabilitate Kant's idea of the cosmopolitan 'world-civil-society' (*Weltburgergesellschaft*), which is not simply an expansion of the citizenship of a nation state to the citizenship of a global trans-national state; instead, it involves a shift from the principle of identification with one's 'organic' ethnic substance actualized in a particular tradition to a radically different principle of identification.[4]

The question of political identification is important. We need new forms of identification in order to address problems that may only be solved on a global and not on a national scale because globalized capitalism and digital technology have taken over the wheel. We need to nourish a notion of the world spirit. Not only this, Žižek adds,

> For Kant [...] 'world-civil-society' designates the paradox of the universal singularity, of a singular subject who, in a kind of short-circuit, bypasses the mediation of the particular by directly participating in the Universal. This identification with the Universal is not the identification with an encompassing global Substance ('humanity'), but an identification with a universal ethico-political principle—a universal religious collective, a scientific collective, a global revolutionary organization, all of which are in principle accessible to everyone.[5]

This constitutes a productive position for the present comparative cultural studies enterprise and account of world-class tennis; for that institution may help to embody formally—if tapped into for its subversive qualities—a "global revolutionary organization" for the world spirit.

Another argument in the present tract is that however reductive and brutally simplifying the power of representation, it is exigent. So, the rhetorics of representation cut in both directions. We also say in tandem with Žižek from *Less than Nothing: Hegel and the Shadow of Dialectical Materialism*, "Present antagonisms are not 'readable' on their own terms; they are like the Benjaminian traces which are readable only from the future" (*LN*, 260). The moral-ethical authority of time then might give us a better perspective on representations of tennis matches from one of its golden ages, the period of the late 1970s and 1980s. So today we may give another picture of matters during those days of raging Cold War tennis battles on the stage of Flushing Meadows.

In the global history of sport in the 1980s antagonisms in the tennis system may be seen as a paradigmatic historical concentrate of larger ones in the global system. For tennis stands as one index to understanding the cultural, economic, political and social significance of the basic tensions and contradictions operating during the cultural era of the Cold War. This time was much concerned with violence and representation. As the announcement of an international research project puts it, "Sport during the Cold War was uniquely positioned between high politics, diplomacy and popular culture. It offers an ideal prism onto issues of hard and soft power and the ways in which body culture and the media interacted at times of ideological tension."[6] Tennis is in some modest respects a truly global phenomenon, and so gives us access to a primal history of the 1980s for an historical energy for our present history and so for our 'now-time' of awesome force awaiting its potentialization.

As Deleuze remarks on Spinoza in Chapter 1, "No philosopher was ever more worthy, but neither was any philosopher more maligned and hated", such a melodramatic claim could also be made about the public interpretation of Lendl, as a tennis player, whose original scandalous impact in the Cold War world of tennis in the 1980s was of such a stinging force that the pioneer of modern tennis was met with much incomprehension and outright hostility from a few of his leading edge Western foes including significant parts of the Occidental media. This phenomenon dropped off later in his career when Lendl was no longer so hegemonic, yet there was no true breakthrough per se in toto during his playing career that terminated in an announcement on 20 December 1994. Mark Hodgkinson notes,

> This is what is so compelling about Lendl's story. If there's a myth to be busted about Lendl and his image, it was that he was the great myth-maker, that he had helped to create this caricature of himself. This image of Lendl as a cold, passionless tennis machine was the one he chose to project to the world, and so that's how the world saw him [...].
>
> How could the public, the press and many of his peers have been so wrong about Lendl? How could such a sensitive man have invited so much abusive literature, such an unrivalled trophy cabinet of bile and insults? [...].
>
> In the 1980s, everyone was a Lendl basher. [...]. And there was absolutely no shame in it. (*IL*, 94–95)

These are intriguing facts and queries about the tennis trailblazer from the coal-mining town of Ostrava, Moravia. It may be pointed out that while a chorus of 'Lendl bashers' was rife, the tennis player did then have fans from all over the world. Not "everyone was a Lendl basher". But Hodgkinson's point remains a good one, on which the reader may wish to pause and reflect for herself as to the power of the media in the production of a reality that may travesty historical reality. That Lendl was engaged in self-caricaturization gives his self-presentation an intriguing and cutting-edge performative power of self-fashioning creativity for another inoperative/operative community. This would be one that asks for its redemptive moment. Precisely this is what for some angles of view happened, and what awaits to happen perhaps again.

Lendl's arrival and intervention in professional tennis was felt instantly in how he scored one of his best years in 1982 at age 22 in winning 15 out of 23 tournaments he entered including 22 final round appearances and also achieving a 44 match winning streak of the 106 matches that he won that year (winning contests according to the only source available at a 92% clip). Also, in 1980 and in 1981 he won a top-level 109 and 97 matches respectively (winning 80% and 87% of his matches in these two calendar years, again in the light of the only source that is available). The objective content of the number of matches won is unusual, let alone for someone in their second and third full years on the tour. In 1978, a year in which Lendl won the Junior Singles Event at the French Open and at Wimbledon, he played 16 matches and he contested a further 60 in 1979, so that in a way 1980 was his first or second full fledged year depending on how you look at the statistics. These events and representations are undoubted. He first attained the number one ranking on 28 February 1983 at the age of 22 (he would turn 23 on 7 March 1983).[7]

Lendl shot out of his particular historical moment to score with wonderful precision a direct hit in an evangelical capitalist ideological and practical world of global tennis that brought players together from wildly different cultural backgrounds. His coach in his first six years on tour was a colorful Polish player and unusually for the world of sport lauded as an art collector (he encouraged Lendl's own interest in the posters of the Czech Art Nouveau artist Alphonse Mucha), and former tennis coach too to Pope John Paul the Second, Wojtek Fibak. Fibak in late August 2013 joined forces for a time on the then world number one's tennis coaching team of his Monaco, Monte Carlo neighbor, the Serbian Novak Djokovic.[8]

As for Connors, he went 99-4 in 1974 a truly amazing year in the history of sport and peaked during the 1970s, but held on to be a major force into the early 1980s and famously making the semifinals of the US Open in 1991 as a 39 year old. Connors also won 1256 tennis singles matches number one over Lendl's 1068, which until recently stood at number two (number four is the Argentine tennis great, Guillermo Vilas with 929, and contemporaneously Federer has now passed Lendl's position as the new number two).[9] Lendl won his last professional match at the 1994 US Open aged approximately 34 and 6 months. Federer eclipsed Lendl aged 34 and 10 months.

US tennis writer, historian, and TV broadcaster Bud Collins named Connors "the Brash Basher from Belleville" after the town in which he grew up opposite St. Louis, Missouri and Ivan Lendl "the Ostrava Ghost". Lendl is from Ostrava, Czech Republic, then Czechoslovakia of course. He was known for charismatically but also intelligently having sawdust in his pocket, so as to apply it to his racket handle-grip when necessary to reduce its moisture level before serving. Lendl's early-career argyle style Adidas tennis polo shirts were also pioneering to some observers for the tennis world of fashion, and to others something memorable for being different from the more run of the mill sartorial look on the men's professional tour at the time.

First Lendl had to defeat the 1979, 1980, and US Open titlist John Patrick McEnroe in the semifinals in order to face Connors in the title match.[10] This foregoing endnoted introductory matter to their match covers McEnroe and Lendl on 11 September 1982 at Louis Armstrong Stadium. The profiles are very short, anti-intellectual and depoliticizing. One sees McEnroe's Davis Cup outfit as a form of nationalistic self-representation, over against Lendl's Adidas argyle diamond shirt. It is a full house and then some with people sitting in the aisles. Lendl had won a record in the history of tennis to that time 1.238 million dollars in prize money in 1982 going into this match one sees noted on the screen at one point. See here minute 93 and also minutes 98–105 (eight minutes total) from the US Open 1982 Men's singles final on CBS Sports.[11]

To return to our principal pathway and subject, the 1982

US Open final took place on 12 September in Louis Armstrong Stadium at the United States Tennis Association National Tennis Center in New York City. There is both the actual sporting event, and the parallel media event, with the latter affecting the transmission and production of the former. The ambient milieu includes Connors tapping into a nationalistic frenzy and the primal drives of the spectators eager for some Cold War blood. Thus, the ideological as well as the physical and chemical conditions are on the side of Connors in this atmosphere of athletic and communal excitement. The environment in the stadium also instances what Peter Sloterdijk communicates, "Perichoresis means that the milieu of the persons is entirely the relationship itself."[12] Here we have a state of 'perichoresis'.

Minutes 10 to 12 of the match illumine that Lendl's earnings that calendar year would exceed more than two million dollars, at the time the most ever for a tennis player in a single year, making Lendl a capitalist hero. This constitutes a paradoxical truth given the player's geographical background from the communist East.[13] At minute 93 of the match the smash from Lendl almost hits Connors, who wags his fingers at Lendl rather imperiously. This was arguably good tennis from Lendl, but Connors uses his own gesture for his tactical purposes, and it also plausibly shows his dreams of a certain grandeur. To play for one minute from minute 98 of the match we hear, "One more" as the announcers enthuse "now he comes" we hear and "this is Jimmy Connors" may be noted.[14] These pronouncements are notable for their uncritical adulation and fixation on the national sports icon, James Scott Connors. The extremely brutal if not blind violence of the ideological conditions are to be noticed. We also hear of Patti Connors, "Mrs. Jimmy Connors trying to stay calm impossible" and at minute 99 the Connors enthused broadcast booth notes for us how "Jimmy loves to play to the crowd" and "it's always got to be a downer for the opponent". This is true and shows the representational nature and personal effect of the system of tennis on performance. It is a personalist and so a very politicized thing, even if the media strives a certain depoliticization of matters to hide its hidden or disavowed ideological projects and built-in disavowed presuppositions and preferences. The roar in the stadium is deafening as we hear from the CBS booth: "oh oh!"[15]

At minute 100, the notable Australian tennis player and broadcaster John Newcombe avers that a Lendl forehand "ripped through the line almost took the line with it". One here recalls the phrase that evokes thoughts of the basic law of our world, competition, "Lendl's Law: Forehands speak louder than words" a known Adidas poster of Lendl from that early period of time 1982/1983 in his career where he embodied a blaze of sartorial and athletic passion if not even commodity fetishism for others in what he wore, Adidas; this lattermost thing is a wonderful paradox for someone from communist Czechoslovakia. But the poster also communicated a good deal more than these ideas, to which we shall return. From minute 102 "and here we go showtime" we hear again from the booth of CBS sports. One may discern the representational nature of entertainment culture and that of the show exemplary of the spectacle society effect. In a viewing experience from minute 105 and following on that point of departure about 3 minutes later we encounter, "They love him in New York", in a display from the crowd of patriotism if not of symbolic violence, and a form of socio-psychological intimidation, if not a psychic lynching of the player from the East. In winning the champion's trophy for the tournament, Connors also thereby shows how "a certain violence characterizes every actual possession"[16] not only in how one actually comes to possess something, but also in the authority that the act of possession wields for the possessor. Connors prevails in this first contest of two back-to-back with Lendl in a US Open men's singles final, 6-3, 6-2, 4-6, 6-4.

Now to the much-anticipated rematch, the 1983 US Open

Final in Louis Armstrong Stadium, which contains 20,575 people for this Cold War battle in ideological and competitive blood; this is all it will hold with 18,430 who have paid to gain entry. It is thus a venue with remarkable energies from the crowd, from the two players, from the media, from the specters of history and more. For the tournament, Connors is the number three seed behind McEnroe at number one, and Lendl at number two.

Set two, point one, in which at the close we hear from the broadcast booth of "a nervous frustrated smile right there from Ivan Lendl". Lendl's nervousness is pointed out time and again. Not once is this observation made about Connors in the present writer's viewing. Should we not resist this simplification? Again sensitive nervousness for the country boy from Ostrava gives us a clichéd representation of the country-communist country versus the city-capitalist boy Connors from near St. Louis, Missouri and New York's adopted cultural figure and tennis protagonist.

Represented in attendance at this match are such US notables as the media figure Johnny Carson from *The Tonite Show*, the TV journalist Walter Cronkite and Diane Sawyer another TV journalist from *CBS News*. Note the McDonald's insignia on Connors's tennis shirt, which illustrates his Americanomania dimension and representation, and so by extension an insignia as an index and agent of American power and violence, be it positive or negative, emancipatory, or coercive and hegemonic. Lendl wears his then famous diamond argyle Adidas tennis shirts adding to his somewhat hard-edged if not dour demeanor, which was encouraged by his cosmopolitan coach, Wojtek Fibak.

In the first 90 seconds from this endnoted link,[17] a "great final great crowd on hand and they are certainly being entertained," notes famed US announcer Pat Summerall. This representation of sports as a popular cultural form of entertainment does not, however, tell the whole story. For there is an athletic, ideological and representational war going on here. Also in another claim from US tennis legend and broadcaster Tony Trabert, "they are not playing what we call pitty pat tennis, are they?" Yet in one more mention, "this is like a heavyweight bout this one," states Pat Summerall. This remark underscores the brutal competitive nature of the struggle out on court, and how it may be seen as an epiphenomenon of the inorganic and antagonistic nature of all social articulations in the system of advanced capitalism. The ideological violence of this state of war goes unchecked and unavowed. This partly accounts for the popularity of sport, for it provides a self-historicization of its era in terms of the operation of, "The 'hard real' of the 'logic of [...] capital'"[18] (Žižek) in the 'hard real' of capital media events for capital is here the motor on which the title match is also in multiple ways played. Though I disagree with Alain Badiou in a way for the categorical nature of his attitude, he writes aptly for us here in another context, "And the rest? The elephant that is capital? This is the hard surface of concrete on which the real match is played. Do not mistake it for [Björn] Borg's game."[19] Yet we see both tennis and capital in a dance in our present Chapter 9, one wherein tennis has something to teach us about the power of big capital and of how to renegotiate it.

Lendl serves set point at 4:30 in the endnoted link only to double fault; 5-3 Lendl is up in the third set and "the psychological inner battle continues" remarks Newcombe; Connors asks them to wipe it: a tactical operation to be sure. This all refers to Lendl's double fault at set point and to what it precipitates a game later after that both from the booth and from Lendl's opponent.[20] The match we are told in a TV representation and broadcasting constitutes the sixth time that two players have met in back-to-back years for the US Open title going back to Johnson vs. Tilden 1919–20, [Parker vs. Talbert 1944–45, Anderson vs. Cooper 1957–58, Emerson vs. Laver 1961–62 and Borg vs. McEnroe 1980–81.] The continuity of Lendl-Connors with these prior figures shows the autopoietic/self-organizing nature of tennis as a subfield of sports as a social system.

The Lendl-Connors rivalry is one of the more tense and tetchy in tennis history and ranks high as far as number of meetings go. Connors dominated early and Lendl later on. Their career numbers are remarkable. For Lendl it seems that the hardest and bitterest experience possible in these two clashes helps to conduct a later flowering in his tennis career. His historical-theoretical defeat from Connors, and from the castratory force of the social milieu in which he played, open out onto another historical chapter for the sport. The massive repression to which Lendl was subject unleashes a different career attuned to the potentials of what through an active intelligence could be done in a field of attention: the global stage of world tennis.

The status of these two classic tennis matches? Consider for purposes of argument these words on sport generally from German scholar Wolfgang Welsch, "Sport can display all the dramatic traits of human existence. In this lies its symbolic dimension. Think of a 10,000 meter race. You can witness the tactical battle between the opponents […]."

> The crucial point is that *all this is created uniquely by the performance and the event itself*—it does not follow from the implementation of a script. […] the athletes' performance is creative in the highest sense. […]. Sport is drama without a script. […].
>
> In this respect sport appears more artistic still than many of the arts […]. The freedom and event character of sport's production of meaning is eminently artistic.
>
> Sporting events act out most basic features of the human condition, and the way they do this is marvellously self-creative. In so doing sport is sport semantically intense and intrinsically artistic. In this respect I see every reason to view sport as art.[21]

These claims are valid as a peculiar set of paradoxical truths that make it impossible/possible "to view sport as art" and of how it displays so many coordinates of human experience in powerfully symbolical ways. Importantly too, as Jean-Luc Godard argues in Chapter 9, sport cannot lie; there are the empirical results; you cannot fake it representationally as you can in a work of art. If you are a big name in cultural production, your signature mediates commodity fetishism for example and so aesthetic merit may not be the reason for winning a book contract or prize. In a way watching a championship level tennis match constitutes an honest popular entertainment and culture experience, something that Connors-Lendl provide for the open forms of a live tennis match for those in attendance and for a live TV broadcast in which the viewer and listener must interact with the screen to make sense of the happenings.

So, the 1982 US Open broadcast on the major television network CBS took place between 31 August and 12 September 1982. It was the 102nd edition of the tournament. The 103rd and 1983 US Open occurred between 30 August and 11 September. These matches are notable for the way in which the overall home court advantage of Connors would seem to have played one, if not the decisive part in the outcome. It strikes me that for all the Cold War-ness of the two battles, it is Connors who surely deserves credit for playing as well as he did given his greater age of 30 and 31, to Lendl's 22 and 23, albeit Lendl's successes outside the grand slam events early in his career remain one of the stunning achievements in the history of the game. Connors benefited from the reception of the crowd and representation of tennis overall (including in the media, which helps to constitute the media-saturated ideological environment of the officials, tournament organizers and of course much else besides) in his native cultural soil. Connors was given a surge of force from such agents. Connors has admitted as much of late namely that the crowd helped him to win these two matches. But what is also signal is how later Lendl seemingly was able to learn from these earlier defeats and sublate them. For example, in the 1985 US Open he was finally to prevail in his fourth consecutive US Open final over John Patrick McEnroe in straight sets in his first of three titles there (he also won five year end Masters tournaments in NYC in the 1980s en route to making a record nine consecutive finals at the then end of the year best of five sets matches tournament).

The 1982 encounter was the first of eight straight appearances in the US final by Lendl, and the sixth final for Connors and fourth title. The contest illustrates Žižek's thought that "radical antagonism can only be represented in a distorted way" (*LN*, 357) in how the US media constantly harped about Lendl's ostensive high-level sensitivity and oftentimes too to Connors's redoubtable mien and mode of being. The match provides a sculpture of events to come also in Jimmy vs. Ivan part two in 1983, which proves another exemplary occasion to see tennis as an embodiment of critical thought. Connors would also win this clash 6-3, 6-7 (2-7), 7-5, 6-0.

We may posit with Žižek about the tennis drive to win major titles that "the drive finds satisfaction not in reaching its goal, but in circulating around it, repeating its failure to reach it. [...]. This shift is deeply Hegelian, forming a kind of 'negation of the negation' [...]" (*LN*, 661). Was this Lendl's mode of accomplishment, so that these early losses did not tell against Lendl so much as constitute a moment of dialectical duress, which helped to propel him to 19 grand slam finals and so many victories all in all? A case can precisely be made for this position. For the community of creative human beings we can tap into sports as a vector of representational meaning and value because it is a matter of mobilizing the revolutionary energies and interests in sports for more political and urgent causes; this is also what makes these tennis matches worthy of mention. The achievement of the outsider from the East Lendl in the narrative of global tennis makes his a sterling example of what dedicated efforts, an ironical-playful humor, athletic discipline and a negative tennis community can spawn.

The cover words of *Sports Illustrated* from 15 September 1986 shows Lendl's encroachment in a national championship was taken as an affront: "THE CHAMPION THAT NOBODY CARES ABOUT: Ivan Lendl Wins The Open" a media event in which the US press transforms a second straight US Open Lendl title into a media/representational loss. The cover shows Lendl wiping his hands with sawdust, a signature Lendl moment. Yet it is a masterstroke of Lendl interpreted in an act of miscrecognition and misunderstanding, and of Cold War representation in the 1986 ideological space and system. A blind and ferocious hostility to the complex whole of world society? Superficial and unappreciative comments to make for a violent attack? Shallow claims? One notable fact is that after such a reception Lendl went on to even finer peaks of achievement. This attack indexes a strange inability to appreciate what is truly novel in one of the decisive achievements of modern tennis. It also displays all sorts of excluded perspectives, itself an effect of the operation of violence. It is well known for example that during the 1980s Lendl was more appreciated by tennis insiders than by most others. Or what of persons of other national-cultural stripes? The besieged citadel of American tennis would have none of this though, as far as the representational decision makers at *Sports Illustrated* go, who are with all due respect part and parcel of the official American ideological template. The brutal representation was necessary to deal with the trauma of the posited (if not necessarily at all) ideological and national outsider. So here one may see how (national) community operates as a bullying mechanism and mediates injustice.

Another paradox about Lendl is that he was able to become even more American in his value ideals than most Americans in taking on board such American values as self-discipline and application to achieve one's aims in one's life process for moral-ethical and for practical excellence and outcomes. This conquering individuality helps Lendl to effectuate a cut in the history of tennis, for he and his team largely launch the contemporary game.

In addition to Borg, Connors, Mats Wilander, Boris Becker and Stefan Edberg, McEnroe is one of Lendl's main rivals in the 1980s. McEnroe avers in a February 1987 *Tennis Magazine Yearbook* with the front image of Lendl and a caption that reads "Why You Should Like This Man, World no. 1, Ivan Lendl": "Nobody gives a damn about Lendl, and that's the bottom line. I could have no personality and be more popular than him."[22] McEnroe's I do not give a damnism mentality and attitude here is agonistic and hostile. In the same article by contributing editor Barry Lorge we also read that "Lendl is not tormented by the mistaken impression so much of the public has of him, but being a perfectionist, he would like to be judged on accurate impressions. It is time for the court of public opinion to reconsider its verdict."[23] This is understandable for someone who "won 386 matches and 39 tournaments between 1980 and 1983 without capturing a Grand Slam title."[24] The ideas of self-discipline and concentration are what were so essential to Lendl's career, which is why he wrote in a missive to *The New York Times* in September 1986: "One of the reasons I have accomplished so much in tennis is that I am a firm believer in hard work [...]. Part of that effort includes total concentration that makes me look impassive most of the time on the court. But that's not really the case. Right now, I am one of the happiest people in the world."[25] This expression of happy bliss from Lendl may surprise some, but again it is a question of ideological values and perceptions.

At the same time, in spite of all the negative remarks from Connors and McEnroe during this period of time, we still read even during this 1980s era from tennis professional Rick Meyer: "If you talk to the players, he's not unappreciated [...]. What he's done is incredible. The guy has put in so much work. The other players say, 'What an unbelievable effort!'"[26] The article indeed dialecticizes (problematizes) the dominant perceptions of Lendl, and yet in spite of such remarks the change in public perception of Lendl did not really change much at all at the time of his retirement due to a back injury on 20 December 1994. Lendl's last match was played in the second round of the 1994 US Open and it was one in which he had to retire due to injury.

To return to the tennis imaginary of the 1980s, one of the posited catastrophes of modern men's professional tennis is Lendl's failure to win any of his first four grand slam final appearances, and these two classic finals between two greats testify to the fact. As far as these two Cold War era matches go, the media apparatus and fan element themselves were part of this phenomenon. Connors was able to play to the New York crowd perhaps better than any other player in the history of the storied tournament and his accomplishments at the event are remarkable including 12 straight semi-final appearances and title match victories on three surfaces grass, clay and hard court. Several years later in 1991 as a 39 year old Connors made the semi-finals of the tournament. For many time fans, this was an emancipation and distinctively exemplary. Now-time here prevails for one's duration as a tennis player.

As for the reception and more current treatments of Lendl go, they have somewhat risen since his initial neglect by the Western media during his playing days that were followed by 14 years when he did not hit a tennis ball, which itself is a notable fact for one so assiduous and focused. This was supposedly ascribable to back problems. What was the media to make of this seemingly inaccessible and enigmatic figure? He was a revolutionary in the sport as a progressive conservative, something that at least became represented with his reception in an April 2010 exhibition match against his rival Mats Wilander.[27] Slavoj Žižek writes, "True revolutionaries are always reflected conservatives" (LN, 139). This adage applies to Lendl. Herein lies the beauty of paradox that the world of a self-reflexive 'conservative' functions as a transformative agent.

In the awards ceremony of a match between seven-time grand slam champion and another former world number one Wilander and Lendl in April 2010 at Caesars in Atlantic City, New Jersey, USA, Lendl's symbolic substance and substantial content gain a representation. For Lendl is given a meaning rather different from the early to mid 1980s one. The example of Lendl's career proves a *munus* for the development of professional tennis.

> *Josh Ripple* (Former WTA Tour President and Chief Operating Officer/ Caesars Tennis Classic Event Director):
> I really believe that he was the guy that every male and every female tennis player looked at and said, if I want to be the best in the world, I gotta do what he does.

Here Lendl provides the gift (the *munus*) of example for a whole generation of tennis players in their approach to the practicing-tennis-life. To continue from the same video we hear from

> *Pete Sampras* (Former World #1, 14 Grand Slam Singles Titles):
> You know, you just need to have the whole package, you need the game, you need the heart, and you need the mind. You know, Ivan had it. You know he had a great game, his heart was strong, mentally he was strong.
> *Gary Kitchell* (Tennis Performance Trainer):
> The world, you know, loved Ivan for his greatness. I think in this second time around people are going to get to know Ivan, as a person.
> […].
> *Venus Williams* (Caesars Tennis Host, 20 Grand Slam Titles):
> He was legendary for his mental strength and for his fitness level, definitely he changed men's tennis.[28]

As Williams suggests, Lendl so to say creates the blueprint for the modern version of men's tennis based on an all-court game he called *Hitting Hot*[29] in a book he coauthored with George Mendoza while a player on the subject. He also trained tirelessly making his career an ongoing site of experimentation challenging the conventional habits of how to be a tennis player in multiple regards in relation to training, Rolfing, diet, coaches, stringers, psychologists, etcetera. That the revolutionarily changed knowledge and praxis that original work produces causes mental confusion is a truism of a field such as literature, but it pertains also to the tennis heritage. To well admire what is impressive seems to require broad-mindedness.

One spirit circulating between Connors and Lendl is that of world historical global Empires, of the capitalist and of the communist ones. From a psycho-historical perspective it might teach us that popular cultural energies provide a more true globality emerging if not attaining the status of a feat of achievement. The real meaning of these two matches then is how things will turn out for the larger context of their popular cultural legacy and of how that will be appropriated and interpreted for another experience of the commons and of radical creativity on a global scale well beyond the modest confines of a sport such as tennis.

As popular culture producer-creators, Connors and Lendl deserve consideration within an historical perspective, which teaches us something about their respective ideological worlds. The remarkably unsympathetic reception and representation of Lendl in the US press in the 1980s underlines that which many ahistorical journalists disavowed: the painful lessons of history to which one is subject. In so doing, they display what Pierre Bourdieu mentions of the journalistic field that "they must avoid the quagmire of intellectual complexity."[30] This is especially relevant if as Bourdieu argues "intellectual discourse remains one of the most authentic forms of resistance to manipulation and a vital affirmation of the freedom of thought."[31]

I here wish to pose a question. In the US media representations of these two championship tennis matches, what of the idea of a certain nationalistic narcissism that refuses any sincere criticism but instead passes over into pseudo-criticism and representation? Television is for Bourdieu "such a formidable instrument for maintaining the symbolic order."[32] The symbolic order is the basic social reality in which we live that is constituted for theoretical psychoanalysis by language. Furthermore, these matches may be said to conduct xenophobia and what Bourdieu terms "the fear-hatred of the foreigner"[33] for system-complicit behaviors.

One fruit of Ivan's teachings came at the 2012 Olympic games where his tennis disciple Andy Murray prevailed to win the Gold medal in men's singles tennis for the United Kingdom. Then came the first grand slam victory for a Briton in 76 years with Murray's win over Novak Djokovic in a long match at the US Open in September of 2012 (4 hours and 54 minutes long, which tied the record length of a US Open men's singles final in 1988 in a five set duel between Lendl and Wilander). A weighty and assertive personal assurance of Murray's future prospects Lendl even gave before the match. Murray gave Lendl credit in his post-match victory speech in interview with Mary Carillo. So, some recognition-representation for Lendl occurs some 18 years after his last professional tour match at Flushing Meadows at the 1994 US Open. In a comment on the linkage between Lendl and Murray, Mark Hodgkinson informs us that,

After winning the 2013 BBC Sports Personality of the Year Award, he allowed his clothing suppliers, Adidas, to release an image of him with the line, 'Not bad for a man with no personality'. It's wrong about Murray, and it's wrong about Lendl. And it matters that it's wrong. Laugh along at jokes about Lendl, but the false perception of him is colouring and distorting the public's opinion of him, and his place in the tennis pantheon. [...]. To a degree, Lendl is still affected by the crowds in the 1980s having questionable taste in tennis players. (*IL*, 103)

The whole problem of a corrupted taste and sensibility then comes to the fore indeed in the public interpretation of matters, including of the reception of 1980s tennis players including overall its most successful male player from this era, Lendl. What we seem to need thus is a more general and global cultural sensibility that would be more international and so shared in order to tap into the phenomenon that was Ivan at the height of his creative tennis prowess and powers.

For an encounter from 2009, Paul Kimmage writes in "The Ivan Lendl Interview", "*PK*: You've never done an autobiography? *IL*: And I never will. *PK*: Why not? *IL*: Why yes? *PK*: Because you are one of the most interesting and most misunderstood sportsmen of all time. *IL*: But isn't that how you keep the mystique, he grins."[34] Absent representation may then be the most powerful kind? Silence as violence? Freedom as freedom from...? Lendl also remarks that some names would have to be mentioned, and he does not see why some people would have to be hurt. He thus will have no truck here with the destructive violence of representation. This is charitable of him and shows a capacity to take the higher moral-ethical road. Also, we read from Kimmage in the same interview, "Another significant influence on your life was growing-up in a communist state. Is it true that you watched the Soviet tanks rolling into Prague?"

IL: Yeah, I remember my parents were in Prague for club matches and I was with my grandparents in another town. They came to pick me up and we went home on the train and at every station there were tanks aiming at the trains.

PK: That must have been terrifying?

IL: Well, it wasn't terrifying because you are only eight. My parents were very upset and I was warned not to use words like 'occupants' or to laugh or spit or say anything against them. People went to jail for using words like that. That's another reason I wouldn't write an autobiography — people here just wouldn't understand. People in Hungary and Poland and the former Soviet republics would understand but people in California? Are you kidding me? They have no idea what it was like.

PK: 'During those formative years here, your relationship with the media was strained,' I suggest. 'And your relationship with the fans suffered as a result of that.'

IL: 'Well, let me tell you about the media,' he says. 'Because there was no freedom of speech in communist countries, I had to be careful what I said and didn't upset the agreements or arrangements I had because if I was home they could have taken my passport and I would never have travelled again; would never have been heard of again. But the first question was always, 'Would you like to live here? When are you going to defect?' Well, what can I say? There was no answer I could give and that's how it started.'[35]

Early in his career, Lendl was walking into a minefield with the Western press for reasons unknown to them. The interview continues thus: "*PK*: The clichéd projection of you here was that you were robotic and devoid of personality, the embodiment of the caricature communist, 'Ivan the Terrible'. *IL*: Yeah. *PK*: That wasn't very fair was it? *IL*: No, definitely not..."[36]

Following on from this, we read of a Cold War item to my mind. Lendl as a Cold War casualty? It is a part of the problem anyway.

PK: In September 1986, you won the US Open and made the cover of *Sports Illustrated* for the first time. The headline was

'The Champion that nobody cares about'.

IL: Yeah, I have not spoken to them since and I never will. It was totally uncalled for in my opinion.

PK: That must have been incredibly hurtful?

IL: It was unpleasant but there is no rhyme or reason for the way things unfold sometimes.[37]

Lendl reveals something of the terror and anxiety that one may feel in being misrepresented by the media. Also, Lendl's attitude here toward the media world is one of basic modesty, playful irony and of the *munus* (of the gift) of equanimity for the negative inoperativity of their interrelation (the US media discourse on Lendl and of their destructive-inoperative connection with one another). As for playing some of the tennis greats from his era, such as Connors and McEnroe, or as Kimmage puts it, "What was it like coming from Czechoslovakia and having to pit your wits against guys like Connors and McEnroe, who were loved here?"

IL: Well, I'm not sure I agree with that statement.

PK: What? That they were loved.

IL: 'Yeah,' he laughs. 'I think, whenever you played the No. 1 player in their own country, it was difficult, but you had to learn to deal with it. It was very satisfying, when you had 20,000 people cheering against you, to hold the trophy and smile. That always appealed to my perverted sense of humor.'[38]

"20,000 people cheering against you" indeed was the state of affairs it would seem in the first three of his US Open finals against Connors in 1982 and in 1983 and contra McEnroe in 1984. It was finally in his fourth consecutive US Open men's singles final in 1985 that he prevailed over his long-time foe McEnroe in straight sets. McEnroe was unable to counteract Lendl's gains in tennis that brought in its train his incendiary laser groundstrokes and all-court attacking game.

Autopoietically, the succession Borg-Connors-McEnroe-Lendl effectuates a collective revolution in the sport. Each pushes the other past the other, with Lendl being pushed to the edge to make resourceful maneuvers not yet seen. The athletic and cognitive giftedness of Lendl would initiate and bring about the common history of modern tennis based on power, fitness, nutrition and a more analytical and scientific approach. The constellation of players for which the period is remarkable reaches one peak in Lendl's critique of tennis that owed as much to the high standards that the first three mentioned great champions set as it did to Lendl's qualities and background. A continuous development of the twentieth century came in no small part thanks to the modalities of Connors and of Lendl, two of the brightest stars the sport has known in these moves and plays of identification and representation.

The problem of representation remains that of power and of a certain violence, be it material, symbolic, good or bad depending on the context including who controls the representations and for whose benefit and purpose. Are we aware of how sensitive things are here? In a revealing paradox Lendl ends up becoming more American than many if not most American-born nationals in his embrace of certain value ideals and freedoms. He went from nervy sensitiveness within a certain subjective phantasmagoria of early 1980s US Open finals in which different cultures are thrown together to represent himself as one of the most pioneering and persevering of players; this all shows the liberation from a certain lack of self-belief and much perhaps to do with his class and economic background, his class inscription in a class informed and structured world society.

Lendl's creative resistance and so form of counter-power in a world ruled by power to a certain "sucking up" as Lendl once put it in interview, put the whole text of the US public ideology in question as well too as a violent appropriation the US media mobilizes. At an elementary psychological observation one's substantial identity was under threat in the 1982 and 1983 ideological conditions as seen from the micro-practices of ideology that were operative in two title-level tennis matches and in their media representation. If as Lacan notes, the truth is a set of méconnaissances (misrecognitions) then the USA TV and journalism media interpretation of Lendl provide fodder for this critical Lacan-thought.

Daily experience on the professional tour of men's tennis as a form of knowledge would come for Lendl who would proceed to win 8 of his next 16 grand slam finals (he would lose the next one too at the 1983 Australian Open to Mats Wilander). The perhaps disavowed economic part of Lendl as a person from Ostrava, Czechoslovakia made it possible that he had in many ways surpassed Borg, McEnroe and Connors. The electrifying New York City crowds were able to feed into a representational frenzy of American can-do energy that made for a pretty harsh environment for the outsider from central Europe and pretty sympathetic for the native-born Connors. It was on the cards that in these matches that condense many contradictions Connors would be difficult to defeat. Playing in front of the US crowd was an education but not in the usual sense for Lendl who had to spin so much out of his own guts and of those around him to become a pioneering figure.

In this violent clash of cultural styles from the US representation, Lendl comes across as a cadaverous extraterrestrial; the abrasive but exciting climate at the final with the original Cold War era tennis characters of Connors and of Lendl make these matches in need of an even greater politicization; their fantastic complexity needs to be radicalized to give us a general frame that transcends local ethnic stereotypes and worlds. The Connors-Lendl constellate and real subjectivity make the status of violence something really mysterious too in the magical spectacle of these aging tennis matches; one rolls in for speculative purposes and knowledge, Esposito's incisive claim that, "Violence is actually community's most intrinsic expression. We might even say that that violence is the inside of the community that has grown to the point of destructively boiling over outside itself."[39] This accurately describes the lifeworld of both of these 1982 and 1983 matches and of their respective environments.

Violent pigeonholing through definition is inadequate; namely, to define something via representation is reductive. Yet for all that we need representation, for it makes a difference in the practical world. One can only hope that one's substantial identity will not get smashed into the ground; for figures of revolutionary subjectivity on TV it is the case that their contributions will give them a symbolic mandate that will not allow itself to be deleted by the symbolic violence of the representational image and word (the society of the spectacle as we like to say now). Even an event on stage such as a grand slam tennis final cannot evade the consecration that comes with the interventionary force of the good form of violence that is the power of liberation. The idea of excessive intensity resonates here for Connors and Lendl were both players of amazing intensity, something that our chosen clashes between these two figures give us for our generalized cultural memory that remains an ongoing project of the present. The reality of these matches is fledged fully because it concentrates in its small compass so many basic contradictions and tensions in the emerging world society at the time.

False and bogus representations and the brutal mediatization of matters are seriously underestimated. These basic tensions between Connors (as spoiled child and as superstar) and Lendl in the battle days of the Cold War that militate against a good form of community, if not conduct a bad community, give way over time to a more cultivated tennis audience in which the objective power relations that structure the field make Lendl seem rather both more and less like a fish on dry American land and

Connors one in blue USA water. The invisible power relations of representation and violence as forms of power in media mediation are now easier to discern after this 35-year period of time. This I hope has now been thrown into sharper relief. The conative agency of an intersubjective common space and common location lies in wait to expose an international audience and specific worldly correlate that might come to pass by means of painful labor and with greater awareness of the political, economic and media practices of violence and representation, so that we emerge with an expanded awareness of the processes of cultural production. This would by a logical extension, give us more ground to stand on, for thinking a creative and resourceful commons, hopeful existence, and imaginative intelligent creation for practices in the symbolic substance of individual and collective experience as so many cardinal achievements of meaning and knowledge.

Chapter 9

The Unconscious, Athletic Identity and a Whole Galaxy on Stage; or, the 1984 French Open, John McEnroe contra Ivan Lendl[1]

Ivan Lendl (L) presents the cup (The Musketeers' Trophy/La Coupe des Mousquetaires) received from René Lacoste (unpictured) after winning the 1984 men's singles final against John McEnroe at Roland-Garros (R) (Photograph: © JOEL ROBINE/AFP/Getty Images)

This chapter brings fresh evidence to one of the finest tennis matches of the Open era, or indeed in tennis history: the 1984 French men's singles final between Ivan Lendl and John McEnroe. The problem of the athletic inferno and/or lost paradise of community will thus be explored. For this match brings into sight and serves as an exemplary situation to discuss problems of community and the creative life. First, McEnroe declares in a book published 18 years after the event:

> It was the worst loss of my life, a devastating defeat: Sometimes it still keeps me up at nights. It's even tough for me now to do the commentary at the French [...].
>
> [...]. Whatever the reason [...] when push came to shove, I couldn't beat Ivan Lendl in the final of the French Open in the

greatest year I ever had, the greatest year any tennis player had ever had. I blew a two-sets-to-love lead [...].

It was a total disaster.[2]

–John McEnroe on the 1984 French final, which he lost 6-3, 6-2, 4-6, 5-7, 5-7[3]

McEnroe receives this loss as an irremediable trauma. In McEnroe's more recent *But Seriously* (2017), he opens with a Prologue precisely on evil nightmares he still has about this match, "let me be clear: nothing could EVER EVER EVER make up for what happened that day,"[4] and does have some complimentary things to say about his rival Lendl including his coaching of Murray, his historical influence on the game, and his capacity still to this day in spite of all the other things the American has done, to provoke competitive feelings in McEnroe. Being surely here is shared. Or, as McEnroe puts it in an Afterword to *But Seriously*: "It's funny that after all these years of chasing other possible identities—as an art dealer, a rock guitarist, a TV talk-show host, even a politician—here I am, back where I started, finding new ways to compete with Ivan Lendl! 'John McEnroe, Mr. Tennis.' But if that's my destiny, then I'm happy with it."[5] Picture 3 is worth a thousand words. It sends a chill down the spine for its historical and breathtaking transcendental character. McEnroe's and Lendl's earthly destinies intersect and meet without meeting so to say. So, for McEnroe a calamitous kairology continues ad nauseam with the historical memory of his tennis career on clay on the day of this memorable match of all-out open radical conflict and struggle: athletically, psychically, spiritually and more. McEnroe misrecognizes his antagonist insofar as one does not see much if any credit given from McEnroe to Lendl's "spirit" for his notable comeback.

Now consider this thought from Benjamin, "Would it be empathy with exchange value that first qualifies the human being for a 'total experience'?"[6] That is, to consider questions about a new identity and community, would an exchangeable popular cultural studies item for consumption and symbolic capital on the stock exchange of life experiences, such as a grand slam tennis final, teach us as much if not more, and be more interesting in some regards, than many an élite object of focus? In this context exchange value mediates a form of experiential truth. In a passage from Žižek,

> Recall Walter Benjamin's notion of revolution as redemption through repetition of the past: apropos the French Revolution, the task of a true Marxist historiography is not to describe the events the way they really were [...]; the task is rather to unearth the hidden potentiality (the utopian emancipatory potential) which was betrayed in the actuality of revolution and in its final outcome (the rise of utilitarian capitalism). (*LN*, 464)

That is, would a return to the rare event of the four hour and eight minute long 1984 French men's singles final be a chance to bring back to view coordinates, lessons and radical contingencies that might yet come into our vision for the first time, so that we may act accordingly and differently for new individual and collective potentialities and emancipations for projects of community and (de)creativity? In this way, so as to escape from, correct and redeem missed opportunities and failed emancipations about things that really matter beyond a sporting event, a tennis match might yet teach us some basic and valuable strategies for how to create and to exist in common.

It is the sunrise of the *now-time* of a new day, a global-cultural moment, with all the city razzmatazz and myth of Paris, France, the capital of cosmopolitan world citizenship, featuring two tennis players who in their simple and tormented if not nonesuch intensity make them seem as if they could be two characters out of a novel in that wide-ranging chronicle and cycle of prose texts of early to mid nineteenth-century Parisian and French life, Honoré de Balzac's *La Comédie humaine*. The present object of focus, the men's singles final of the 1984 French Open Championships, is one of the top four prizes in the world of tennis along with the Australian Open, Wimbledon and the United States Open. Here we have a face-off of uncommon depth, energy, feeling and daring athleticism on both sides of the net in a title match on la terre battue (the red clay) at Stade Roland-Garros featuring an American tennis icon (he would later become US Davis Cup captain for 14 months) and a Czech one (Lendl became a US citizen in 1992 to become a dual national) to make for a trans-hemispheric clash that also brings out the brutally competitive nature of our communal life under populist late capitalism. Antinomic relations and basic antagonisms curiously are as much, if not more blindingly evident, under popular and mass culture occasions such as a professional tennis match as against a high culture poem, novel or film.

In the 1970s and 1980s the cultural status of tennis in the United States differed from then Czechoslovakia where tennis was taken as a class élite sport—in that free access to courts and a democratic level of participation was possible. Tennis has since undergone a change in the Czech Republic, where ease of access to the sport is at a more affordable level and so more widespread.

Perhaps counterintuitively, this 1984 French Open final constitutes one of the epochal sporting events of the 1980s, partly because of the nature of the players and event involved and that it took place during the Cold War era wherein the ontology of national belonging was so important. Indeed, what interests me here is also how NBC constructs the championship round as a transatlantic super-spectacle in a broadcast on Sunday 10 June 1984 with their studios in New York City at Rockefeller Center serving up "Breakfast from the French Open". For against its own profit driven intentions in so many regards the NBC cultural production allegorizes what a global community might begin to look like. Indeed, this chapter explores how out of mutual competitiveness between two tennis players in an historic match something greater emerges, a disavowed world community and collective creativity. The chair umpire for the title contest is veteran Frenchman Jacques Dorfmann.

For some this match defines and inaugurates a new epoch of professional tennis. It is one of tennis history's unacknowledged wonders of the impossible/possible and inoperative/operative community. The extremely skillful hands at net of McEnroe playing at the topmost peak of his abilities at the age of 25 in his veritable anno miraculo. McEnroe had won all 36 of his matches and all six of the tournaments he had played that year to that date of time (losing only five sets in 1984 and in addition winning 42 straight matches going back to 1983), and would go on to have the best record year-wise of any professional ever, 82-3 (a 96.5% winning percentage). McEnroe would go on to defeat Jimmy Connors in a drubbing in the 1984 Wimbledon Final (he had a mere two unforced errors in a 6-1, 6-1, 6-2 performance and upended Lendl too in straight sets in the final of the 1984 US Open after the famed Super Saturday session that saw both Lendl and McEnroe pushed to five set victories over their respective semi-final opponents, Pat Cash and Connors). Variously described as a tennis genius to a super-brat, the New York City native and former Stanford University star, McEnroe brought attention wherever he went as much for his breathtaking abilities on court as for his temper tantrums at umpires, cameramen and fans. Meanwhile the tall and lanky Lendl who revolutionized the sport of tennis with a gifted and laser forehand, would gallantly endeavor to win Wimbledon, but would never succeed despite two final and a further five semi-final appearances. If McEnroe is one of, if not the greatest of players to never win the French, then Lendl may well be among, if not the finest player to never triumph at Wimbledon: on top of seven appearances in the final four he earned two Queen's Club titles in 1989 and in 1990 (the principal pre-Wimbledon tune up tourney with according to many the sport's highest quality grass courts).[7] Hodgkinson notes that in the light of the nature of the grass courts at the time, and Lendl's strong suits, "His view has long been that [...] appearing in two finals at the All England Club, and reaching the semi-finals at five other Wimbledons, was much more of an accomplishment for him than featuring in eight successive US Open finals" (*IL*, 288). This illumines Lendl's intriguing view on his career performance at Wimbledon.

The standard doxa is that Lendl was a bit of an enigma to the public interpretation, preferring to leave his emotions elsewhere and psychic life hidden from view, and focus on the tennis; how intensely focused Lendl was and became increasingly especially following on the coattails of this career altering match. English critic and novelist John O. Bayley once told me in a personal communication (in Oxford, England in February 1992 at a dinner with him and with his spouse Iris Murdoch, both of whom said that they liked Lendl) that Lendl was perhaps something like "a sphinx with nothing standing behind him". Hence the question was sometimes asked if not explicitly, what was standing behind "the sphinx"? A powerful void that would be a most powerful power or an empty container without content? Or something else altogether that would solve the puzzle? With the chronological advantage of the passage of time, now he is considered a breakthrough figure, and one who opened up a new page for modern tennis in how he trained (he worked with psychologists in the dark to enhance his powers of concentration, was the first player to have both a nutritionist and a physiotherapist, and was arguably among the fittest of athletes in any sport in the world at his peak from 1985–87), and in the objective fact that he played in 19 grand slam finals (a record since eclipsed by Federer and now also the Mallorcan/Spaniard Rafael Nadal and the Serbian Novak Djokovic).[8]

Lendl remains the only modern Open era tennis player (post-1968) to have won 90% or more of his matches on tour for five different years: 1982, 1985, 1986, 1987 and 1989. Also in the Open period Lendl (1981–91) shares a record with Sampras (1992–2002) for appearing in a grand slam final in 11 consecutive years and tied at number two with Rafael Nadal (2004-17) behind Federer (2001–15) for consecutive years 14 behind Federer's 15 in which one ATP tournament or more was won (Lendl 1980–1993).[9]

Yet entering this 1984 clash, Lendl had lost four straight major finals, including two in which he was the favorite to win over Jimmy Connors at the US Open, in another he lost an intriguing five set contest contra Sweden's Björn Borg in the 1981 French Open final (it would be Borg's last grand slam title) and he lost the 1983 Australian Open final to Mats Wilander. We define the contemporary tennis situation as an effect of "The Lendl Break" or of "The Lendl Cut". Something changed in the professional community of tennis after Lendl in regard to mental and physical preparation, and in a number of habits on court, including changing one's rackets due to a lower string tension after x number of games played. This is why one can speak of the Lendl *munus* of an enhanced *communitas* to the world of tennis as was already argued in Chapter 8, for he made the sport more professional.

McEnroe and Lendl were arguably two of the more articulate and intelligent players on tour; both were brilliant tactically on the court, and yet this match was given a billing in advance as another soon to be choked by Lendl who had become earmarked by some as the "Czechoslovchokian" for not being able to win the big title matches in grand slam finals, even though he enjoyed notable successes on tour up until this time, including two end-of-year Masters titles in 1981 and 1982 (he would go on to win five titles in nine consecutive finals from 1980-88). He also had major accomplishments and winning streaks in the lesser tournaments from 1981-83, but he had not yet broken through on the biggest of stages.

NBC's Dick Enberg notes at one point with a US football metaphor in the 1984 French Open men's singles final match to colleague Bud Collins on air that Lendl "might get out in the open, Bud, and never be tackled; he certainly has great skills."[10] Following on from this tournament this was precisely what happened. Lendl would go on to win 54 more tournaments as well as seven more majors in 14 finals. For the record in the Open era as for contests between major players, Djokovic and Nadal have met 50 times (26-24), Djokovic-Federer 45 times (23-22), Nadal-Federer (23-15) and in fourth come the Lendl-McEnroe duels with 37 contests (21-15 in finished matches), and in fifth place is a tie with Connors-Lendl tallying 36 battles (13-22 for completed matches), as well as Djokovic and Murray (25-11).[11]

If the stylistically inventive at net McEnroe wins this match, he has a chance to win the grand slam in 1984 (the Australian Open at that time was played in December on grass), which he may well have done, and furthermore would in the event be considered up to that time perhaps one of the two or so most accomplished tennis players in history, along with his spiritual mentor (and one of whom he was compared to by some observers even as a teenager) the Australian "Rocket" Rod Laver who won the grand slam in both 1962 and 1969, the last player to do so to be sure albeit Agassi, Federer, Nadal and Djokovic have since achieved a career grand slam wherein one wins one of all four of the majors (and Agassi and Nadal the career golden slam with their respective Olympic Gold Medals). McEnroe had never won the French Open going into the title match, and this was his only appearance in the final of the most prestigious clay court tournament in the world.

I now shift registers to challenge an ideological attitude. That is, the anemic disposition of scholars who dismiss popular culture such as sport. So, here I am concerned to attack such an ideological stance. To the contrary, an engagement with the body is needed. While certain distinguished minds may disparage pop-cultural items such as tennis, it cannot be said of such figures as the English literary critic John O. Bayley, the French philosophers Deleuze and Derrida, the French film-maker Jean-Luc Godard, the US literary critic and theorist J. Hillis Miller, the English novelist Iris Murdoch, the Scottish scholar of French literature Graham Robb and the US philosopher Hugh J. Silverman who the present writer knows have some interest in tennis (whether as player or as fan).

Godard for instance says in interview,

> My one and only dream is to compete at the French Open dressed in an overcoat, sporting heavy shoes and smoking, and maybe reading this text by Fréderic Prokosch on Bill Tilden 'Une Sarah Bernhardt'. "Well, let me tell you something, my boy. Tennis is more than a simple sport. It is an art, like ballet. Or like a stage play. That moment I enter the court I feel like Anna Pavlova. Or Adelina Patti. Or even Sarah Bernhardt. I see the footlights in front of me. I hear the crowd whispering. I feel a cold shiver. Win or die! It's now or never! It's my life's crucial moment. But I'm old, my boy, old. My legs are giving out on me. Will the last act be tragic?"
> *Your dream is to compete at the French Open—and win?*
> Obviously![12]

This is moving for its passion and enthusiasm. Other cultural figures could be brought in here for illustrative purposes. German-born US scholar Hans Ulrich Gumbrecht has written a classic on sports (not tennis) *In Praise of Athletic Beauty* (2006), which I commend to the interested reader. Contemporary French writer Serres suggests here of the disciplines of philosophy and of the bodily:

> The body is far from behaving as a simple passive receptor.

Philosophy should not offer it to the given of the world in its recent repulsive manifestation, sitting or slumped over, apathetic or ugly. It exercises, trains, it can't help itself. It loves movement, goes looking for it, rejoices on becoming active, jumps, runs or dances, only knows itself, immediately and without language, in and through its passionate energy. It discovers its existence when its muscles are on fire, when it is out of breath—at the limits of exhaustion.[13]

How true are these observations. We may dig deeper.

In Bataille sport constitutes one fulcrum for the *numen*, the sacred precisely because it is non-utilitarian and so is coextensive with the energy of the stars in his notion of the general economy.[14] Matters are more complicated as Bataille argues in conceptualizing an edifice that contests the closed and restricted economy of money and of work that grounds our societies. One must depose the idea that sports is simply regressive and part of corporate capital full stop in our oligarchic and plutocratic financial system. We must attack our neurotic societies at the point of the physical body by reorganizing both. Not only this, as many scholars argue the notion of the intellectual itself seems rather insubstantial. If the distinguishing feature of human being is that we use our hands as French critic Gérard Genette, inter alia, point out, what distinctions could we make between hitting a tennis volley or forehand, and writing a sentence? This is not to say that the two spheres of attention are comparable or exact but that these manual/physical activities themselves are reductive labels.

I endorse these abovementioned declarations against the idée reçue of the intellectual. Our bodies need self-care, as much as our intellects. These are not just Spinozan (recall the thematic of the parallelism of the mind with the body), Artaudian or Deleuzoguattarian suggestions (the Body without Organs): it is clear without having to invoke the authority of these names.

Consider the thought produced by ancient Greece and the relation that epoch had to the body. Was this good or bad? I leave it for the reader to decide. Perhaps it is still too difficult to adjudicate. Yet the prospect remains tantalizing.

This discussion on the choreography of the unconscious, of athletic identity and of a galaxy on stage will admit the subterranean if not always explicit influence of Lacan's corpus of texts, with special reference to his 1953–78 *Seminar*, into its elaboration of the sparks of the elephant in the room that is for Lacan the unconscious in the formation of the self and of identity in the constitution of cultural pair connections. Here we make the surprising convergence of McEnroe and Lendl. The adventures of this journey of self, of identity, and of the unconscious and of its concomitant enlistment or mirroring of the other cultural figure ("the unconscious is the unconscious of the other"—Lacan) is informed by the phenomena of ideal example, opponent, mentor, correspondent, double or even of exact opposite, all of which are permeable to the effects of "the unconscious as the desire of the other" (Lacan) and of how as Lacan argues on multiple occasions, subjects are essentially othered. Whence the unconscious' chthonic power.

While the parameters of this chapter do not allow for a detailed elucidation of our chosen paired cultural linkage, this demonstration nevertheless drives home the whole core of the magnetic field of identity vis-à-vis the mentor-opponent figure with some textual supports above all from the 1984 French final as a way to discuss the filaments and lineaments of identity and of self, and of how they radiate out onto the plane of the mentor-opponent in one's own signifying elaboration. Further than this, the mechanisms of the unconscious and of how they operate in the interstices of the structural relationship between our athletic-cultural figures as a formation effect also traverse the frontier of our presentation.

However, to self-problematize, why include pop-cultural

figures and identities such as McEnroe and Lendl, however fascinating they may seem only to some in the subfield of popular culture of tennis? Yet this tennis rivalry has not yet been properly formalized in print culture. There is a documentary film on the two in German online, and that screened on the cable channel ARTE, but nothing substantive in print to my knowledge in any language.[15] The focus of McEnroe's recent *But Seriously* suggests more than is usually the case on this rivalry yet it necessarily remains less than thoroughgoing.

Psychoanalysis permits us to understand Lendl and McEnroe in newfangled ways. Subtle issues require a fine-tuned and refined theory. Perhaps a certain passionate radicalism is here at stake. Where is the energy going? What of this timeless unconscious? The 1984 match itself is of an unusual density and intensity. These are both complex persons if not indigestible for some. How are we to describe and thematize this? What is the special essence of this match? The empirical symbolical order includes tennis as an institution. That recognition is always misrecognition seems to inform McEnroe-Lendl in their various misapprehensions and distortions about one another (although for this observer more on the side of the publicly verbose McEnroe, than on that of the more reticent in public Lendl). McEnroe won the junior singles title at Roland Garros in 1977 and Lendl in 1978. Lendl took control of their earliest nine matches (McEnroe winning their first two matches in 1980 and Lendl all seven of their matches in 1981 and 1982); McEnroe came back to overtake Lendl (10-2 in 1983 and 1984 and overall 12-9 until the end of 1984) with Lendl then in ascendancy in the second half of their respective careers from 1985–92 (Lendl 12-3 and overall 21-15).[16]

The foundational imposture by some scholars of anti-sport claims needs unmasking. Roland Barthes writes, "At certain periods, in certain societies, the theater has had a major social function: it collected the entire city within a shared experience:

the knowledge of its own passions. Today it is sport that in its way performs this function. Except that the city has enlarged: it is no longer a town, it is a country, often even, so to speak, the whole world; sport is a great modern institution case in the ancestral forms of spectacle."[17] Paris, June 10, 1984 is a splendid example of a theatrical event for the whole world.[18] McEnroe from the capitalist West contra Lendl from the communist East; it was a battle in which weaponry of multiple kinds are part and parcel of the various forms of cultural meaning of the match. For Barthes in a volume on sport, "The spectators' choral manifestations punctuate the duration of the match. By its massive exclamations the crowd comments on the spectacle. Every moral value can be invested in the sport: endurance, self-possession, temerity, courage. The great players are heroes, not stars."[19] In this context, McEnroe recalls of the match, "When I was introduced on Center Court at Stade Roland Garros, I got the greatest hand I'd ever received at the start of a match—a huge roar!" (YCS, 175). As for the idea that players were more like gladiators than mere stars during one golden age of tennis appears the case with McEnroe and with Lendl who played with other mythical figures in this era, such as the abovementioned Björn Borg from Sweden (he won in his short career an unprecedented 11 of the 27 grand slam tournaments in which he entered) and again the winningest player in tennis history, James Scott Connors from the US (he won 109 career singles titles with Lendl coming in third with 94, McEnroe fourth with 77, Nadal fifth with 75, Djokovic sixth with 68, and Borg tied with Sampras for seventh each tallied up 64; Agassi garnered 60 singles titles, which trails Guillermo Vilas who held a singles trophy 62 times). Roger Federer who is now second with 97, Nadal, Djokovic, Sampras and Agassi are five major players who came after this particular golden age of the Open era of the sport in the 1970s and 1980s that was inaugurated in 1968 and that saw the computer rankings system in place from 1973.[20]

The name and city of Paris signifies the summit of cultural bliss in the humanist tradition, and so it was for some on this late Spring Sunday of 1984. Also, for Barthes, "Then sport returns to the immediate world of passions and aggressions, dragging with it the crowd, which came precisely to seek purification from it. Sport is the entire trajectory separating a combat from a riot."[21] As for these exciting observations, this match precisely was a super heavyweight title fight of world tennis and the intense focus of the Parisian crowd was palpable. There is something dramatic and memorable about a Grand Slam final, in part because one's place in tennis history is assured for both players regardless of the outcome. The fans were completely into the 1984 French Final clash. It was a taut and atmospheric ambient milieu. Furthermore, for Barthes, "In sport, man experiences life's fatal combat, but this combat is distanced by the spectacle, reduced to its forms, cleared of its affects, of its dangers, and of its shames: it loses its noxiousness, not its brilliance or its meaning."[22] Precisely it is television as the spectacle of power and the power of the spectacle that we get here, albeit in a relaxed and intelligent mode it would seem compared with many tennis broadcasts especially those of more recent vintage. The match was called by Dick Enberg (1935–) and Bud Collins (1929–2016).

Barthes argues of sport,

First, it must be remembered that everything happening to the player also happens to the spectator. But whereas in the theater the spectator is only a voyeur, in sport he is a participant, an actor. And then, in sport, man does not confront man directly. There enters between them an intermediary [...] a ball. And this thing is the very symbol of things: it is in order to possess it, to master it, that one is strong, adroit, courageous. To watch, here, is not only to live, to suffer, to hope, to understand but also, and especially, to say so—by voice, by gesture, by facial expression; it is to call the whole world to witness; in a word, it is to communicate. Ultimately man knows certain forces, certain conflicts, joys and agonies: sport expresses them, liberates them, consumes them without ever letting anything be destroyed.[23]

This providing of an explosive occasion of 'communication' perhaps explains the enthusiasm for spectator sports. It is an evental form of life-enhancing and life-furthering non-self-identity that does not self-destruct. One must try to grasp this idea firmly in hand. Sport is a democratic participative operation.

McEnroe recounts of an exhibition finals duel in November 1979 in Milan, Italy (though he may actually be referring to a match held in November 1981 in Milan)

> I wiped Lendl out in the first set [...]. Halfway through that set, I could see his shoulders slump—I could tell he'd given up, and now he was dogging it. He was just standing there, barely even trying.
>
> [...]. I said, 'Listen, Ivan, you're acting like a pussy. Get out there and start playing. You wimp!' [...].
>
> In the second set, he again played an abysmal game, putting virtually no effort into it. I gave it to him again, totally roasted him: 'You're a quitter, man.'
>
> 'Sergio!' He called Sergio Palmieri, later my agent, used to be the tournament director there—'Sergio, you tell him to stop that! He can't talk to me like that!' And I still wouldn't let up.
>
> I often wonder why I didn't just let him make a complete ass of himself in that match. Because then, all of a sudden, Lendl started playing harder than I'd ever seen him play before. I'd gotten him so worked up that he wound up beating me! (YCS, 152–53)

A perhaps disavowed spirit of McEnroe felt responsible, if not even an ethical duty for his fellow player, and in so doing he helped him find his way. It illumines the psychoanalytic notion that identity is given as a gift from the other on the basis of a challenge and even defiles laid down by the other that one must fulfill and contest to avoid embarrassing the other who set the said challenge and offered up the perhaps even rude rebuke(s). McEnroe here taps into community as *avec* as *cum*; or, as the back of an Esposito-text argues community is "a void, a debt, a gift to the other that also reminds us of our constitutive alterity with respect to ourselves" (*COD*, back cover). Whence McEnroe gives a blank check to the Czech-born Lendl. Esposito in a discussion of Jean-Jacques Rousseau: "Community appears to be definable only on the basis of the lack that characterizes it. It is *nothing other* than what history has negated, the nonhistoric backdrop from which history originates in the form of a necessary betrayal" (*COD*, 16). This could also describe the unsung McEnroe-Lendl historical linkage that the cultural history of the sport of tennis disavows in comparison with some other leading rivalries in the Open era. As such, Lendl-McEnroe mediate community.

McEnroe continues, "Maybe because of his background, Ivan was always going into strange sulks and weird head trips. Sometimes the victim was his opponent; for a long time, it was just as often himself."

For quite a while, he had a reputation for choking away big matches.

Once he decided to work on his mind, body, and game, however, he started cutting a wide swath through professional tennis. As much as I may have disliked him, I have to give Lendl credit: Nobody in the sport has ever worked as hard as he did [...] his dedication—physical and mental—was incredible, second to none. (*YCS*, 154–55)

As a physical and mental agent, Lendl dramatically improves.

The ordeal of this French match helped; for it is well known in tennis lore that a physician told Lendl he could have had a heart attack out there and died (he was vomiting horribly after the match). Health was a motivating factor for him to change his training and conditioning regime. The self-injury of inadequate fitness (despite his successes hitherto) made this necessary. His so-called mysterious "head trips" also vanished. The Lendl revolution was now underway after scoring a few top-level years on the tour in his short career. These are all lessons for the construction of athletic and other forms of creativity and community.

Important factors are personal attributes, class and physical stratification and situational features (Lendl as an Easterner playing in the West, etcetera). Lendl came from a family of physical élites if not so much of economic ones as was the case with McEnroe; both of Lendl's biological parents were notable tennis players. Both fathers for McEnroe and for Lendl were lawyers, but the economic conditions and the relation to capital of their respective families were different. I saw Lendl's tennis club when I visited Ostrava in November 2010 to observe Lendl play Björn Borg and Mats Wilander in an exhibition match, the first time Lendl had played in his native town for more than three decades, and it was clear that however pleasant, this club was not what McEnroe would have had access to given his family's relation to (Western) capital.

McEnroe opens the door for Lendl to walk through to new life when he loses his cool early in the third set. McEnroe's error is one Lendl makes him meet with the harshest penalty. As for McEnroe on his temper tantrums: "On a tennis court, you're out there all alone. People ask why I get so angry. This is a big part of it. I'm out there on the line, by myself, fighting to the death in front of people who are eating cheese sandwiches, checking their watches, and chatting with their friend about the stock market" (YCS, 29). McEnroe also it seems had a certain tortured creativity; his skills were remarkable, not least because he did not rehearse to the same extent that Lendl did to win his majors, though he claims he tried weight lifting and much else besides during his six-months long 1986 sabbatical after losing to Brad Gilbert at the year end 1985 Masters. For the record McEnroe won 7 grand slams losing also 2 finals to Lendl, 1 to Borg and 1 to Connors, and Lendl triumphed in 8 and lost 11 in total to Borg, Connors, McEnroe, Wilander, Boris Becker and Stefan Edberg—perhaps the most colorful list of slam final rivals of any Open era player. It was that emotional tirade in the third set that critically if not fatally hurt McEnroe in this match. McEnroe became more and more upset by a cameraman whose headset was emitting noise. Finally when it was 1-1 and with a mini break point for McEnroe against Lendl's serve, McEnroe strolled over to the cameraman and screamed something into his headset. Lendl recovered to win his serve in this game and then after going down 1-2 McEnroe smashed his racket out of fury and frustration on the sidelines before he sat down. Lendl then followed by breaking McEnroe's serve in the very next game in a set in which Lendl prevailed 6-4; this was only the sixth set that McEnroe had lost the whole year. The reader may wish to watch the relevant clip of McEnroe going berserk.[24] In minute one of 9:41 in this clip McEnroe turns to red hot lava, which as suggested above contributed to his downfall in this hotly contested match; all Lendl needed was a small opening for his fearsome clay court skills to take hold, and McEnroe gave him that creative opportunity.

Lendl and McEnroe share a maniacal attention to detail, and are unusual athletes. McEnroe in his great touch, and Lendl in the vertiginous precision and impressive power of his ground strokes and consistency. Though, in a certain way the historiographical codification of the being of their self-identities should be negated in favor of the supervening reality of an unconscious (Lacano-Freudian) that stands outside of time and which makes of them co-creative agents. Ultimately we are addressing shared human destinies: that we have a multiple identity shared with others that percuss and reverberate our own life narrative. McEnroe again on his rival, "As much as I hate to give Lendl credit, he became a great champion. And in a way, he has me to thank for it, I think. I goaded him into it" (YCS, 156). Even if McEnroe may exaggerate the case, this is true in a certain sense. Note the classic idea from Baltasar Gracián that our opponents are the ones who make us renowned: "The greatness of many has been fashioned thanks to malicious enemies" (POAP, 32). This is because the friend-enemy distinction is a false one as Friedrich Nietzsche instructs us to think. We are the conative energies of others.

The stage play-actors for our present event, Lendl and McEnroe, had both been compiling accomplishments for several years with each winning millions of dollars in the process. But a French title is the beyond of value for a tennis player who has never won it (and many top-level players have not, from Connors to McEnroe to Becker to Edberg to Sampras and we could continue). The cruelty of tennis, of the passage of the power of time, would also pinch McEnroe who would never win the French. You do not get any closer than that: 5-7 in the fifth set after being up two sets to love and a break in the fourth set when he was five points away from the championship. McEnroe has every reason to view it as a catastrophic personal loss. But as I argue the puzzle of identity in a truer sense makes both players winners in this battle for the ages.

Sport as a remarkable phenomenon? Consider again Barthes, "What is it then that men put into sport? Themselves, their human universe. Sport is made in order to speak the human contract."[25] It is the communicativity of matters that tennis occasions for 'the human contract'. Here Luhmann's systems theory teaches us that

communication is the mechanism that constitutes society

as an autopoietic system and processes it in these terms. The negation of communication is itself communication, and hence the expression of society. [...]. Communication becomes the basic structure of society, where the relationship between communication and society is circular [...].[26]

So in a way sport mediates society. Further than this, we learn that "Luhmann sets a view of a world that temporalizes, differentiates, and decentralizes all identities" for "Identities are products of past events";[27] this is true. Also interesting about this match is that many concerned at the time seem to have forgotten about it, which accords to what "Luhmann says of memory that its true function for society consists not of storage, but rather of forgetting."[28] This paradox constructs society.

Raw energy and entertainment value shoot through a four-hour long plus tennis battle. True to his ranking, McEnroe's early play in sets one and two is sublime, which he wins handily with his elegant play, hitting lines with clinical precision, and playing perhaps better than most anyone has ever played on clay. Indeed many a seasoned commentator argue that those first two sets are the best clay court tennis ever played by a non-specialist of la terre battue in a French final. McEnroe was in the marvel of the zone. In the third set, none too early, the sheer force of Lendl's ground strokes becomes truly phenomenal. From here this then aged into one of the all-time matches of clay court tennis. The intensity and concentration of both players was also uncommon. What grabs my attention here is how Lendl comes back to win the next three sets in a rather polite if extreme effort that nearly did him in; a conative force prevails.

Early in the second set Collins remarks that "McEnroe's confidence is as high as the Eiffel Tower." Indeed, McEnroe avers, "It's the only match in which I ever felt I was playing up to my capabilities and lost" (YCS, 180). This is extraordinary, and even mythical, at least for students of tennis historiography. For

Lendl though it was abrupt and revolutionary in a good way. It has made of this match an historical concentrate, a Benjaminian monad and dynamic instance of time for one's emancipatory potentials and self-redemption if not even for the whole history of humanity as a paradigm or example for the power of building universality and community. Consider here that we may for purposes of argumentation make being defeated something like being killed, when we read that according to Esposito, for the English philosopher Thomas Hobbes, "What men have in common [...] is their generalized capacity to be killed: the fact that anyone can be killed by anyone else. This is what Hobbes sees in the dark depths of the community; [...] nothing remains for us except to 'immunize' us beforehand and, in so doing, to negate the very same foundations of community" (COD, 13). By extension, it is hardly surprising that the brutally competitive system of tennis has made it challenging for Lendl-McEnroe to avoid immunizing themselves against one another even if respect exists on both sides.

Is modern and postmodern tennis subjectivity by default a spirit of bourgeois subjectivity? Perhaps. Perhaps not if it is reductionist. What if Richard Rorty is right that we need to bourgeoisify? Perhaps that is not correct. Concretely, however, this seems at least superficially accurate; for we live in a bourgeois era and are educated in the bourgeois university. Clearly though in the final accounting, tennis escapes easy definitions and labels so as to be part and parcel of the inherent incompleteness of reality as contemporary quantum physics teaches. As a category, tennis awaits its completion.

Lendl and McEnroe fade into and cross each other. The violence of McEnroe's comments and critique provoke the incomplete Lendl who feels the appalling trivialization of his destiny, and proves that you can never know the net outcome given the unfinished nature of things and of people. On the nineteenth-century Danish philosopher Søren Kierkegaard's tombstone one reads, "THAT INDIVIDUAL" but that does not eliminate self-other relations, perhaps it even intensifies them for forms of inter-individuation. The co-functioning of identity is what we get with Lendl-McEnroe. A challenge to the current organization of knowledge. We may also broach the idea of "the non-identical individual" from Theodor Adorno's critical philosophy as what Lendl enlists in this match and also in his career to avoid a certain reductive comprehension of his person as tennis player. In any case, there appears to be a competitive trading of identities between McEnroe and Lendl in this internecine tennis combat.

Admittedly though why should we talk about persons whose symbolic place (their material wealth) goes beyond 99% of the population? But they are also illustrative of the commerce, globality and psychology of tennis, among much else besides. Both of our players have a dark side, something in each of them that transcends whoever "they" supposedly are. McEnroe exploding with violence. Lendl going on these self-destructively strange "head trips" as McEnroe notes. And of course we are in a state of war in our late capitalist universe. Perhaps Lendl's backgrounding did not prepare him for an individual professional sport in the hardline capitalist West? It is hard to know. One could even argue the opposite, that it was growing up in the Stalinist East that made him so desirous of success, but that all the grand slam finals that he played in were played in the capitalist West did not necessarily help him even if it made some of those finals intrinsically interesting from a transcultural viewpoint.

The non-relation between McEnroe and Lendl make them exemplary of the inoperative community; consider Esposito, "the community is made possible only by the lack of a relation among its members" (COD, 46). Thus the paradoxical non-relation sort of relation that constitutes a negative community, which may also function as something regressive and progressive, depending on the context.

Is the world of tennis part of the ruling oligarchy as a discipline and activity that both confirms and continues the power of the ruling classes? Though there is a pinch of truth to that, a more radical line of reasoning would say the question is too universal for that reductive line of reasoning. All the same "the emancipation from class will be the emancipation of all of humanity,"[29] as Alain Badiou argues. Both McEnroe as well as his backgrounding from Ostrava, Czechoslovakia push Lendl over the edge. He was hungry. He had *desire* in superabundance, that which Spinoza calls and Lacan concurred as "the true essence of human being". Not only economic or libidinal causes, but also intersubjective recognition (including with one's internal alter self), and the Nietzschean one of excellence (to do what you do as equally excellently as your mentor does idea only here it applies to an opponent) Lendl and McEnroe were as subjects striving and aiming.

If, as Žižek argues, "God is thus the tragic impotent observer"[30] then the Roland-Garros tennis gods were unable to aid McEnroe. Lendl's singularity resides in how he did not turn off the lights. He dealt with the adversity of being down with grace, tenacity and courage, and these attributes allowed him to achieve another subjectivity via his opponent McEnroe, paradoxically in an ontology in which being is shared. This is vital because we must go to first things first. Ironically it was an Easterner who appropriated the Occidental heritage of individualist rationalism. This is one of the paradoxes of the instituter of modern tennis.

Another issue to address is fashion: its systemic aspects and linguistic dimension. Lendl wore Adidas gear that became part and parcel of his public person and cultural identity. In this way, Lendl became an icon for reified consciousness proving perhaps that reification can also be a form of power, and in Lendl's case a signature of not only name brand commodity fetishism and phantasmagorical merchandise, but also of high level disciplined professionalism. So the idea of false reifications is a generalization that need not always apply. Reification after all can be a good thing. For it may instill a noble quality of value and of meaning to something that conducts respect, care and attention toward the object. Worth noting here are the Adidas tennis rackets Lendl used in the first half of the 1980s.[31] These rackets became an emblem of Lendl's cutting-edge approach to tennis, and of the power revolution he ushered in to the sport with incomparably fast groundstrokes. Lendl as tennis agent in one of the sport's heydays became the human tennis machine that mobilized the awesome power of the ontological idea of drive from Žižekian psychoanalysis.

Lendl was also a trailblazer insofar as, "In the early twentieth century fashion houses commissioned sports champions to endorse their product. In the twenty-first century fashion designers created ranges for sportswear companies. Two giant sportswear companies, Adidas and Nike, revolutionized activity wear by employing top designers and the latest technology [...]."[32] Lendl was as much known for his Adidas racket and signature argyle tennis polo shirt that he wore in the early 1980s through the French Final of 1984 (and his later versions of Adidas shirts from 1985 and after) as he was for his tennis prowess. Roland Barthes's *Système de la Mode* (1967)/*The Fashion System* (1983) here springs to mind as a relevant cultural analysis to note.

Lendl's taciturnity on court was part and parcel of what Nancy calls "the taciturn restraint of a superlanguage [...]."[33] Lendl is contrariwise off court; consider for example his appearance on *The David Letterman Show* from 1986. Anecdotally, when the present writer saw him practicing with his Australian coach Tony Roche at Wimbledon in 1992 before his fourth round match against Goran Ivanisevic you may not recognize the joviality of the man compared with his on court demeanor.[34] In his silent way of being there seemed to reside a hope for changing the course of not only the sporting, but also of the cultural conversation. The cycle of fire that was Ivan Lendl's forehand in the early to mid 1980s comes to mind here with a poster, "Lendl's Law: Forehands speaker louder than words." The picture shows Lendl hitting through a forehand with flames of fire emanating from his signature Adidas tennis racket. The whole poster speaks the scene. This silence of being that was Lendl at this time in his career was of course also a function of his experiences growing up in Czechoslovakia during the totalitarian period of so-called normalization. Yet another silence denotes the silent revolution that Lendl was effectuating for tennis history.

Also impressive about this cultural form of a tennis match that constituted an example of *now-time* and of the *dynamic instant* that we have been tracing, was that it broaches and mediates through its Parisian inflected scenes a notion of cosmopolitan worldwide state identity. It points toward the social symbolic substance of international citizens for world citizenship. It also registers the future global subject in incubation. What British historian Maurice Keen calls "the chivalric virtues of courage and endurance"[35] both McEnroe and Lendl display to a greater or lesser degree. However, chivalrous standards of civilized conduct are not seen by McEnroe when he storms off the stage during the awards ceremony. Here McEnroe's agonistic behavior and arrogance shine out. This match blows things open for Lendl, for it paves the way for his 1985 US Open final victory over McEnroe that consolidates his number one ranking and heralds a five-year period when he rules the men's tennis world. For Lendl the weight of the world is lifted. His great promise achieves some recognition. In a learning curve, Lendl plays set five with a new vehemence that broke McEnroe's 42 match winning streak (unlike in 1981 when Lendl lost the fifth set, 1-6, as a 21 year old in the French Final to the great Swede Borg in the last appearance he would make at Roland-Garros after winning six championships by the age of 24). Lendl wins the fifth set 7-5.

Lendl's realism about tennis was a good 20 years ahead of his time, which explains why he is seen as a foundational figure for contemporary tennis. But it did take that much time for many observers to move beyond the imbecilic remarks and misunderstandings to which Lendl was subjected. Lendl's hard-edged realism came paradoxically enough from the communist East (and so was hard won) even as the realism of late financial capitalism continues on apace. One may discern in Lendl who was healthily destructive of the status quo, Benjamin's idea of, "The destructive character [who] is always blithely at work"[36] and who "tolerates misunderstanding; he does not promote gossip [...]."[37] Lendl suggests as much himself when he remarks in an interview this volume cites that he will not do an autobiography.

Now the whole issue of the social world as a world at war in our competitive bourgeois societies certainly exists; though this is incomplete, for as I argue the construction of athletic identity is transindividual. Finally it is McEnroe who also wins for he provokes Lendl and lifts him to another level. By being an ass, by being that proverbial character out of Shakespeare's *A Midsummer Night's Dream* he somehow showed how hating is a form of loving. Crazy? Perhaps. But truth lies in paradox, if we are to believe many a thinker not least one of the noted psychoanalytic thinkers since Lacan, Žižek.

Considerations of theoretical psychoanalysis and energy aside, the match is good entertainment, as well as a metaphor for reflection on the nature, and on the destiny, of the human person as a cooperative and shared being. As a pair cultural connection there is none more uncomfortably compelling in modern tennis, even Borg-McEnroe for all its sublimity lacks dimensions that make this Lendl-McEnroe rivalry rather more visceral, violent, primal, and even rather more Freudian, Nietzschean and Marxian. The Connors-McEnroe rivalry is another for the world tennis archive, though both are red, white and blue born Americans, whereas for this interpreter, Lendl and McEnroe share topmost intensity, yet are at the same time decidedly different in their respective histories.

This match reveals that we are multiple. The moral agency of time makes Lendl a paternal figure in tennis history. The cultural and paradigmatic power of tennis allows us to see the real matter of competitivity and the impossible/possible community at hand in our experience of the everyday; it reveals how it is necessary to liberate untapped potentials and energies for a becoming global common identity irreducible to a self or essentialist ontological unit.

This narrative of failed and of taken opportunities invites the question: what can theater tell us about identity? What is impossible/possible? What truth can be communicated? Breath, heartbeats, sweating, shouting, energy, gestures, time: what of it all in the construction of the silhouette of self and of an identity irreducible to a vain and greedy self outsourced by the powers of representation in our market economy of rampant megalomania, of abuse of power and of resigned cynicism. What of world communication in this global-cultural moment of a tennis match? What of worldwide trade, ecology, war, communion? What of the paradoxical "un-power" dimension (a good form of power for Nancy, Lacoue-Labarthe, Blanchot and the present writer in *The Dialectics of Late Capital and Power: James, Balzac and Critical Theory*, 2007) to identity since we already know about its clichéd power aspect? What of the power of the decision to provoke the other as McEnroe did to Lendl in Milan?

What more precisely—to return to our psychoanalytic narrative—of the unconscious structure of subjectivity? The psychodrama of this match shows us that psychology is drama. And that the synergy of dreams and discipline go hand in glove with explosions of energy that de-reify the human being for a form of freedom wherein the other ignites the matter that is the other's unconscious as one's own. This chaotic and untamable power of the unconscious, this unbound form of energy and of elements, create an assiduous athletic mode of being in the Lendl-event and phenomenon.

McEnroe is unable to get out from under the reified, commoditized and capitalized self. If McEnroe could he would see that this intersubjective and transindividual victory by his arch rival was his own as well. As Heidegger, Nancy and others would argue in concerto Being is always being-with, including for us here by extension for athletic identity in a becoming global community. The splendor of an identity irreducible to a self is what a market existence does not permit. In this regard McEnroe's logic goes hand in hand with the trend of globalization and not of what Jean-Luc Nancy rightly argues we really require "the creation of the world".[38] This is regrettable as we need to get beyond the totalitarian self. Even if one wishes to find McEnroe culpable (McEnroe himself does more recently for his ill-chosen behavior at the 1984 French in a special show attached to the 2017 French Open) one must locate causality as well to the historical social system that has produced him, and to which Luhmann would argue he has been banished with little (if any) individual agency. Yet once again it is a paradox. When in cooler hours McEnroe says that, "I've never watched that match once. I can't bear to. […]. It's too sickening to me" (YCS, 179) it points to a certain reified, commoditized, and even monadic mode of reality part and parcel of an overly credulous if not even religious and cultish capitalist ideology. The radical negativity of this loss haunts McEnroe's bourgeois-competitive-capitalist brain and individual imaginary. Instead McEnroe could again consider how in the cooperation that was the co-articulation of the match he helped to inspire his opponent Lendl in 1979. There was/is a true spirit between Lendl and McEnroe that remains disavowed.

We require a way of reconceiving identity wherein its truth resides in the other's truth. All else is naked aggrandizement.

Identity is a cooperative process in which the other is intersubjectively recognized (whether positively or negatively). Against this background, world understanding itself would be enhanced if we could imagine identities based on the truth of the opponent's position. Thereby we might engender what Stiegler calls "fields of transindividuation".[39] We need a transindividual understanding of the being of identity.

Yes: albeit in the final of a major tournament, it was just a professional men's tennis match. But the explosive nature of the occasion, the constellation of rôles, the ambient milieu, the historical clash of ideological worlds (for example the Cold War facet of the encounter), and much else besides make it a precious legacy so as to formalize things that really matter, such as notions of community and creativity. The red clay clash created a tremendous stir at the time, even if most people have now forgotten about it that is paradoxically as Luhmann would remind us, precisely the point. The traumatic entry of Lendl into the domain of men's tennis came from his atypical background from the communist East, Ostrava, Moravia. The power of his identity may be seen in McEnroe's very reaction to his stunning defeat and usurpation as king of tennis in due course at Lendl's hands. Yet what Žižek writes of as "the Void of subjectivity"[40] is the lesson that the advanced capitalist brain and the late capitalist identity have yet to cognize. Still this void is far from nothing. The creative nature of athletic identity and the creativity of the will itself in an athletic endeavor such as a draining even life-threatening sporting contest is that it allows an exciting opportunity to reflect on these issues. The cosmological allegory of a tennis match is seen here stage center. And how we can create the luster of marble out of nondescript stone remains for experience to reveal. To see the real problems is to see that they are bound up with new notions of subjectivity that would be co-creative, explosive, cooperative and nobly effortful. This would inform the output the mighty power of that which in a fashion is the only thing that really exists individuals in their tangled being-withness with others.

Those images from Paris 10 June 1984 that continue to haunt the cultural imaginary in the world of tennis are a reminder of what it might mean to return on our path in the dance-play, the athletic-play, that is human life and of its extraordinary and unlikely powers. A gift to the universe would be to take the intensive charge of energy and intensity of our chosen athletes and the evental quality of the occasion (spectators, city, ambient milieu, etcetera) and to transform all this for the conative power of a summons to existence, creation and community, which count for infinitely more.

From this world society match we gain a source of inspiration that teaches us that a final that flowed through the world and across time today might instruct us on how we can establish identities that will enact similar qualitatively different activities. The trophy of a person's identity might be rewon by rethinking it afresh with the politics of respect of the other, and of transindividuality. Such things are incongruous in an age of self-congratulatory self-marketing designed to annihilate the other through the power of representation if not exploitation. However, well measured and cognized depths of the unconscious offer a glimmer of hope that they need not remain lying low in the dungeon, but something with a more dialectical intention, where in our example the structure of the Lendlian subject becomes an intense drama of growth. The sparks of the unconscious might give us spiritual eyes to become who we are if they are only apprehended via the other opponent or mentor or of some combination of the two.

Interpretation itself is an act and a sign of the unconscious; so, what else have we here been pondering? The confluences of the wonderfully different Lendl and McEnroe both enable us to reflect on the wider matter and implications of the limits of nations, of individuals, and of self-identities in this primal fire of a tennis match from the transferential energy and stars of Stade Roland-Garros in one spiritual capital of the liberal West, Paris. For some fans and historians of tennis, this match continues to occasion wonder as a plain miracle of being-with, even if it has of yet to be recognized as such, by our enameled and not quite spiritual enough eyes. It remains a terra incognita. Perhaps one day we might see things a bit more in the optic of the whole globe, if not of the whole galaxy.

When Bill Macatee introduces the match for Roland Garros classics for the Tennis Channel in the US he closes his introduction to the broadcast of the Lendl-McEnroe conflict thus: … "His most formidable rival Ivan Lendl. Perhaps the only thing greater than their stylistic contrasts, was the extraordinary outcome." Indeed that Lendl would topple McEnroe was for many a totally unforeseeable development. For the explosive finality and unlikeliness of the ending of the match constructs a striking and memory-laden dynamic of the emancipatory and miraculous instant.

In a transmission from NBC sports in the USA, we witness from the historic broadcast

> *Dick Enberg*: John McEnroe, USA, the favorite today to win the French Open title. The complete player, McEnroe in the semis against Jimmy Connors displayed his total weaponry, a big serve 12 aces to none, plus countless service winners. […]. Oh yes, there is the naughty side, the angry, the rough, and the rude McEnroe, whether hitting balls at photographers or yelling at officials, or verbally volleying with fans.
>
> *John McEnroe*: Keep that thing off! Off! How many times do I have to ask!?[41]

The idea surfaces of McEnroe as spoiled child. In this account his behavior was alternatively or concomitantly for the majority of observers monstrous, shocking, manipulative, predatory and a form of gamesmanship; for a minority seemingly without intellectual refinement, his behavior was prodigious, wondrous, marvelous and performance enhancing. The coverage continues thus

DE: The complex McEnroe meets 24 year old Ivan Lendl of Czechoslovakia [...]. Lendl has never won any of the grand slam events this is his fifth chance. He has moved methodically through this tournament, losing only one set in six matches, his win over Wilander most impressive and most rewarding because he now has another chance to win one of the big four! [...].

Bud Collins: Merci, Richard [...]. Tony [Trabert] we are surrounded by champions here in the tribunal. I might point out René Lacoste in the white shot [sic shirt] and hat and Jean Borotra who were champions in the 1920s. But, Tony, 1955, why has this court been such quicksand for American men since then?

Tony Trabert: Bud, I wish I knew, I guess we have not had a complete player [...]. So, I think John is going to do it today. He's playing very well. [...].

BC: As Davis Cup captain of the United States, you've sat beside the court with him many times, will his temper be a factor today?

TT: Normally his temper ends up helping him. Unless he lets it get away

completely. [...]. The players are coming out now. But I think it will not have an ill-effect on his play.[42]

However, as above-indicated it may have been McEnroe's volcanic rage during that third set over the microphones from the press that cost him dearly. Lendl may have rallied anyway, we shall never know with any surety, yet that Lendl did do so on this the record is clear.

Let us now return to this match in its unfolding, which the crowd opens with a dynamic instant of intersubjective intensity

> *BC*: Well I think this crowd should hype the adrenalin! Thank you, Tony Trabert, Dick Enberg!
>
> *DE*: Alright, Bud, there they are, McEnroe, he's at the peak of his game, unbeaten the last 42 matches. He's won all six championships that he's entered this year; now he's after his first French final. Lendl: grand slam greatness has eluded him. He has 39 career championships, but never one of the big four. They're separated by a year, McEnroe 25, Lendl 24; they both won here as juniors and we'll have the match in just a moment.
>
> *DE*: It's a beautiful day, an elegant crowd, and they're ready; you have that sense that they're here, and they've picked their favorite, and ready to vocalize.[43]

As posted on the live coverage, the conditions are close to ideal for the match, "MATCH CONDITIONS Temperature: 82 degrees Humidity: 52% Wind: SW-7 SUNNY" an event that will prove the energy of a cultural memory and a spectacle for the tennis imagination if not beyond. During the second game of the first set with Lendl serving to tie 1-1 (which he does) we hear Enberg speak of Lendl

> *DE*: He's been shut out in those grand slam opportunities, but he's won 39 tournaments in his rather brief career. You get the feeling that when Lendl finally captures that elusive first grand slam title that it might really send him off on a run. He needs to believe in himself.[44]

Current knowledge claims that Lendl won 40 tournaments between Houston 1980 and Luxembourg 1984 before the French Open that year. What Enberg describes would indeed prove prophetic, for Lendl would win 94 tournaments and eight major championships out of 19 finals in a storied career. Enberg's words about Lendl's "rather brief career" resonate, for they give us to speculate what he would have done had he reached such heights as he did in this match sooner. Set one:

DE: It's 5-3 McEnroe serving to win the set.

BC: And Lendl showing some of that burn that he talked openly about a year ago. He and McEnroe have never been on each other's dance cards. Last year when Lendl felt that McEnroe was intimidating umpires and lines people, he said if they don't do something about McEnroe, I will, implying that he would take the law into his own hands, and perhaps McEnroe into his own hands. It didn't happen, but there's not been good feelings.

DE: Wojtek Fibak the coach of Lendl on the left [shown].

BC: And his wife Eva…

BC: John McEnroe Senior [shown wearing an NBC Sports cap].[45]

Lendl's coach and McEnroe's father are important elements to both players. DE: "The third call against Lendl in this set. He obviously is bothered by what he feels is preferential treatment."[46] McEnroe wins the first set 6-3. We now fast forward to after the tennis miracle has happened on court.

In the post-match broadcast on NBC Sports from award-winning Enberg and broadcaster-journalist from *The Boston Globe* Collins, we hear the following dramatic words after the coverage of the awards ceremony in which Lendl raises La Coupe des Mousquetaires/The Musketeers' Trophy

DE: As you see Lendl in that classic pose, the trophy that will mean so much to him. He'll have many other championships, but this will be the one he'll probably remember most. René

Lacoste with him. Let's go down now to Bud Collins.

BC: Thank you, Dick Enberg. This is the stuff the mixture of limestone and brick dust, where so many Americans have been buried. It didn't seem it would happen again, but it has. Ivan Lendl on leaving the court after the presentation ceremony was vomiting, terribly nervous. I'm sure he's spent much more than he's spent in a match before. John McEnroe we don't know. Bob Basche is in the locker room trying to bring both of them out. [...]. For Lendl the first question I would have said to him was: Well, here's one question I can't ask you: Why can't you win the big one? We've all done that a few times with Ivan; perhaps it seems like a cruel question to ask a man who has won millions of dollars and about 90% of his matches on a tennis court. [...]. Everybody put him down as a front runner, a slugger, a guy who got on top of you and knocked your brains out, but once the crunch came, he wasn't ready. Today you saw crunch after crunch after crunch, particularly in the fifth set, he was down 15-40 in that seventh game, and he didn't collapse.[47]

Ethically Lendl did not give in and yield, and thus showed the immunizing power of bravery and fortitude or inner strength and ethical joy and ideas when required. Moreover, this is outstanding tennis journalism from Collins working at the peak of his powers as TV journalist. Here Collins confesses to Enberg that he is uncertain where the match changed

BC: But I think you can pinpoint that seventh game, we joke about it often, the critical seventh, with the score tied three all. McEnroe had come back saved a couple of games himself 15-40 and John missed a forehand passing shot that he might have had, he missed another forehand in a rally from the baseline. And once Lendl got to what Alasdair [...] called the sanctuary of deuce he was a different man, and he never looked back.

DE: Well done, Bud. Ivan Lendl not only has won his first grand slam title, but erased another thought, he does have the heart, he can fight back, and he has the trophy to prove it today.[48]

A commercial break occurs at this point; then Enberg returns from Paris. At this stage, we meet Lendl himself.

BC: Ivan Lendl has come down, he's barefoot, but rather happy, I would say. [Ivan makes a deep guttural laugh.] Ivan there's one question I no longer can ask you, why can't you win the big one?

Ivan Lendl: Well I'm glad, Bud, so you can't give me a hard time anymore; that's why I tried so hard today.

BC: Ivan, I've never seen you try harder. [...]

BC: Why do you think you won, why?

IL: I thought I played pretty good tennis. I was fighting hard, and I really wanted to win.

Here an inflamed desire and a striving Spinozaesque conative force both win out.

BC: You really wanted to win.

IL: I think so.

BC: Have there been other times when you did give up?

IL: No, not really. But you know, I just was in better shape today than some other times, and I could run a little longer.

BC: You were ready to win. Congratulations, here he is the French champion. Ivan Lendl.

IL: Thank you.

BC: Dick Enberg.

DE: Thank you, Bud, and Ivan Lendl obviously under some physical duress for Lendl to take the time to visit with us. We appreciate that. And certainly the crowd did here at Roland-Garros. They cheered his tremendous comeback down two sets to win this 1984 French Open. Weatherman cooperated, Paris was ready, the fans enjoyed, and Ivan Lendl wrote a marvelous script […].[49]

Lendl as tennis author thus may be said to exemplify "spirit" in representing the value ideals of courage, steadfastness and cunning or resourcefulness in the light of the German idealist philosopher's words, JG Fichte (1762–1814), "One may describe spirit […] as a capacity for raising ideas to consciousness, a capacity for representing ideals. In contrast, lack of spirit would be described as an incapacity for representing ideals […]".[50] Hodgkinson affirms the importance of Lendl's spirit: "For all Fibak's years of instruction, it wasn't [sic; it was] Lendl's spirit that changed the match and with it started his collection of grand slam titles" (IL, 154). This idea of a figure mediating ideals remains a bastion of true spirit value. A certain valid courage, genius of talent and spiritedness then may be said to shoot through Lendl both in his playing and coaching prime. This may occur not only when Enberg broadcast his heartfelt words after match point of the 1984 French final "Ivan Lendl has finally won a grand slam championship and he showed great courage in rallying from two sets down to accomplish it" but also when Murray won his majors and gold under Lendl's coaching guidance.

As for McEnroe as spoiled child, during the awards ceremony, Lendl remarked after shaking hands with a great figure in the tennis past René Lacoste: "I just would like to say that I am very happy that I won my first grand slam tournament here in Paris and I will be back next year. Thank you." McEnroe then left the scene without so much as a word. In response, the crowd booed and jeered.

We move to a post facto interview with Lendl about winning

the 1984 French: "*PK*: How did it feel when you had done it? *IL*: I don't remember any of it." Consider here for one's speculative knowledge also McEnroe's comment above on the disaster that was this match for him and Blanchot's words that we discussed above to describe the experience of reading *Finnegans Wake*: "Patience can neither be advised nor commanded: it is the passivity of dying whereby an I that is no longer I, answers to the limitlessness of the disaster, to that which no present remembers" (*WD*, 14).

> *PK*: You must.
>
> *IL*: I don't remember any of it. A friend of mine said to me a few years later, 'You looked really tired in that locker room'. I said, 'What are you talking about? You were not even there'. But apparently he was.
>
> *PK*: Did you celebrate that night?
>
> *IL*: No, I was too tired.
>
> *PK*: There was no joy? No elation?
>
> *IL*: Sure I was elated, of course I was elated but... you play for yourself. You don't play for your parents or for your coach, you play for yourself.
>
> *PK*: But you didn't celebrate?
>
> *IL*: No.
>
> *PK*: Did you drink?
>
> *IL*: No.[51]

Here we glance into a philosophical and intelligent approach to tennis and to a 'general ascetology'. In a volume on 250 great tennis matches Julien Pichené devotes three pages that are worth reading to the current match under our critical purview.[52] Incidentally, Andy Murray, who was then coached by Lendl, says close to the same thing as Lendl did in the above interview about the 1984 French, for when asked about the last parts of his winning match against Novak Djokovic in the 2013 Wimbledon

Final in the post-match interview on court with Sue Barker who asks, "How much of that last point do you remember" and he says, "I have no idea what happened. I really don't know what happened. It was... I don't know how long that last game was. I don't know. I can't even remember. I am sorry. I was concentrating."[53] This concordance between Lendl-Murray has to the present writer's knowledge not been noted until now.

Indeed, the emancipatory potential of a revolution began again with Lendl's appointment as Andy Murray's coach on 31 December 2011, which in its first act lasted until 19 March 2014. As Lendl's former coach the Australian Tony Roche prophetically put it when the hiring was announced, "Andy Murray's new coach Ivan Lendl is a grossly misunderstood character who will break the mould of great players being pitiful coaches, the Czech-born eight-time major winner's former mentor Tony Roche has said." Roche also commented, "I am pretty sure Andy has struck a bit of gold here" and added, "I mean, he was just a giant of the game. He didn't want anything to do with it for 15 years. I'm happy he's back for Andy's sake and also our sport's. People have always had the wrong impression of him. First of all, he's a very intelligent guy, very smart about tennis but just very intelligent in general. He's a fun guy, you know, great company, someone who was completely different to the person you saw on the court. That was his office between those lines and he went out there with a job to do."[54] These claims might have weight with the reader given the stature of the important former player and coach Roche. Some assessments rate Roche as one of if not the finest tennis coach on the men's tour in the past several Open era decades; he also coached Federer, among others. Lendl himself in spite of his relatively brief stint with Murray has also been cited as high as among the top five coaches in this period.

Before joining the coaching ranks again with Murray there was for a time, The Ivan Lendl International Junior Tennis Academy.[55] The institution was unique for its emphasis on cultivating academic, life and tennis skills. As such, it may provoke future-oriented figures of existence, creation and community. For as the 1984 men's singles final taught us to realize once more, as Žižek puts it, "from time to time, miraculous Acts occur which announce another dimension."[56] Assuredly, this constitutes a stained-glass form of virtue of strong and imaginative creativity as game-playing in the grounding and subtending present account of the present work of a cultural *kairology*. The Ivan Lendl International Junior Tennis Academy dissolved itself in January 2015 for financial reasons. A society more sensitively attuned to the uniqueness of the experiment that it constituted may have supported it for longer, but as an attempt it may inspire other such academies in the future.

Opening the immunizing power of vistas and tennis frontiers via radical athletic creativity constitutes one reboot for unleashing regenerated forms of the communal/creative life. For these weighty matters we need to dare a higher expectation, even as we recognize with Nancy from Chapter 2 that real community is on some fundamental level inoperative/operative; it is thereby impossible/possible. Furthermore, these insights need remarking to yield fruit for the interpretation of the untamed popular culture energies and phenomenon of the *munus* the gift of the 1984 French men's singles final and after for its influences beyond for activating the powers of the creative and communal dimensions of life. As we leave this gladiatorial war of attrition, and of the danger of death on a Colosseum-like clay court tennis arena, it is *now-time*, messianic power that we have at our disposal, which awaits its practical and intelligently creative exercise, practice and realization: a new community provoked by athletic creativity, which is also hard at work practicing and exercising for novel institutings and establishings. The athleticization of community and the creative life also conducts a general ascetology, immunology and economy for realizing the flash of the power of the impossible: liberty and justice for community and the creative life. Such an objective would reach out for the highest of human aspirations. This closes our account of creative and communal work accomplished at a material-bodily level in 'a 1984 tennis match that as a resource and an example of spiritual power and spirituality changed and transformed the (tennis) world. It also informs our argument by giving us an expanded sense of community as embodied in conflict and tension on limestone and crushed brick for another global coordination of knowledge.

Chapter 10

Tennis Conclusions

It is time to close Part III of our comparative cultural-studies analysis and theory of the immunizing power of community and the creative life, and so to draw together the threads of our overall argument. This study has brought fresh evidence to expand perspectives on creative work, self-discipline, training, humor and community. These qualities have been shown to reside in the fabric of our figure's forms and modes of being, and their projects, and the aim here has been to reveal these cultural phenomena as resources of hope for individual and social transformation. This is all to upturn convention and contest the longstanding fiasco of a *kairology* for another modality/mode of existence, of creation, and of the commons, still to be brought into play. Even if one cannot offer a blueprint for the foregoing, one can proffer forms and examples of the abovenoted, and register their effects on experience, meaning and value, to constitute the subversive countermovement and counterprocess of transformative agents, figures, forms, movements and structures for our world society. This society is firstly made up of individuals in their concrete actuality and ontic existence. Two passages will enliven our considerations about ennobling values and the power of failure and loss to mediate new realities. Exhibit one is from an early 1980s *Tennis Magazine* advertisement:

'It's not all headlines and glory. It's disappointment and pain. It's loneliness and learning to conquer yourself. It's wanting the best of yourself and for yourself. That's me. Ivan Lendl.'
We're with you all the way.
Adidas

Exhibit two is another from Lendl in 1987, "I only wish I could have back the years when I was twenty to twenty-four."[1] In other words, Lendl would like to regain those years from 1980 until his French triumph in late Spring 1984.

Moving forward, the oft-triviality of the cultural models on offer in our spectacle society merit a dialectical reversal and sublation, to which this study aspires to contribute. Viewed in this way, the shock of adventures of existence, creation and the commons await a ripening with the interventionary help of an emancipatory revolution that would give us a new direction, tone and tonality. To discover this in Spinoza's wake down to Lendl in what is joyful and moving would enable us to accomplish our individual and collective mission as forms and figures of the life process. After this subversive emancipation, existence and creation would return for community relations to the absolute maximum in paradoxically simple freedom, dignity and integrity. This would serve forms of solidarity, compassion, discipline, knowledge work, joy, humor and passion. These in turn would create conditions for an enhanced life world and experience and for the universality that we share cooperatively.

For Alain Badiou we are after what he calls a "laicized grace". Badiou defines it thus:

> what I call laicized grace describes the fact that, in so far as we are given a chance of truth, a chance of being a little bit more than living individuals, pursuing our ordinary interests, this chance is always given to us through an event. This evental giving, based absolutely on chance, and beyond any principle of the management or calculation of existence—why not call it a grace? Simply it is a grace that requires no all-powerful, no divine transcendence. What interests me in Saint Paul is the idea—very explicit in his writings—that the becoming of a truth, the becoming of a subject, depend entirely on a pure event, which is itself beyond all the predictions and

calculations that our understanding is capable of.[2]

Such a "laicized" grace would speak to the highest hopes of the creative life and of community. Did not McEnroe precisely give Lendl that chance in Paris in 1984? And did not Lendl give Andy Murray also this opportunity, if not also Murray, Lendl? Given its unlikelihood, the two-act program of Lendl-Murray is all the more noteworthy for its Shakespeareanization of things (recall the article on Lendl in the Introduction) with regard to community and the creative athletic life. This is thus by extension as a general basic mimetic lesson the 'now-time' of real possibility and the 'dynamic instant' of revolutionary agency and force. One might also be inclined to talk about the Virgilization of things too insofar as the Lendl-Murray connection has certain resonances with that between Virgil-Dante in *The Divine Comedy*; in both scenarios it is the elder figure who helps to show the way for the younger pupil and creative disciple who himself strives to achieve his own version of community and the creative life as yet another among the creative ones, the ones who thereby also pave the way for others to do things differently but also excellently. Somewhat as God and Adam stretch out a hand to one another in Michelangelo's painting in the Sistine chapel so too did Virgil and Dante and Lendl and Murray connect the dots to constellate a community-relation.

Murray has become a consequential Lendlian, and a pioneer of Scottish tennis and for the culture of cosmopolitan world tennis. Murray did well under the *munus* (the gift) of Lendl's tutelage making the 2012 men's singles final of the Wimbledon tennis championships and winning Wimbledon in 2013 thereby ending a 77 year drought for a British player to win at SW19 in southwest London. In 2012 Murray won the Olympic Gold Medal in men's singles in London, which also took place at Wimbledon, and also the US Open men's singles title in New York City, which broke a 76 year gap of time in which a British player did not win a major tournament. Murray made it to but lost in the final of the 2013 Australian Open men's singles final at Melbourne. As a teacher-coach Lendl's blend of humor, discipline and steadfastness rubbed off on his student, Murray.[3] To be sure, on the last day of winter in the northern hemisphere of 2014 Murray and Lendl parted ways. From the first day of spring 2014 Murray was on his own.

Simon Briggs writes that as a transformative figure Lendl "was more than a coach to Murray: he was a totem." Briggs adds of Lendl's "phenomenal record as Murray's coach" and of how, "His 2¼ years with Murray may come to be seen as a brilliant anomaly: the moment when a legend of the game picked up a racket after the best part of two decades away from the sport and steered his charge to a series of career breakthroughs, before stepping back off the ATP Tour. Their achievements together have certainly undermined the theory that great players do not make great coaches." Briggs adds, "And that lesson has since prompted a swathe of other former grand slam champions [...] to find coaching placements of their own. But it is hard to imagine that any of them will have as dramatic an impact as Lendl." Briggs writes too, "In the words of sports psychologist Don Macpherson: 'When Murray looks up at his team and his monkey mind is just about to shout abuse, he suddenly sees the brooding, unsmiling Lendl, and the monkey backs down every time... out of respect.'" Briggs concludes: "Since the partnership started in the build-up to the 2012 Australian Open, Murray has won 83 per cent of his matches when Lendl has been in attendance, and just 69 per cent when he has been absent. Whoever takes up the mantle will have one hell of a tough act to follow."[4] This surely is the factual case. The endnoted links give some popular media accounts of the historic power of the creative athletic-intellectual community of the Murray-Lendl linkage. Following the injunction of this media account the author of this monograph stands up and claps;[5] for in the foregoing Chris

Oddo writes, "No matter whose decision it ultimately was [...] the only sensible reaction is to get up and start clapping, because what Murray and Lendl achieved together was truly historic and impressive." It is indeed as if Lendl deconstructed and shocked Andy Murray's world in order to awaken it and to reveal its redemptive possibilities.

In one tennis podcast, a journalist compared the Lendl-Murray split to the breakup of the Beatles. Mats Wilander claimed that Lendl had done more for Andy Murray than any tennis player has ever done for another player. Hyperbolic or not, these index how the divorce was experienced. Tennis great Becker has credited Lendl with helping to inspire him to take on the coaching job of Djokovic from late 2013 to late 2016, and a bevy of others have followed too in Lendl's wake including Magnus Norman coaching Stan Wawrinka from 2013, Edberg coaching Federer in 2014 and 2015. From 2014, Sergei Bruguera coaches Richard Gasquet, Michael Chang mentors Kei Nishikori, and Goran Ivanisevic instructs Marin Cilic, which was taken over by Jonas Björkman in 2017. McEnroe served as a consultant coach for Milos Raonic during the 2016 Wimbledon and in 2017 Agassi coached Djokovic at the French Open and Wimbledon and is expected to continue the connection into 2018. In December 2016 Carlos Moya began coaching Rafael Nadal, and with the already announced departure at the end of 2017 of the great coach Toni Nadal from Rafa's camp, Moya will perhaps take on an increasingly important rôle. As Briggs already noted above, Lendl-Murray have thus set in motion a logic for a different model of athletic identity and community that includes paired connections that combine past legends and present stars for fresh present and future-oriented possibilities. In this model of subjectivity, the self is a lack or a gap psychoanalytic style, and subjectivity too is shared or folded from and on one to another.

Lendl-Murray constitute a paradigm for the community of friendship and of the creative and intelligent athletic life. Briggs writes about Murray's then newly appointed coach the French former women's world number one Amélie Mauresmo that occurred 15 minutes before the start of the 2014 French Open men's singles final between Djokovic and Nadal on 8 June.[6] Thus, on the 30-year anniversary of the noteworthy Lendl-McEnroe clash (albeit technically two days shy of that) saw an anticipated coaching appointment of Mauresmo from Murray, the first time that a leading male tennis player hired a female coach. In May 2016 Murray-Mauresmo severed their professional relations; Murray led Great Britain to its first Davis Cup title in seventy-nine years in 2015, was at the time of the professional break from Mauresmo the world number two, and so in a good position to make a go for the number one ranking.

Lendl rejoined Murray's team on 12 June 2016 where Murray won the 2016 Aegon Tennis Championships at The Queen's Club in London on 19 June for a record fifth time against Milos Raonic who had as a coaching consultant for the tournament McEnroe; before the awards ceremony took place, in which Murray raised the heaviest trophy in men's professional tennis, coach Lendl left the stands to use the restroom and so later watched the ceremony from the balcony. Murray in looking at his coach's empty seat, could not resist the wry comment: "It was nice of Ivan to stick around for the presentation." So at least the energy of humor lives on in the second Lendl era with Murray. Murray played the 2016 French Open with assistant coach Jamie Delgado and reached the final, the first Briton to do so since Fred Perry in 1937, where he lost to Novak Djokovic in four sets. Murray also thus became the first British player since Perry to appear in the final of all four majors. After winning Wimbledon for a second time in 2016, Murray won the Gold medal in the men's singles competition at the Olympic Games in Rio de Janeiro in August 2016, and was after winning the Paris 1000 Master's event on 6 November 2016 the world number one from 7 November 2016 until 20 August 2017. Sir Andrew Barron Murray, OBE Kt also won the year-end ATP World Tour Final in late 2016, and in the New Year's Honours list 2017 was knighted for his services to tennis and to charity. He received an OBE in October 2013 after winning Wimbledon in July of the same year.

Do we realize the immensity of what we are aiming at? For it is where our global and individual hope, for self, and for collective redemption reside, and that still remains to be written and accomplished as a move in the dynamic instant and in the now-time of messianic time. Indeed, as Žižek writes, "Heisenberg, Bohr, and others, on the contrary, insisted that this incompleteness of our knowledge of quantum reality indicates a strange incompleteness of quantum reality itself, a claim which leads to a breathtakingly weird ontology."[7] It follows that we have to innovate a new ontological form of human community. Relatedly, Žižek reminds us in his paradoxically atheistic version of Christianity, which means that secularization accords to an actualization of the Holy Spirit, which is par excellence, community: "Christ already had returned as the Holy Spirit of their community. The very meaning of Christ's death is that the work to be done is theirs, that Christ put his trust in them" (*MC*, 283). More exactly, for Žižek, "The specificity of the Holy Spirit, the apocalyptic emancipatory collective" (*MC*, 283) means that community as Holy Spirit as some sort of liberated togetherness awaits its day for our own ontological interventions. This would be for a fuller ontological reality that would accord with emancipatory figures of creativity and community in our day to day and ethical activities. Because the universalist project of the West remains a Christian project, it makes a transformation of the Christian tradition all the more expedient and needful.

The community of radical creativity awaits a dialectical sublation of the solid historical realities of class exploitation and of economic debasement. That arch-totem figure of the advanced capitalist individual must be given the awareness of what constitutes a true materialism. We need perhaps even a belief in 'unbelief' in the 'big Other' (of its fundamental inexistence) of the money god for example. Indeed for an arresting counter- and more mature late capitalist figure it would be beneficent if as Žižek puts it "a true materialism joyously assumes the 'disappearance of matter' the fact that there is only void" (*MC*, 92). For we agree in concerto with Žižek, "It is our wager that only the materialism of void and multiplicity [...] is the materialism that, as Hegel would have put it, reaches the level of its notion" (*LN*, 94). Materialism awaits its true messianic power for both those within and for those informed by a transformation of a spirit of the Christian tradition.

US author Francis Scott Fitzgerald wrote in *The Last Tycoon*, "There are no second acts in American lives", but an adopted American the Czech-born Lendl proves otherwise in his efficacious mentorship of, and well-written second script and so too the *munus* (donation) of his initiatory community relations with Andy Murray, from 31 December 2011 to 19 March 2014.[8] The announcement in June 2016 of another Murray-Lendl era had much of the tennis world standing on its head. Brian Phillips formulates a nice hypothetical point about the end of the first go of the Murray-Lendl linkage in which the bond and team experience were co-created by each, and only then to be deconstructed by Lendl in perhaps a conscious/unconscious attempt to teach the following lesson: "It's a hard world, you guys. You can't count on player-coach relationships to cheer you up. The only thing you can count on is yourself. Wait, could that be what Murray and Lendl are trying to tell us here? Could... could Ivan Lendl now be coaching us all?"[9] In this light, the 'big Other' aspect of the big name tandem itself of Lendl-Murray cannot be relied on with any surety other than its historical exemplariness. We are ourselves the messiah again both individually and collectively, and so need with the creativity of intelligence and of will, to work accordingly, toward our emancipation and redemption. That is the basic lesson of one tradition of Christianity, of Benjamin's theology of our contemporaneity, of much recent theoretical psychoanalysis, and of the Murray-Lendl linkage. With regard to the lattermost dynamic, one may note in concert with Esposito that "community *resides* precisely in its own withdrawal" (*COD*, 102) making it an historical necessity that Murray be left by Lendl to his own devices in order truly for Murray to extend the link's lessons. Hodgkinson reflects in his account,

> It was the tennis divorce that no one [...] had been predicting. If it's highly irregular for a coach or employee to be the one who precipitates the end of a working relationship [...] it's rarer still for a tennis couple to split up because they had been so successful.
>
> [...]. Maybe you can even trace it to a hug, to that moment during the wait for the prize giving ceremony when Murray climbed up to his guest box and the first person he embraced was Lendl. By then, Murray had already won the Olympics and the US Open, but it was the victory on the Wimbledon grass that had given the project a sense of completion. (*IL*, 320–21)

These points from Hodgkinson perhaps hit the nail straight in the center. What if a newfangled commons were to have a second act with a start from zero in the utter freedom of a re-beginning? What if the practice and exercise of existence and creation were to come stage center in a more mature version of post capitalist commons that would overcome the current impasses and deadlocks of our world capitalist society, which can never truly become a global capitalism for it will also be mediating that final resting point? It is a paradox that it would be such figures as the tennis player from outside the West, Ivan Lendl, who embraced both capitalism and new tennis technology and methods, and became one of their more visible exponents and late twentieth-century heroes, would provoke such a thought in us; but that is the truth and beauty of paradox and of the dialectical process.

However, there is yet another way to read this and it is via Žižek's reading of Spinoza, which contains some pertinence on Lendl's relation to Murray,

> Spinoza's ontology is one of full immanence to the world, I 'am' just the network of my relations with the world, totally 'externalized' in it. My *conatus*, my tendency to assert myself, is thus not an assertion at the expense of the world, but a full acceptance of being part of it, my assertion of the wider reality within which alone I can thrive. The opposition of egoism and altruism is thus overcome: I fully am not as an isolated Self, but in the thriving reality of which I am a part.[10]

Lendl himself overcame the distinction between brutal egoism and pacific altruism by flying Murray's flag for a two-year or so period of time 'in the thriving reality' that they both inhabited. And as we note this duo has been relaunched for a double go.

The gap that separates our contemporaneity without community, and a rebuilding of community, must take the true measure and value of such valuable lessons in innovative knowledge work, discipline, creativity, and community, as the foregoing pages teach us to know, in the service of and for, a turning-point toward fascinating and complex communities, people, and creativities. This whole complex dynamic remains a radically open structure. We need to reconceive our collective mission and destiny for the foundations of a new science of the world that may emerge from the old and of what is new within the old. We must not misconstrue our true interests here, and fall easy prey to the egotism and exploitation of the world. It is not a question so much of self-identity as identity with others, and of a truly dramatic and improbable dialectical reversal of the brutally egotistic and exploitative logic of the aged capitalist system. This is then the halfway point. We need to find another footing. Consider in this context, Žižek on Hegel: "'tarrying with the negative', of enduring the power of the negative [means] the subject *does NOT survive* the ordeal of negativity, he *effectively* loses his very essence, and passes over into his Other."[11] And enter Roberto Esposito: "That we are *mariners* has no other meaning than this: our condition is that of a voyage that takes us far away from ourselves" (*COD*, 107). This is true if we are to attain our possible ripening amidst real-world complexities. May all of the immunizing mariners among us thrive!

At stake here are our life substance and substantial content, both as persons and as societies. The above investigations illuminate that we need to turn ourselves around, amidst the chaotic power of today's tensions, antagonisms, contradictions, and conflicts we tarry over and endure in the negativity in our shared mortalities and lives. The awesome force and gift or *munus* of the 'dynamic instant' and of capacious 'now-time' is upon us. Where are we going? For this, we each of us need courageously to persevere to find our *clinamen* for our swerve to tap into the power and force of the drive, for community, and for acts of creation in light, as this text has argued, of "*the New of the past itself*" (Žižek). For the model of temporality in the present study, the paradoxical revolutionary possibilities of the past for the present are what remain an inspiring element. We have to travel back into our past to discover our future.

To further complete ontological reality, the productive and curative rôles of creative work, discipline, play, drive and revolt may mediate more imaginative, intelligent, and spiritual ways of individual and of collective life as well as a "world-civil-society" (Immanuel Kant). We are still at the dawn of such a global culture, and of its possible positive newness, mediated by the politics of the flash. Badiou writes that, "All confidence is abandonment and discipline."[12] By extension, to attain our self and other creative world community, we plunge with abandon into a forceful and purposeful journey of exercise and practice.

In this model, we advance from the known to the unknown, where all things are possible including the miraculous and the impossible for the now of community and creative existence.

Gaps remain. But it is precisely in such gaps that the long-acute need of a new community and creativity may be born, a studio and an environment for transactions with the conative force of inspiring others, not least in our popular culture account, la Tour Eiffel from the venue of the 1984 French Open men's singles final as one such other. In the final accounting, this would all be in the service of the individual and of the community in the *communitas* of life to arrive stage center in the exercise and practice of a truly world society. This is because after a lifetime of thinking and wandering as Mariners there would be a relentless reworking, restating, refocusing and crystallizing of this most crucial point: the making possible of the impossible for the achievement of community and the creative life. For the surprising paradox of the event would be so violent that it would shock community and the self back to the intelligence of the liberated creative life and so too of the genuine possibility of the convincing power of the impossible: collective agency and radical creativity to realize new forms of liberty, justice and equality.

If we consider the matter more carefully, highly (im)possible, hugely powerful, passionate, practicing, exercising, thinking and committed lives and communities lie in wait in a general economy of possibility. *Now-time* is thus upon us if we can only discover, awaken and seize it as the *munus* the gift, challenge and task of a sublation of the impossible: to vindicate the value-ideals and practices of community and the creative life that would enable society by extension to facilitate and to support forms of collective and of self-improvement. It has been the creative objective of this critical book to breathe new life into such notional possibilities. A breakthrough awaits a possible rendering of the impossible: the joy of living and knowing still uncreated radical creativity and community in the changed environment of today and after. A cooperative and creative effort is thus what we require. And the shortest way may not be the best one. For Žižek "at its most radical, freedom is the freedom to change one's Destiny."[13] With a broader, more panoramic vision, and with the release of the historical energies as displayed in the foregoing chapters, the gift of such a task, taken on board in the flash of sudden discovery and wonder, awaits our present history.

By an act of daring, will, knowledge—and a dose of predestination and secular grace—the impossible community and creative life will thus prove possible. Our constellation of figures and their deeds illustrate such a feat of immunizing power and coherence standing behind our efforts for the making of the ideals of contemporary community and forms of the creative life as achievements of meaning and knowledge. The above going chapters and exemplary figures stand as a provocation of the potential energy of cultural memory for individual and collective transformation. We may conclude that self- and collective-overcoming would attest and provide witness to the impossible; self- and collective-liberation to overcome a polarizing neoliberal capitalism and digital technology on the edge structure of progressive struggle for a new substantial community that would give space and agency for creative modalities of life: intellectually, politically, socially and spiritually.

We may now go further in our decreative and dedicated efforts to realize and to comprehend the meaning of myriad forms of community and the (de)creative life for *homo politicus*. This quest for our shared universality may be imaginatively richer than what was previously estimated. The planned enterprise of a collective and self-redemption may thus find a place in a potent blend of freedom and necessity for the dialectical sublation of a positive world-whole connection and cosmic spirit. This creative overcoming of things as they now are may start on the tar of the tennis courts and of the streets alike for new knowledges and shared futurity. If the impossible remains impossible then we will have yielded our best chances for a radical reconfiguration and sublation (*Aufhebung*) of empty forms of community and the creative life. Therefore, cultivating and mobilizing the intersubjective and sublational force and magic of the power of the impossible/possible miracle may institute novel forms in the galaxy of (de)creative community and universality.

Notes

Introduction

1. Giorgio Agamben, *Nudities*, trans. David Kishik and Stefan Pedatella (Stanford: Stanford University Press, 2011) 7. Hereafter cited as *N*.

2. Peter Sloterdijk, *In the World Interior of Capital: For a Philosophical Theory of Globalization*, trans. Wieland Hoban (Cambridge, UK: Polity, 2013) 264.

3. Slavoj Žižek, *Living in the End Times* (London: Verso, 2010) 185.

4. Julia Kristeva, *This Incredible Need to Believe*, trans. Beverley Bie Brahic (New York: Columbia University Press, 2009) 33–34.

5. Peter Sloterdijk, *You Must Change Your Life: On Anthropotechnics*, trans. Wieland Hoban (Cambridge, UK: Polity, 2013) 34.

6. Peter Sloterdijk, *Nietzsche Apostle*, trans. Steven Corcoran (Los Angeles, CA: Semiotext(e), 2013) 41.

7. Bernard Stiegler, *Taking Care of Youth and Generations*, trans. Stephen Barker (Stanford: Stanford University Press, 2010) 25.

8. Alain Badiou, *Conditions*, trans. Steven Corcoran (London: Continuum, 2008) 148–49.

9. See J. Hillis Miller, *The Conflagration of Community: Fiction Before and After Auschwitz* (Chicago: University of Chicago Press, 2011) as well as his *Communities in Fiction* (New York: Fordham University Press, 2015).

10. Baltasar Gracián, *The Pocket Oracle and Art of Prudence*, trans. with an intro. and notes Jeremy Robbins (London: Penguin, 2011) 3. Hereafter cited as *POAP*.

11. Roberto Esposito, *Communitas: The Origin and Destiny of Community*, trans. Timothy Campbell (Stanford: Stanford

University Press, 2010) 7. Hereafter cited as *COD*.

12. Slavoj Žižek, *Disparities* (London: Bloomsbury Academic, 2016) 19.

13. Rex P. Stevens, *Kant on Moral Practice: A Study of Moral Success and Failure* (Macon, GA: Mercer University Press, 1981) 105.

14. Slavoj Žižek, *Less than Nothing: Hegel and the Shadow of Dialectical Materialism* (London: Verso, 2012) 1010. Hereafter cited as *LN*.

15. Mark Hodgkinson, *Ivan Lendl: The Man Who Made Murray* (London: Aurum, 2014) 64. Hereafter cited as *IL*.

16. Michel Serres, *The Troubadour of Knowledge*, trans. Sheila Faria Glaser and William Paulson (Ann Arbor: University of Michigan Press, 1997) 92.

17. Julia Kristeva, *The Sense and Non-Sense of Revolt: The Powers and Limits of Psychoanalysis*, volume 1, trans. Jeanine Herman (New York: Columbia University Press, 2000) 7.

18. Lutz Koepnick, "Aura Reconsidered: Benjamin and Contemporary Visual Culture" pp. 95–120 in *Benjamin's Ghosts: Interventions in Contemporary Literary and Cultural Theory*, ed. Gerhard Richter (Stanford: Stanford University Press, 2002) 100.

19. David S. Ferris, *The Cambridge Introduction to Walter Benjamin* (Cambridge, UK: Cambridge University Press, 2008) 42.

20. Giorgio Agamben, *Potentialities: Collected Essays in Philosophy*, ed. and trans. with an intro. Daniel Heller-Roazen (Stanford: Stanford University Press, 1999) 245.

21. Leland de la Durantaye, *Giorgio Agamben: A Critical Introduction* (Stanford: Stanford University Press, 2009) 23. Hereafter cited as *GA*.

22. Michael Löwy, *Fire Alarm: Reading Walter Benjamin's 'On the Concept of History'*, trans. Chris Turner (London: Verso, 2005) 32.

23. Xan Brooks, "Wimbledon won't be the same without Ivan

Lendl". *The Guardian.* 22 June 2014. 23 June 2014 <http://www.theguardian.com/sport/shortcuts/2014/jun/22/wimbledon-wont-be-same-without-ivan-lendl>.

24. Fabio Vighi, *On Žižek's Dialectics: Surplus, Subtraction, Sublimation* (London: Continuum, 2010) 109.

25. Löwy, *Fire Alarm: Reading Walter Benjamin's 'On the Concept of History'*, 33.

26. Walter Benjamin, "On the Concept of History," in *Selected Writings, vol. 4: 1938-1940*, ed. Howard Eiland and Michael W. Jennings, trans. Edmund Jephcott and Others (Cambridge, MA: Harvard University Press, 2003) 397.

27. *Fire Alarm: Reading Walter Benjamin's 'On the Concept of History'*, 95–96.

28. Michael Polanyi, *Personal Knowledge: Towards a Post-Critical Philosophy*, enlarged edition with a New Foreword by Mary Jo Nye (Chicago: University of Chicago Press, 2015) 143.

29. Michael Polanyi, *Knowing and Being: Essays by Michael Polanyi*, ed. Marjorie Grene (Chicago: University of Chicago Press, 1969) 108.

30. Plotinus, *The Enneads*, trans. Stephen MacKenna, abridged with an intro. and notes John Dillon (London: Penguin, 1991) 421.

31. Plotinus, *The Enneads*, 424.

32. Slavoj Žižek and Boris Gunjević, *God in Pain: Inversions of Apocalypse*, Boris Gunjević's chapters translated from the Croatian by Ellen Elias-Bursać (New York: Seven Stories, 2012) 100.

33. Sloterdijk, *You Must Change Your Life: On Anthropotechnics*, 451–52.

34. Žižek and Gunjević, *God in Pain: Inversions of Apocalypse*, 102.

35. *God in Pain: Inversions of Apocalypse*, footnote 2, 129.

36. *God in Pain: Inversions of Apocalypse*, 268.

37. St. Augustine, *Concerning the City of God against the Pagans*,

trans. Henry Bettenson, with a new intro. GR Evans (London: Penguin, 2003) 924.

38. Charles Taylor, *Sources of the Self: The Making of the Modern Identity* (Cambridge, MA: Harvard University Press, 1992) 182.

39. Taylor, *Sources of the Self: The Making of the Modern Identity*, 182.

40. Michel Serres, *Times of Crisis: What the Financial Crisis Revealed and How to Reinvent our Lives and Future*, trans. Anne-Marie Feenberg-Dibon (New York: Bloomsbury, 2014) 42–43.

41. Walter Benjamin, "On the Concept of History", *Selected Writings, Volume 4, 1938-1940*, trans. Edmund Jephcott and Others, ed. Howard Eiland and Michael W. Jennings (Cambridge, MA: Belknap Press of Harvard University Press, 2003) 390.

Chapter 1

1. A first airing of this chapter was given on 1 June 2012, "Expression, the Fold, and the Spinozan Opportunity of Existence qua Deleuze", for a panel, "Deleuzian Futures: expression, indifference, event, fold", William Watkin, chair (panel also included Dany Nobus and Sean Bowden) at the 36th IAPL Conference "Archaeologies of the Future: tracing memories / imagining spaces", 28 May–3 June, Tallinn, Estonia. Plenary speakers Jacques Rancière, Erkki-Sven Tüür, and Sofi Oksanen. A second version of the piece "Forms of Immortality: Expression, the Fold, and the Spinozan Opportunity of Existence qua Deleuze and Žižek" was presented on the invitation of Christopher Norris at a Philosophy Research Seminar Series at the Cardiff branch of the Royal Institute of Philosophy, Cardiff, Wales, UK, 31 October 2012. A later version was delivered "On Spinoza and Contemporary Culture" on the invitation of Ivan M. Havel

at the Center for Theoretical Study of the Czech Academy of Sciences, Prague, Czech Republic, 22 November 2012.

2. Karl Jaspers, *Spinoza* from *The Great Philosophers: The Original Thinkers, Volume II*, ed. Hannah Arendt, trans. Ralph Mannheim (New York: Harcourt Brace Jovanovich, 1966) 34.

3. For one book-length account see, Erik S. Roraback, *The Philosophical Baroque: On Autopoietic Modernities* (Leiden, The Netherlands: Brill, 2017).

4. Gilles Deleuze, *Spinoza: Practical Philosophy*, trans. Robert Hurley (San Francisco: City Lights, 1988) 6. Hereafter cited as *SPP*.

5. Benedictus de Spinoza, *The Ethics* from *A Spinoza Reader: 'The Ethics' and Other Works*, ed. and trans. Edwin Curley (Princeton: Princeton University Press, 1994) 3–4. Hereafter cited as *TE*.

6. Roberto Esposito, *Immunitas: The Protection and Negation of Life*, trans. Zakiya Hanafi (Cambridge, UK: Polity, 2011) 16.

7. Gilles Deleuze and Félix Guattari, *What is Philosophy?*, trans. Hugh Tomlinson and Graham Burchell (New York: Columbia University Press, 1994) 59–60.

8. Slavoj Žižek, *Organs without Bodies: On Deleuze and Consequences* (New York: Routledge, 2004) 45.

9. Žižek, *Organs without Bodies: On Deleuze and Consequences*, 42.

10. Gilles Deleuze and Claire Parnet, *Dialogues*, trans. by Hugh Tomlinson and Barbara Habberjam (London: Athlone, 1987) 15.

11. *Dialogues*, 15.

12. Gilles Deleuze, *Expressionism in Philosophy*, 180. Hereafter cited as *EP*.

13. Gilles Deleuze, *The Fold: Leibniz and the Baroque*, foreword and trans. Tom Conley (Minneapolis: University of Minnesota Press, 1993) 22.

14. Steven B. Smith, *Spinoza's Book of Life: Freedom and Redemption*

in the 'Ethics' (New Haven: Yale University Press, 2003) 147. Hereafter cited as *SBL*.

15. Mari Ruti, *The Call of Character: Living a Life Worth Living* (New York: Columbia University Press, 2014) 173.
16. Warren Montag, *Bodies, Masses, Power: Spinoza and His Contemporaries* (London: Verso, 1999) 121.
17. Montag, *Bodies, Masses, Power: Spinoza and His Contemporaries*, 122.
18. *Bodies, Masses, Power: Spinoza and His Contemporaries*, 122–23.
19. Deleuze and Guattari, *What is Philosophy?*, trans. Hugh Tomlinson and Graham Burchell, 48.
20. Slavoj Žižek, *The Parallax View* (Cambridge, MA: MIT Press, 2006) 123.
21. Marcus Pound, *Žižek: A (Very) Critical Introduction* (Grand Rapids, MI: William B. Eerdmans, 2008) 7–8.
22. Pound, *Žižek: A (Very) Critical Introduction*, 10.
23. Michel Serres, *Times of Crisis: What the Financial Crisis Revealed and How to Reinvent our Lives and Future*, 42–43.

Chapter 2

1. A first airing of this chapter took place on 6 November 2004 "Jean-Luc Nancy, Being-in-Common, and the Absent Semantics of Myth" at an international conference of the ACUME project, "Mythologies, Foundation Texts and Imagined Communities", Prague, Czech Republic, 5–7 November 2004. The piece was then published as "Jean-Luc Nancy, Being-in-Common, and the Absent Semantics of Myth" in *Time Refigured: Myths, Foundation Texts & Imagined Communities*, ed. Martin Procházka & Ondřej Pilný. Prague: Litteraria Pragensia, 2005, 121–35. Grateful acknowledgment to the editors for permission to use this earlier material in reworked form. A revised version of this original publication was presented on, "City of Cosmos;

or, Community and Communication" 17 July 2010, on the invitation of Barbara Weber for an international conference, "Understanding the Other/the Stranger/the Foreigner", University of Regensburg, Regensburg, Germany.

2. Maurice Blanchot, *The Writing of the Disaster*, trans. Ann Smock (Lincoln: University of Nebraska Press, 1995) 41. Hereafter cited as *WD*.

3. Jean-Luc Nancy, preface, *The Inoperative Community: Theory and History of Literature, Volume 76*, foreword Christopher Fynsk, ed. Peter Connor, trans. Peter Connor, Lisa Garbus, Michael Holland, and Simona Sawhney (Minneapolis: University of Minnesota Press, 1991) xl–xli. Hereafter cited as *IC*.

4. Antonio Negri and Michael Hardt, *Multitude: War and Democracy in the Age of Empire* (New York: Penguin, 2004) 278. Hereafter cited as *MWD*.

5. Christopher Fynsk, foreword, *The Inoperative Community: Theory and History of Literature, Volume 76*, by Jean-Luc Nancy, xi.

6. Fynsk, foreword, *The Inoperative Community: Theory and History of Literature, Volume 76*, xv–xvi.

7. For purposes of historical contextualization and the power of comparison, the Frankfurt School social theorist Max Horkheimer (1895–1973) writes: "The National Socialist regime rationalizes the mythical past which it pretends to conserve, calling it by name and mobilizing it on behalf of big industry. Where this archaic heritage did not explode the Christian form and assume Teutonic features, it gave to German philosophy and music their specific tone. The mythology in National Socialism is not a mere fake, but the spotlight thrown upon this surviving mythology liquidates it altogether." from Max Horkheimer, "The End of Reason" pp. 26–48 in *The Essential Frankfurt School Reader*, ed. by Andrew Arato and Eike Gebhardt, intro. by Paul Piccone

(New York: Continuum, 1982) 43. So, a certain vulgarization of the masses and 'massing' of the mass mind prevailed with the advent of the system of Nazi power, which went hand in hand with Nazi myth.

8. Jean-Luc Nancy, *Being Singular Plural*, trans. Robert D. Richardson and Anne E. O'Byrne (Stanford: Stanford University Press, 2000) 37–38.

9. Maurice Blanchot, *The Unavowable Community*, trans. Pierre Joris (Barrytown, NY: Station Hill, 1988) 11.

10. Étienne Balibar, *Politics and the Other Scene*, translations Christine Jones, James Swenson, Chris Turner (London: Verso, 2002) 170.

11. Balibar, *Politics and the Other Scene*, 142.

12. For an elucidation of the concept of the 'Body without Organs' see Deleuze and Guattari's chapter "6. November 28, 1947: How Do You Make Yourself a Body Without Organs" pp. 149–66 in *A Thousand Plateaus: Capitalism and Schizophrenia*, trans. and foreword Brian Massumi (Minneapolis: University of Minnesota Press, 1987).

13. Jacques Derrida, *Le toucher, Jean-Luc Nancy* (Paris: Galilée, 2000); Derrida, *On Touching—Jean-Luc Nancy*, trans. Christine Irizarry (Stanford: Stanford University Press, 2005).

14. Pierre Joris, translator's preface, *The Unavowable Community*, by Maurice Blanchot, xiii.

15. Roberto Esposito, *Two: The Machine of Political Theology and the Place of Thought*, trans. Zakiya Hanafi (New York: Fordham University Press, 2015) 209.

Chapter 3

1. A first airing of this chapter was given on 29 August 2006, "James, Nancy, and the Concept of Freedom", for a panel "James, Post-structurality and After", ESSE-8, Senate House, London, UK, 29 August–2 September 2006; other participants: Annick Duperray (Convener, Provence), Cornelius Crowley

(Paris 10) and Adrian Harding (Provence). A second effort was a paper given on 22 October 2010, "Forms of Community, Freedom, and Duplicity; or, Double Registers in James's *The Ambassadors* (1903)" for a panel "Duplicity and Double Registers", 21–23 October 2010, the second international conference of the European Society of Jamesian Studies, "Henry James and the Poetics of Duplicity", the American University of Paris, Paris, France.

2. Leo Bersani, *A Future for Astyanax: Character and Desire in Literature* (Boston: Little, Brown and Company, 1976) 132.

3. Slavoj Žižek, *The Puppet and the Dwarf: The Perverse Core of Christianity* (Cambridge, MA: MIT Press, 2003) 95.

4. Pierre Macherey, *A Theory of Literary Production*, trans. Geoffrey Wall, with a new intro. Terry Eagleton and a new afterword by the author (London: Verso, 2005) 93.

5. Quotations from Nancy's *The Experience of Freedom*, trans. by Bridget McDonald, with a foreword by Peter Fenves (Stanford: Stanford University Press, 1993); the linguistic original appeared as *L'Experience de la liberté* (Paris: Galilée, 1988). Further references to this text are denoted in parentheses as *EF*.

6. Anselm Jappé, *Guy Debord*, trans. Donald Nicholson-Smith with a foreword TJ Clark and a new afterword by the author (Berkeley: University of California Press, 1999) 159.

7. Henry James, *The Ambassadors*, ed. with an intro. Harry Levin (London: Penguin, 1986) 214–16.

8. Ezra Pound, "Henry James" in *Literary Essays of Ezra Pound*, ed. with an intro. TS Eliot (New York: New Directions, 1918) 296.

9. Jean-Paul Sartre, *Critique of Dialectical Reason, Volume 1, Theory of Practical Ensembles*, trans. Alan Sheridan-Smith, ed. Jonathan Rée, foreword Fredric Jameson (London: Verso, 2004) 105.

10. Jacques Rancière, *The Ignorant Schoolmaster: Five Lessons in*

Intellectual Emancipation, trans. with an intro. Kristin Ross (Stanford: Stanford University Press, 1991) 58.

11. Jean-Pierre Dupuy, *Economy and the Future: A Crisis of Faith*, trans. MB DeBevoise (East Lansing: Michigan State University Press, 2014) 129.

Chapter 4

1. An initial airing of this chapter "Heretical Capital: Walter Benjamin's Cultic Status in Cultural and Theoretical History" was presented at the 12th Colloquium of American Studies on "Cult Fictions, Film and Happenings", Palacký University, Olomouc, Czech Republic, 4–9 September 2005. Plenary lecturer: Werner Sollors, Harvard University. The talk was then revised for publication as "Heretical Capital: Walter Benjamin's Cultic Status in Cultural and Theoretical History". Editor: Arbeit, Marcel, inter alia, *The Moravian Journal of Literature and Film*. Volume 1, no. 2 (Spring 2010), 5–18, published by Filosofická Fakulta, Palacký University, Olomouc. Grateful acknowledgment is paid to the editor of this journal for permission to reuse the older material here in modified form.

2. Theodor W. Adorno, "A Portrait of Walter Benjamin" in *Prisms*, trans. Samuel and Shierry Weber (Cambridge, MA: MIT Press, 1967) 229.

3. Adorno, "A Portrait of Walter Benjamin", 230.

4. "A Portrait of Walter Benjamin", 232.

5. "A Portrait of Walter Benjamin".

6. "A Portrait of Walter Benjamin", 233.

7. "A Portrait of Walter Benjamin", 241.

8. Hannah Arendt, ed. and intro., *Illuminations*, by Walter Benjamin, trans. Harry Zorn (London: Pimlico, 1999) 8.

9. Arendt, ed. and intro., *Illuminations*, by Walter Benjamin, 9.

10. Arendt, ed. and intro., *Illuminations*, by Walter Benjamin, 11.

11. Arendt, ed. and intro., *Illuminations*, by Walter Benjamin, 33.

12. Arendt, ed. and intro., *Illuminations*, by Walter Benjamin, 47.

13. Susan Buck-Morss, *The Dialectics of Seeing: Walter Benjamin and the Arcades Project* (Cambridge, MA: MIT Press, 1989) 222. Hereafter cited as *DS*.

14. Martin Jay, *Refractions of Violence* (London: Routledge, 2003) 24.

15. *Refractions of Violence*, 116.

16. Beatrice Hanssen, *Walter Benjamin's Other History: Of Stones, Animals, Human Beings, and Angels* (Berkeley: University of California Press, 1998) 6.

17. Hanssen, *Walter Benjamin's Other History: Of Stones, Animals, Human Beings, and Angels*, 29.

18. *Walter Benjamin's Other History: Of Stones, Animals, Human Beings, and Angels*, 66.

19. *Walter Benjamin's Other History: Of Stones, Animals, Human Beings, and Angels*, 123.

20. Carol Jacobs, *In the Language of Walter Benjamin* (Baltimore: Johns Hopkins University Press, 1999) 3.

21. Gregg Lambert, *The Return of the Baroque in Modern Culture* (London: Continuum, 2004) 70.

22. Jacobs, *In the Language of Walter Benjamin*, 11.

23. *In the Language of Walter Benjamin*, 40.

24. Pierre Missac, *Walter Benjamin's Passages*, trans. Shierry Weber Nicholsen (Cambridge, MA: MIT Press, 1995) 2.

25. Missac, *Walter Benjamin's Passages*, 10.

26. Richard Wolin, *Walter Benjamin: An Aesthetic of Redemption*, with a new Introduction by the Author (Berkeley: University of California Press, 1994) xv.

27. Wolin, *Walter Benjamin: An Aesthetic of Redemption*, 59.

28. *Walter Benjamin: An Aesthetic of Redemption*, 159.

29. *Walter Benjamin: An Aesthetic of Redemption*, 195.

30. *Walter Benjamin: An Aesthetic of Redemption*, 217–18.

31. Leo Bersani, *The Culture of Redemption* (Cambridge, MA: Harvard University Press, 1990) 54.

Chapter 5

1. This chapter was first aired as "The Necessary Autopoiesis and Politics of Patience and of Strangeness of *Finnegans Wake*" 14 May 2006: XLVIe Congrès de la SAES, 12–14 May 2006, Université de Nantes, Nantes, France.

2. Walter Benjamin, *Selected Writings, Volume 1, 1913-1926*, ed. Marcus Bullock and Michael W. Jennings (Cambridge, MA: Belknap Press of Harvard University Press, 1996) 284.

3. Jacques Rancière, *Short Voyages to the Land of the People*, trans. James B. Swenson (Stanford: Stanford University Press, 2003) 123.

4. James Joyce, *Finnegans Wake*, intro. John Bishop (London: Penguin, 1999) 47. Hereafter cited as *FW*.

5. Eco, *The Aesthetics of Chaosmos: The Middle Ages of James Joyce*, trans. Ellen Esrock (Cambridge, MA: Harvard University Press, 1982).

6. Daniel W. Smith, "Introduction, 'A Life of Pure Immanence': Deleuze's 'Critique et Clinique' Project" in *Essays: Critical and Clinical*, by Gilles Deleuze, trans. Daniel W. Smith and Michael A. Greco (Minneapolis: University of Minnesota Press, 1997) xxv, xxviii, xxxvii, xli, xlvi.

7. Thomas à Kempis, *The Imitation of Christ*, trans. with an intro. Leo Sherley-Price (London: Penguin, 1952) 40. Hereafter cited as *IOC*.

8. Edward Said, *Beginnings* (London: Granta, 1985) 261.

9. Sheldon Brivic, *The Veil of Signs: Joyce, Lacan, and Perception* (Urbana: University of Illinois Press, 1991) 23.

10. Jacques Rancière, *On the Shores of Politics*, trans. Liz Heron (London: Verso, 1995) 70.

11. Søren Kierkegaard, *Papers and Journals: A Selection*, trans. with intro. and notes Alastair Hannay (London: Penguin, 1996) 511.

12. Theodor Adorno, *Minima Moralia: Reflections from Damaged Life*, trans. EFN Jephcott (London: Verso, 1974, thirteenth

impression 2002) 29.

13. Herman Rapaport, *Heidegger & Derrida: Reflections on Time and Language* (Lincoln: University of Nebraska Press, 1989) 233.

14. Kevin Hart, *The Dark Gaze: Maurice Blanchot and the Sacred* (Chicago: University of Chicago Press, 2004) 192–93.

15. Harry Burrell, *Narrative Design in* Finnegans Wake: *The* Wake Lock Picked (Gainesville, FL: University Press of Florida, 1996) 5.

16. Giorgio Agamben writes in "Bartleby or On Contingency", "The interruption of writing marks the passage to the second creation, in which God summons all his potential not to be, creating on the basis of a point of indifference between potentiality and impotentiality. The creation that is now fulfilled is [...] a decreation in which what happened and what did not happen are returned to their originary unity in the mind of God, while what could have been but was becomes indistinguishable from what could have been but what was not." In *Potentialities: Collected Essays in Philosophy* (Stanford: Stanford University Press, 1999) 270.

17. Niklas Luhmann, *Observations on Modernity*, trans. William Whobrey (Stanford: Stanford University Press, 1998) 112.

18. Niklas Luhmann, *The Reality of the Mass Media*, trans. Kathleen Cross (Stanford: Stanford University Press, 2000) 7.

19. Niklas Luhmann, *Art as a Social System*, trans. Eva M. Knodt (Stanford: Stanford University Press, 2000) 24.

20. Luhmann, *Art as a Social System*, 74.

Chapter 6

1. Esposito, *Immunitas: The Protection and Negation of Life*, 26.

2. Brian Davies, *The Thought of Thomas Aquinas* (Oxford: Clarendon Press, 1992) 8.

3. Jean-Pierre Dupuy, *The Mark of the Sacred*, trans. MB

DeBevoise (Stanford: Stanford University Press, 2013) 48.

4. For a rich account of the life and work of Thomas Aquinas see GK Chesterton, *St. Thomas Aquinas* (Mineola, New York: Dover, 2009).

5. Georges Bataille, *On Nietzsche*, trans. Bruce Boone, intro. Sylvère Lotringer (London: Athlone, 1992) 124. French original, *Sur Nietzsche*. Hereafter cited as *ON*.

6. Georges Bataille, *Guilty*, trans. Bruce Boone, intro. Denis Hollier (Venice, CA: Lapis, 1988) 161. French original *Le coupable*. Hereafter cited as *G*.

7. Jean Baudrillard, *Paroxysms: Interviews with Philippe Petit*, trans. Chris Turner (London: Verso, 1998) 21; linguistic original *Le Paroxyste indifférent: Entretiens avec Philippe Petit*.

8. Baudrillard, *Paroxysms: Interviews with Philippe Petit*, 40.

9. *Paroxysms: Interviews with Philippe Petit*, 49.

10. Georges Bataille, *Inner Experience*, trans. with an intro. Leslie Anne Boldt (Albany: SUNY Press, 1988) 28. French original *L'expérience intérieure*. Hereafter cited as *IE*.

11. Peter Sloterdijk, *Spheres, Volume 3: Foams, Plural Spherology*, trans. Wieland Hoban (South Pasadena, CA: Semiotext(e), 2016) 433.

12. Leo Bersani, *The Culture of Redemption* (Cambridge, MA: Harvard University Press, 1990) 113.

13. Bersani, *The Culture of Redemption*, 113.

14. Georges Bataille, *The Accursed Share: Volume 1*, trans. Robert Hurley (New York: Zone, 1991) 76–77.

15. Michael Richardson, *Georges Bataille* (London: Routledge, 1994) viii. Hereafter cited as *GB*.

16. Martin Heidegger, *What is Called Thinking?: A Translation of 'Was Heisst Denken?'*, with an intro. J. Glenn Gray (New York: Harper, 1968) 4.

Chapter 7

1. A first airing of this chapter was given on 13 November

2009: "The Dialectics of Existence and Creation; The Real of *Invisible Man* (1952)" at the *16th Olomouc Colloquium of American Studies, Black Odyssey Continued*, 12–14 November 2009, Palacký University, Olomouc, Czech Republic. The text was then revised for a presentation 14 May 2012, "The Dance Between Existence Creation and the Commons in Dante's *Commedia*, Dostoevsky's *Notes from Underground* and Ellison's *Invisible Man*" for a conference "Reading a Symptom: Literary and Psychoanalytical Perspectives", 14 May 2012, University of Tel Aviv, Tel Aviv, Israel.

2. Michel Serres, *The Troubadour of Knowledge*, trans. Sheila Faria Glaser and William Paulson (Ann Arbor: University of Michigan Press, 1997) 92, 96.

3. Alexandre Leupin, *Lacan Today: Psychoanalysis, Science, Religion* (New York: Other, 2004) 16–17.

4. Leupin, *Lacan Today: Psychoanalysis, Science, Religion*, 17.

5. Eugenio Montale, "Introduction", *The Divine Comedy*, by Dante Alighieri, notes Peter Armour (New York: Knopf, 1995) 31.

6. Montale, "Introduction", *The Divine Comedy*, 12–13.

7. Hans-Georg Moeller, *The Radical Luhmann* (New York: Columbia University Press, 2011).

8. Jason Powell, *Jacques Derrida: A Biography* (London: Continuum, 2006) 10.

9. Powell, *Jacques Derrida: A Biography*, 10.

10. *Jacques Derrida: A Biography*, 5.

11. *Jacques Derrida: A Biography*, 5.

12. Peter Sloterdijk, *Critique of Cynical Reason*, trans. Michael Eldred, foreword Andreas Huysen, *Theory and History of Literature, Volume 40* (Minneapolis: University of Minnesota Press, 1987) 194.

13. Simon Critchley, *Ethics-Politics-Subjectivity: Essays on Derrida, Levinas & Contemporary French Thought* (London: Verso, 1999) 51.

14. Sloterdijk, *Critique of Cynical Reason*, 320.

15. Ralph Ellison, *Invisible Man* (New York: Vintage, 1952) 7. Hereafter cited as *IM*.

16. In Henri Mondor, *Vie de Mallarmé* (Paris: Gallimard, 1941) 687, as cited by Vincent Kaufman from his essay "Angels of Purity" trans. John Goodman in *Guy Debord and the Situationist International: Texts and Documents*, ed. Tom McDonough (Cambridge, MA: MIT Press, 2002) endnote 11, 311.

17. Mustapha Khayati, "Captive Words (Preface to a Situationist Dictionary)", trans. Tom McDonough in *Guy Debord and the Situationist International: Texts and Documents*, ed. Tom McDonough (Cambridge, MA: MIT Press, 2002) 173.

18. Martin Heidegger, *Being and Time: A Translation of 'Sein und Zeit'*, trans. Joan Stambaugh (Albany: SUNY Press, 1996) 120/128.

19. David Kishik, *The Power of Life: Agamben and the Coming Politics (To Imagine a Form of Life, II)* (Stanford: Stanford University Press, 2012) 110–11.

20. Kishik, *The Power of Life*, 114.

21. *The Power of Life*, 115.

22. Hans-Georg Moeller, *The Radical Luhmann* (New York: Columbia University Press, 2012) 8.

Chapter 8

1. This chapter was first aired on 10 November 2012, "A Fully Fledged Reality: James Scott Connors versus Ivan Lendl in the Men's Singles Finals at the 1982 and 1983 United States Tennis Open", for the 16th Prague-Constance Workshop on "Violence and Representation", 9–10 November 2012, Charles University, Prague, Czech Republic.

2. Bill Dwyre, "Lendl lets everyone in on jokes". *Los Angeles Times*. 29 August 2007. 2 March 2009 <http://articles.latimes.com/2007/aug/29/sports/sp-dwyre29>.

3. <http://www.atpworldtour.com/News/Tennis/2013/08/34/ Heritage-No1-Celebration.aspx>. Web. Accessed 16 June 2016.
4. Slavoj Žižek, *Interrogating the Real*, ed. Rex Butler and Scott Stephens (London: Continuum, 2005) 14.
5. Žižek, *Interrogating the Real*, 14.
6. Uncredited, "Cold War, Call for Papers: The Global History of Sport in the Cold War / Wilson Center", October 31, 2012. 29 August 2017. <http://www.aisseco.org/cfp-the-global-history-of-sport-in-the-cold-war/>.
7. Wikipedia contributors. "Ivan Lendl career statistics." *Wikipedia, The Free Encyclopedia*. Wikipedia, The Free Encyclopedia, 28 Jul. 2017. Web. 10 Sep. 2017. <https://en.wikipedia.org/w/index.php?title=Ivan_Lendl_career_statistics&oldid=792728400>.
8. See for example, Malcolm Folley, "Murray is so good his rival's taken on the Pope's coach! Djokovic recruits Polish veteran in bid to make up ground on Brit." *Mail Online*. 1 September 2013. 2 September 2013 <http://www.dailymail.co.uk/sport/tennis/article-2407990/US-Open-2013-NovakDjokovic-recruits-coach-Pope-John-Paul-II.html>. As Folley puts it of Djokovic, "But the success Murray has had against him, in New York and London, has clearly forced his hand as he seeks an answer to the alchemy of Ivan Lendl." See also Simon Briggs, "US Open 2013: Novak Djokovic hoping a bit of Andy Murray's Ivan Lendl magic will rub off via Wojtek Fibak." *Telegraph*. 2 September 2013. 2 September 2013 <http://www.telegraph.co.uk/sport/tennis/usopen/10282142/US-Open-2013-Novak-Djokovic-hoping-a-bit-of-Andy-Murrays-Ivan-Lendl-magic-will-rub-off-via-Wojtek-Fibak.html>. In early 1980s tennis lore, Wojtek Fibak was instrumental in getting Lendl to hit every shot he could with topspin instead of with slice especially the backhand and also taught Lendl not to show any emotion on

the court, something that became part and parcel of Lendl's on court stone face image. As Fibak puts it, "Last week, he was practicing with Andy on the next court and I was so proud because Ivan hasn't missed a ball, [...] I said, 'Wow, Ivan you are playing so well, I am so proud'. He said, 'No, no', but I can see he is happy. Deep, flat, strong, beautiful forehand. Steady backhand. I said, 'Wow, I am proud to be part of that machine'. It's more than 25 years since we worked together and the guy, his tennis was very modern, it didn't look like from some other era. Chapeau." Ivan Lendl as tennis machine that would augur the future of the game Fibak underlines.

9.   Wikipedia contributors. "ATP World Tour records." Wikipedia, The Free Encyclopedia. *Wikipedia, The Free Encyclopedia*, 9 Sep. 2017. Web. 10 Sep. 2017. <http://en.wikipedia.org/wiki/ATP_World_Tour_records>.

10. Here we get a sense of the complex dynamic before the match: "US Open 1982 Men's Singles Semi-Final Lendl vs. McEnroe". DVD. Disc 1. Or see, <http://www.youtube.com/watch?v=8WT4mtCwbno>. "Lendl vs McEnroe Semi Final - US Open 1982 - 01/12". 27 March 2011. 20 April 2011. Note especially the first nine minutes of the 10:27 that constitute this clip.

11. "US Open 1982 Men's Singles Final". DVD. Disc 1 of 2.

12. Peter Sloterdijk, *Spheres I: Bubbles, Microspherology*, trans. Wieland Hoban (Los Angeles: Semiotext(e), 2011) 607.

13. "US Open 1982 Men's Singles Final". DVD. Disc 1 of 2.

14. "US Open 1982 Men's Singles Final". DVD. Disc 1 of 2.

15. "US Open 1982 Men's Singles Final". DVD. Disc 1 of 2.

16. Peter Fenves, *The Messianic Reduction: Walter Benjamin and the Shape of Time* (Stanford: Stanford University Press, 2011) 189.

17. "US Open 1983 Men's Singles Final". DVD. 1 disc. Or see "Lendl - Connors US Open 1983 Final. Set 3 pt 2". *YouTube*.

19 February 2010. 6 May 2011. 7:51 <http://youtu.be/ MEAuHYvB0Pk>.

18. Žižek, *Living in the End Times*, 185.

19. Alain Badiou, *Theory of the Subject*, trans. and with an intro. Bruno Bosteels (London: Verso, 2009) 280–81.

20. "US Open 1983 Men's Singles Final". DVD. 1 disc. Or see "Lendl – Connors 1983 US Open Final. Set 3 pt 5." *YouTube*. 19 February 2010. 6 May 2011. 7:07 <https://youtu.be/ de1RKgNYPbQ>.

21. From: *The Aesthetics of Everyday Life*, ed. Andrew Light and Jonathan M. Smith (New York: Columbia University Press, 2005), 135–155. Wolfgang Welsch (Friedrich-Schiller-University Jena, Germany) "Sport Viewed Aesthetically, and Even as Art?", 145–46.

22. Barry Lorge, Contributing Editor, "Why You Should Like Ivan Lendl", *Tennis*, Vol. 22, No. 10, February 1987, 39.

23. Lorge, "Why You Should Like Ivan Lendl", 43.

24. "Why You Should Like Ivan Lendl", 42.

25. "Why You Should Like Ivan Lendl", 43.

26. "Why You Should Like Ivan Lendl", 42.

27. "Ivan Lendl – The Return of a Champion part 5 of 5". *YouTube*. 12 December 2010. 5 July 2011. 10:15 <http://youtu. be/GONUiquuQvU>. See especially minute 8:30 to minute ten.

28. "Ivan Lendl – The Return of a Champion part 5 of 5". *YouTube*. 12 December 2010. 5 July 2011. 10:15 <http://youtu. be/GONUiquuQvU>.

29. Ivan Lendl and George Mendoza, *Ivan Lendl's 14-Day Tennis Clinic: Hitting Hot*, photographs Walter Iooss, Jr. (London: Star, 1986).

30. Pierre Bourdieu, *On Television* (Cambridge, UK: Polity, 2011, 1998) 3.

31. Bourdieu, *On Television*, 11.

32. *On Television*, 16.

33. *On Television*, 21.

34. Paul Kimmage, "The Ivan Lendl Interview". *The Sunday Times*. 24 May 2009. 10 July 2009. Indirectly accessible at <http://www.thesundaytimes.co.uk/sto/sport/article169694. ece>.

35. Kimmage, "The Ivan Lendl Interview", 24 May 2009.

36. "The Ivan Lendl Interview", 24 May 2009.

37. "The Ivan Lendl Interview", 24 May 2009.

38. "The Ivan Lendl Interview", 24 May 2009.

39. Esposito, *Immunitas: The Protection and Negation of Life*, 37.

Chapter 9

1. I dedicate these lines to the memory of my teacher in a graduate school seminar (from 1994–97 at All Souls College, Oxford) Jacques Lacan theorist and a teacher-scholar of European literature and culture, Malcolm M. Bowie, fellow of the British Academy (1943–2007). This chapter was initially aired on 24 September 2010, "The Unconscious, Athletic Identity, and a Whole Galaxy on Stage; or, the 1984 French Open Final, McEnroe vs. Lendl", for a panel on "The Self, Action and the Unconscious" at a Colloquium at Metropolitan University-Prague on "Nations, Cultures, Individuals and Their Limits", 24–25 September 2010, Prague, Czech Republic.

2. John McEnroe with James Kaplan, *You Cannot Be Serious* (New York: Berkley, 2002) 174–75. Hereafter cited as *YCS*.

3. John McEnroe, *But Seriously* (New York: Little, Brown and Company, 2017) 3.

4. McEnroe, *But Seriously*, 268.

5. "Roland Garros 1984 Men's Singles Final". DVD. Disc 2 of 2. Also see the final nine minutes of this match online on *YouTube*.

6. Walter Benjamin, *The Arcades Project*, trans. Howard Eilend and Kevin McLaughlin, prepared on the basis of the German

volume edited by Rolf Tiedemann (Cambridge, MA: Belknap Press of Harvard University Press, 1999) 801.

7. For one viewpoint on Lendl at the big W, Wimbledon at the All England Lawn Tennis & Croquet Club in London, England see this account, Rajat Jain, "Ivan Lendl: Greatest Grass-Court Player Never to Win Wimbledon." *Bleacher Report*. 25 April 2009. 10 June 2011 <http://bleacherreport. com/articles/162033-ivan-lendl-greatest-grass-court-player-never-to-win wimbledon>.

8. For a revealing interview with Ivan Lendl again see Paul Kimmage, "The Ivan Lendl Interview." *The Sunday Times*. 24 May 2009. 10 July 2009. To quote one portion, here is Paul Kimmage, "why not set the record straight and say, 'This is who I am. These are the events that shaped me. Now make your own mind up'." *IL:* "[...]. To write a proper book I would have to name names, it would hurt some people, and I don't think that's necessary. Secondly, it's not that important to me. I know who I am and my friends know who I am, that's what is important to me. Would it be nice that all the tennis fans know who I am? Yeah, but not at the price of hurting people."

9. Wikipedia contributors. "All-time tennis records – men's singles." *Wikipedia, The Free Encyclopedia*. Wikipedia, The Free Encyclopedia, 15 Oct. 2017. Web. 15 Oct. 2017. <https:// en.wikipedia.org/w/index.php?title=All-time_tennis_records_–_men%27s_singles&oldid=805432493>.

10. "1984 French Open Men's Singles Final". DVD. Disc 2 of 2.

11. Wikipedia contributors. "List of tennis rivalries." *Wikipedia, The Free Encyclopedia*. Wikipedia, The Free Encyclopedia, 15 Oct. 2017. Web. 15 Oct. 2017. <https://en.wikipedia.org/w/index.php?title=List_of_tennis_rivalries&direction=next&oldid=805431876>.

12. Jérome Bureau and Bennoît Heimermann interview with Jean-Luc Godard, first published in *L'Équipe*, May 9, 2001.

Reprinted here in Jean-Luc Godard, *The Future(s) of film: three interviews, 2000-01* (Bern: Verlag Gachnang & Springer AG, 2002) 79.

13. Michel Serres, *The Five Senses: A Philosophy of Mingled Bodies (I)*, trans. Margaret Sankey and Peter Cowley (London: Continuum, 2088) 314.

14. For these theories see Georges Bataille, *The Accursed Share, Volume 1, Consumption*, trans. Robert Hurley (New York: Zone, 1991) and his *The Accursed Share, Volume II: The History of Eroticism & Volume III: Sovereignty*, trans. Robert Hurley (New York: Zone, 1993).

15. The following in French is worth watching on *The Twilight of the Gods*, "McEnroe-Lendl Le Crépuscule des Dieux" on *YouTube* <https://youtu.be/-hdFuOBQF4Q>. 11 June 2017. 16 June 2017. 54:30.

16. Wikipedia contributors. "Lendl–McEnroe rivalry." *Wikipedia, The Free Encyclopedia*. Wikipedia, The Free Encyclopedia, 25 Jul. 2017. Web. 10 Sep. 2017. <https://en.wikipedia.org/w/index.php?title=Lendl%E2%80%93McEnroe_rivalry&oldid=792318301>.

17. Roland Barthes, *What is Sport?*, trans. Richard Howard (New Haven: Yale University Press, 2007) 58–59.

18. See early part of 1984 Roland-Garros McEnroe vs. Lendl. "1984 French Open Men's Singles Final". DVD. Disc 1 of 2. Or see the match on *YouTube* online.

19. Barthes, *What is Sport?*, 49.

20. Wikipedia contributors. "All-time tennis records – men's singles." *Wikipedia, The Free Encyclopedia*. Wikipedia, The Free Encyclopedia, 15 Oct. 2017. Web. 15 Oct. 2017. <https://en.wikipedia.org/w/index.php?title=All-time_tennis_records_–_men%27s_singles&oldid=805432493>.

21. *What is Sport?*, 55.

22. *What is Sport?*, 61.

23. *What is Sport?*, 59, 61.

24. "1984 French Open Men's Singles Final". DVD. Disc 1 of 2. Or see, <http://youtu.be/vx-U6zag_GY>. "Roland Garros 1984 Final – McEnroe vs Lendl 08/23." *YouTube*. 29 December 2009. 5 September 2010. 9:41.

25. *What is Sport?*, 65.

26. Nico Stehr and Gotthard Bechmann, intro., *Risk: A Sociological Theory* by Niklas Luhmann (New Brunswick, NJ: Aldine Transaction, 2002) xvi–xvii.

27. Stehr and Bechmann, intro., *Risk: A Sociological Theory* by Niklas Luhmann, xiv.

28. Stehr and Bechmann, intro., *Risk: A Sociological Theory* by Niklas Luhmann, xxi.

29. Alain Badiou, *Theory of the Subject*, trans. and with an intro. Bruno Bosteels (London: Verso, 2009) 262.

30. Slavoj Žižek, *The Puppet and the Dwarf: The Perverse Core of Christianity* (Cambridge, MA: MIT Press, 2003) 137.

31. <http://www.80s-tennis.com/pages/ivan-lendl.html>. Accessed 16 June 2017.

32. Valerie Mendes and Amy de la Haye, *Fashion Since 1900, New Edition* (London: Thames & Hudson World of Art, 2010) 280.

33. Jean-Luc Nancy, *Multiple Arts: The Muses II*, ed. Simon Sparks (Stanford: Stanford University Press, 2006) 20.

34. See "David Letterman Ivan Lendl 1986." *YouTube*. Web. 6 December 2013. 2 March 2014. 5:18 <https://youtu.be/QEwUMnqG4us>. This video also espouses Lendl's qualities of discipline and focus when growing up; it also includes the first interview with Lendl, "Ivan Lendl, Tennis Legend." *YouTube*. 12 November 2011. 8 December 2011. 11:22 <https://youtu.be/0H2emaQjiDw>.

35. Maurice Keen, *Chivalry* (New Haven: Yale University Press, 1984) 76.

36. Walter Benjamin, *Selected Writings, Volume 2, Part 2, 1931–1934*, trans. Rodney Livingstone and Others, ed. Michael W. Jennings, Howard Eiland, and Gary Smith (Cambridge, MA:

Harvard University Press, 1999) 541.

37. Benjamin, *Selected Writings, Volume 2, Part 2, 1931-1934*, 542.

38. See Jean-Luc Nancy, *The Creation of the World; or, Globalization*, trans. and with an intro. by François Raffoul and David Pettigrew (Albany: SUNY Press, 2007). In this tome a negative understanding attaches to the concept 'globalization' and a positive understanding to 'the creation of the world'.

39. Bernard Stiegler, *Taking Care of Youth and the Generations*, trans. Stephen Barker (Stanford: Stanford University Press, 2010) 148.

40. Slavoj Žižek, *The Fragile Absolute: Or, Why Is The Christian Legacy Worth Fighting For?* (London: Verso, 2000) 43.

41. "French Open 1984 Men's Singles Final". DVD. Disc 1 of 2.

42. "French Open 1984 Men's Singles Final". DVD. Disc 1 of 2.

43. "French Open 1984 Men's Singles Final". DVD. Disc 1 of 2.

44. "French Open 1984 Men's Singles Final". DVD. Disc 1 of 2.

45. "French Open 1984 Men's Singles Final". DVD. Disc 1 of 2.

46. "French Open 1984 Men's Singles Final". DVD. Disc 1 of 2.

47. "French Open 1984 Men's Singles Final". DVD. Disc 2 of 2.

48. "French Open 1984 Men's Singles Final". DVD. Disc 2 of 2.

49. "French Open 1984 Men's Singles Final". DVD. Disc 2 of 2.

50. Fichte, JG, *Early Philosophical Writings*, trans. and ed. Daniel Breazeale (Ithaca: Cornell University Press, 1988) 195.

51. McEnroe played Lendl in New York in February 2011, of which we read from Lendl: "*Q. But you never had that kind of a relationship with McEnroe, where you'd have lunch or dinner together. Has your relationship changed? A.* No. I really don't have one with him. I wish we could. After all this time, you would think it would be reasonable." Stuart Miller, "Q. and A. With Ivan Lendl." *Straight Sets: Tennis Blog of The New York Times*. 26 February 2011. 28 February 2011 <http://straightsets.blogs.nytimes.com/2011/02/26/q-and-a-with-ivan-lendl/>.

52. Julien Pichené, *Carnets de balles: De Laver à Federer en passant par McEnroe, 250 matches indispensables,* préface de Patrice Dominguez (Paris: Publibook, 2010) 118.

53. "Andy Murray's Championship Winning Speech." *YouTube.* 7 July 2013. 7 July 2013 4:54 <https://youtu.be/uapCx5yEbGQ>.

54. By *Telegraph* Staff, "Ivan Lendl has right credentials to lead Andy Murray to grand slam, says former mentor Tony Roche". *Telegraph.* 1 January 2012. 1 January 2012 <http://www.telegraph.co.uk/sport/tennis/andymurray/8986908/Ivan-Lendl-has-right-credentials-to-lead-Andy-Murray-to-grand-slam-says-former-mentor-Tony-Roche.html>.
   Also see Liam Power, "Andy Murray Shares Ivan Lendl Admiration." *SportsMole.* 22 January 2013. 26 January 2013 <http://www.sportsmole.co.uk/tennis/australian-open/news/murray-shares-lendl-admiration_65409.html>. Murray discloses: "Now that I know him and have watched him a lot, he would be the most fun guy to go play. He was incredibly consistent, very rarely played a bad match, he did everything well, served well, good forehand, passed well, moved well."

55. The Web site is now defunct for Lendl's academy but the same day when his split with Murray was announced one could find this online, Jack Cavanaugh, "Ivan Lendl highlights tennis open house." *Bluffton Today.* 19 March 2014. 21 March 2014 <http://www.blufftontoday.com/bluffton-sports/2014-03-19/ivan-lendl-highlights-tennis-open-house#.UznBI62SybI>.

56. Slavoj Žižek, *Did Somebody Say Totalitarianism? Five Interventions in the (Mis)use of a Notion* (London: Verso, 2002) 173.

Chapter 10

1. Paul Fein, *You Can Quote Me on That: Greatest Tennis Quips, Insights, and Zingers* (Washington DC: Potomac, 2005) 213.

2. Alain Badiou, *Ethics: An Essay on the Understanding of Evil*, trans. and introduced Peter Hallward (London: Verso, 2001) 123.

3. Note the Lendl smile here, "Ivan Lendl, the man who turned Andy Murray into a champion". By Jim White. *Telegraph*. 9 July 2013. 10 July 2013 <http://www.telegraph.co.uk/sport/tennis/andymurray/10166724/Ivan-Lendl-the-man-who-turned-Andy-Murray-into-a-champion.html>.

4. "Ivan Lendl and Andy Murray split as coach is unable to commit to the Scot's dates with destiny". By Simon Briggs. *Telegraph*. 19 March 2014. 19 March 2014 <http://www.telegraph.co.uk/sport/tennis/andymurray/10708657/Ivan-Lendl-and-Andy-Murray-split-as-coach-is-unable-to-commit-to-the-Scots-dates-with-destiny.html?fb>. 20 March 2014. See also Malcolm Folley, "Andy Murray's future is clouded in doubt after mystery of break-up with mentor Lendl." *Mail Online*. 22 March 2014. 23 March 2014 <http://www.dailymail.co.uk/sport/tennis/article-2586927/Andy-Murrays-future-clouded-doubt-mystery-break-mentor-Lendl.html>. As Folley notes, "Mats Wilander perhaps best summarised what Lendl has accomplished, when he told the Tennis Podcast: 'You have to consider Lendl as the greatest game-changer ever, as a coach, for what he did with Murray.'"

5. Chris Oddo, "Five Things We'll Always Cherish about the Murray-Lendl Pairing." *Tennis Now*. 19 March 2014. 20 March 2014 <http://www.tennisnow.com/News/Five-Things-We-ll-Always-Cherish-about-the-Murray.aspx>.

6. Simon Briggs, "Andy Murray appoints Amelie Mauresmo as his new coach." *Telegraph*. 8 June 2014. 9 June 2014 <http://www.telegraph.co.uk/sport/tennis/andymurray/10884664/Andy-Murray-appoints-Amelie-Mauresmo-as-his-new-coach.html>. As this article notes, Murray appointed Mauresmo as his new coach a mere fifteen minutes before

the start of the Men's singles final at Roland-Garros in 2014.

7. Slavoj Žižek and John Milbank, *The Monstrosity of Christ: Paradox or Dialectic?*, ed. Creston Davis (Cambridge, MA: MIT Press, 2009) 89. Hereafter cited as *MC*.

8. Tom Perrotta, "Ivan Lendl's Second Act." *Men's Journal.* 17 June 2013. 26 June 2013 <http://www.mensjournal.com/magazine/ivan-lendls-second-act-20130617>.

9. Brian Phillips, "The End of Ivan and Andy." *Grantland: Tennis.* 19 March 2014. 21 March 2014 <http://grantland.com/the-triangle/andy-murray-ivan-lendl/>.

10. Slavoj Žižek, *Absolute Recoil: Towards a New Foundation of Dialectical Materialism* (London: Verso, 2014) 329.

11. Slavoj Žižek, *The Indivisible Remainder: On Schelling and Related Matters* (London: Verso, 1996) 126.

12. *Theory of the Subject*, 331.

13. Slavoj Žižek, *First as Tragedy, Then as Farce* (London: Verso, 2009) 151.

Select Bibliography

Online Publications Consulted

Briggs, Simon. "Andy Murray appoints Amelie Mauresmo as his new coach." *Telegraph*. 8 June 2014. 9 June 2014 <http://www.telegraph.co.uk/sport/tennis/andymurray/10884664/AndyMurray-appoints-Amelie-Mauresmo-as-his-new-coach.html>.

— . "Ivan Lendl and Andy Murray split as coach is unable to commit to the Scot's dates with destiny." *Telegraph*. 19 March 2014. 19 March 2014 <http://www.telegraph.co.uk/sport/tennis/andymurray/10708657/Ivan-Lendl-and-Andy-Murray-split-as-coach-is-unable-to-commit-to-the-Scots-dates-with-destiny.html?fb>.

— . "US Open 2013: Novak Djokovic hoping a bit of Andy Murray's Ivan Lendl magic will rub off via Wojtek Fibak." *Telegraph*. 2 September 2013. 2 September 2013 <http://www.telegraph.co.uk/sport/tennis/usopen/10282142/US-Open-2013-Novak-Djokovic-hoping-a-bit-of-Andy-Murrays-Ivan-Lendl-magic-will-rub-off-via-Wojtek-Fibak.html>.

Brooks, Xan. "Wimbledon won't be the same without Ivan Lendl." *The Guardian*. 22 June 2014. 23 June 2014 <http://www.theguardian.com/sport/shortcuts/2014/jun/22/wimbledon-wont-be-same-without-ivan-lendl>.

Cavanaugh, Jack. "Ivan Lendl highlights tennis open house." *Bluffton Today*. 19 March 2014. 21 March 2014 <http://www.blufftontoday.com/bluffton-sports/2014-03-19/ivan-lendl-highlights-tennis-open-house#.UznBI62SybI>.

Dwyre, Bill. "Lendl lets everyone in on jokes." *Los Angeles Times*. 29 August 2007. 2 March 2009 <http://articles.latimes.com/2007/aug/29/sports/sp-dwyre29>.

Folley, Malcolm. "Andy Murray's future is clouded in doubt after mystery of break-up with mentor Lendl." *Mail Online*.

22 March 2014. 23 March 2014 <http://www.dailymail.co.uk/sport/tennis/article-2586927/Andy-Murrays-future-clouded-doubt-mystery-break-mentor-Lendl.html>.

— . "Murray is so good his rival's taken on the Pope's coach! Djokovic recruits Polish veteran in bid to make up ground on Brit." *Mail Online*. 1 September 2013. 1 September 2013 <http://www.dailymail.co.uk/sport/tennis/article-2407990/US-Open-2013-NovakDjokovic-recruits-coach-Pope-John-Paul-II.html>.

Jain, Rajat. "Ivan Lendl: Greatest Grass-Court Player Never to Win Wimbledon." *Bleacher Report*. 25 April 2009. 10 June 2011 <http://bleacherreport.com/articles/162033-ivan-lendl-greatest-grass-court-player-never-to-win wimbledon>.

Kimmage, Paul. "The Ivan Lendl Interview." *The Sunday Times*. 24 May 2009. 10 July 2009 <http://www.timesonline.co.uk/tol/sport/columnists/paul_kimmage/article6349407.ece?token=null&offset=108&page=10>.

Lendl, Ivan and James Buddell. "Ivan Lendl: The Constant Gardener." Interview: Ivan Lendl spoke to James Buddell. Web. 7 November 2016. 17 November 2016. <http://www.atpworldtour.com/en/news/ivan-lendl-remembers-masters-1980s-murray>.

Miller, Stuart. "Q. and A. With Ivan Lendl." *Straight Sets: Tennis Blog of The New York Times*. Web. 26 February 2011. 28 February 2011 <http://straightsets.blogs.nytimes.com/2011/02/26/q-and-a-with-ivan-lendl/>.

Oddo, Chris. "Five Things We'll Always Cherish about the Murray-Lendl Pairing." *Tennis Now*. 19 March 2014. 20 March 2014 <http://www.tennisnow.com/News/Five-Things-We-ll-Always-Cherish-about-the-Murray.aspx>.

Perrotta, Tom. "Ivan Lendl's Second Act." *Men's Journal*. 17 June 2013. 26 June 2013 <http://www.mensjournal.com/magazine/ivan-lendls-second-act-20130617>.

Phillips, Brian. "The End of Ivan and Andy." By Brian Phillips.

Grantland: Tennis. 19 March 2014. 21 March 2014 <http://grant-land.com/the-triangle/andy-murray-ivan-lendl/>.

Power, Liam. "Andy Murray Shares Ivan Lendl Admiration." *SportsMole.* 22 January 2013. 26 January 2013 <http://www.sportsmole.co.uk/tennis/australian-open/news/murray-shares-lendl-admiration_65409.html>.

Telegraph Staff, By. "Ivan Lendl has right credentials to lead Andy Murray to grand slam, says former mentor Tony Roche." *Telegraph.* 1 January 2012. 1 January 2012 <http://www.telegraph.co.uk/sport/tennis/andymurray/8986908/Ivan-Lendl-has-right-credentials-to-lead-Andy-Murray-to-grand-slam-says-former-mentor-Tony-Roche.html>.

Uncredited. "Cold War, Call for Papers: The Global History of Sport in the Cold War / Wilson Center", October 31, 2012. 4 September 2017 <http://www.aisseco.org/cfp-the-global-history-of-sport-in-the-cold-war/>.

White, Jim. "Ivan Lendl, the man who turned Andy Murray into a champion." *Telegraph.* 9 July 2013. 10 July 2013 <http://www.telegraph.co.uk/sport/tennis/andymurray/10166724/Ivan-Lendl-the-man-who-turned-Andy-Murray-into-a-champion.html>.

<http:/www.atpworldtour.com/>. Accessed 15 October 2017.

<http://www.80s-tennis.com/pages/ivan-lendl.html>. Accessed 26 September 2017.

"Andy Murray's Championship Winning Speech." *YouTube.* 7 July 2013. 7 July 2013. 4:54 <https://youtu.be/uapCx5yEbGQ>.

"David Letterman Ivan Lendl 1986." *YouTube.* 6 December 2013. 2 March 2014. 5:18 <https://youtu.be/QEwUMnqG4us>.

"Ivan Lendl – The Return of a Champion 5/5." *YouTube.* 12 December 2010. 5 July 2011. 10:15 <http://youtu.be/GO-NUiquuQvU>.

"Ivan Lendl, Tennis Legend." *YouTube.* 12 November 2011. 8 December 2011. 11:22 <http://youtu.be/0H2emaQjiDw>.

"Lendl vs McEnroe Semi Final - US Open 1982 - 01/12." *YouTube.*

27 March 2011. 20 April 2011. 10:27 <http://www.youtube.com/watch?v=8WT4mtCwbno>.

"Lendl - Connors US Open 1983 Final. Set 3 pt 2." *YouTube.* 19 February 2010. 6 May 2011. 7:51 <http://youtu.be/MEAuHYvB-0Pk>.

"Lendl – Connors 1983 US Open Final. Set 3 pt 5." *YouTube.* 9 February 2010. 6 May 2011. 7:07 <https://youtu.be/de1RKg-NYPbQ>.

"McEnroe-Lendl Le Crépuscule des Dieux." *YouTube.* 11 June 2017. 16 June 2017. 54:30 <https://youtu.be/-hdFuOBQF4Q>.

"Roland Garros 1984 Final – McEnroe vs Lendl 03/23." *YouTube.* 29 December 2009. 5 September 2010. 9:55 <http://youtu.be/FBk1zyxjre4>.

"Roland Garros 1984 Final – McEnroe vs Lendl 08/23." *YouTube.* 29 December 2009. 5 September 2010. 9:41 <http://youtu.be/vx-U6zag_GY>.

Wikipedia contributors. "All-time tennis records – men's singles." *Wikipedia, The Free Encyclopedia.* Wikipedia, The Free Encyclopedia, 15 Oct. 2017. Web.

15 Oct. 2017. <https://en.wikipedia.org/w/index.php?title= All-time_tennis_records_%E2%80%93_men%27s_singles&oldid=805432493>.

Wikipedia contributors. "Ivan Lendl career statistics." *Wikipedia, The Free Encyclopedia.* Wikipedia, The Free Encyclopedia, 28 Jul. 2017. Web. 10 Sep. 2017. <https://en.wikipedia.org/w/index.php?title=Ivan_Lendl_career_statistics&oldid=792728400>.

Wikipedia contributors. "Lendl–McEnroe rivalry." *Wikipedia, The Free Encyclopedia.* Wikipedia, The Free Encyclopedia, 25 Jul. 2017. Web. 10 Sep. 2017. <https://en.wikipedia.org/w/index.php?title=Lendl%E2%80%93McEnroe_rivalry&oldid=792318301>.

Wikipedia contributors. "List of tennis rivalries." *Wikipedia, The Free Encyclopedia.* Wikipedia, The Free Encyclopedia, 15

Oct. 2017. Web. 15 Oct. 2017. <https://en.wikipedia.org/w/index.php?title=List_of_tennis_rivalries&direction=next&oldid=805431876>.

Wikipedia contributors. "Open Era tennis records – men's singles." Wikipedia, *The Free Encyclopedia. Wikipedia*, The Free Encyclopedia, 9 Sep. 2017. Web. 10 Sep. 2017. <https://en.wikipedia.org/w/index.php?title=Open_Era_tennis_records_%E2%80%93_men%27s_singles&oldid=799801155>.

DVD-Videos Consulted

"French Open 1984 Men's Singles Final". DVD. 2 discs.

"US Open 1982 Men's Singles Final". DVD. 2 discs.

"US Open 1982 Men's Singles Semi-Final McEnroe vs. Lendl". DVD. 1 disc.

"US Open 1983 Men's Singles Final". DVD. 1 disc.

Print Publications Consulted

Adorno, Theodor W. "A Portrait of Walter Benjamin". In *Prisms*. Trans. Samuel and Shierry Weber. Cambridge, MA: MIT Press, 1967. 227–41.

—. *Minima Moralia: Reflections from Damaged Life*. Trans. EFN Jephcott. London: Verso, 1974, thirteenth impression 2002.

Agamben, Giorgio. *Nudities*. Trans. David Kishik and Stefan Pedatella. Stanford: Stanford University Press, 2011.

—. "Bartleby or On Contingency". *Potentialities: Collected Essays in Philosophy*. Stanford: Stanford University Press, 1999. 243–71.

Arendt, Hannah. Ed. and intro. *Illuminations*. By Walter Benjamin. Trans. Harry Zorn. London: Pimlico, 1999.

Attal, José. *La non-excommunication de Jacques Lacan: quand la psychanalyse a perdu Spinoza*. Paris: L'Unebévue éditeur, 2010.

Augustine, St. *Concerning the City of God against the Pagans*. Trans. Henry Bettenson, with a new intro. GR Evans. London: Penguin, 2003.

Badiou, Alain. *Conditions*. Trans. Steven Corcoran. London: Continuum, 2008.

—. *Ethics: An Essay on the Understanding of Evil*. Trans. and introduced Peter Hallward. London: Verso, 2001.

—. *Theory of the Subject*. Trans. and with an intro. Bruno Bosteels. London: Verso, 2009.

Balibar, Étienne. *Politics and the Other Scene*. Translations Christine Jones, James Swenson, Chris Turner. London: Verso, 2002.

Barthes, Roland. *What is Sport?* Trans. Richard Howard. New Haven: Yale University Press, 2007.

Bataille, Georges. *Guilty*. Trans. Bruce Boone, intro. Denis Hollier. Venice, CA: Lapis, 1988.

—. *Inner Experience*. Trans. with an intro. Leslie Anne Boldt. Albany: SUNY Press, 1988.

—. *On Nietzsche*. Trans. Bruce Boone, intro. Sylvère Lotringer. London: Athlone, 1992.

—. *The Accursed Share: Volume 1*. Trans. Robert Hurley. New York: Zone, 1991.

Baudrillard, Jean. *Paroxysms: Interviews with Philippe Petit*. Trans. Chris Turner. London: Verso, 1998.

Benjamin, Walter. "On the Concept of History". In *Selected Writings, Volume 4, 1938-1940*. Ed. Howard Eiland and Michael W. Jennings. Trans. Edmund Jephcott and Others. Cambridge, MA: Harvard University Press, 2003. 389–400.

—. *Selected Writings, Volume 1, 1913–1926*. Ed. Marcus Bullock and Michael W. Jennings. Cambridge, MA: Belknap Press of Harvard University Press, 1996.

—. *Selected Writings, Volume 2, Part 2, 1931-1934*. Trans. Rodney Livingston and Others. Ed. Michael W. Jennings, Howard Eiland, and Gary Smith. Cambridge, MA: Harvard University Press, 1999.

—. *The Arcades Project*. Trans. Howard Eilend and Kevin McLaughlin, prepared on the basis of the German volume edited by Rolf Tiedemann. Cambridge, MA: Belknap Press of Harvard University Press, 1999.

Bersani, Leo. *A Future for Astyanax: Character and Desire in Literature*. Boston: Little, Brown and Company, 1976.

—. *The Culture of Redemption*. Cambridge, MA: Harvard University Press, 1990.

Blanchot, Maurice. *The Unavowable Community*. Trans. Pierre Joris. Barrytown, NY: Station Hill Press, 1988.

—. *The Writing of the Disaster*. Trans. Ann Smock. Lincoln: University of Nebraska Press, 1995.

Bourdieu, Pierre. *On Television*. Cambridge, UK: Polity, 2011, 1998.

Brivic, Sheldon. *The Veil of Signs: Joyce, Lacan, and Perception*. Urbana: University of Illinois Press, 1991.

Buck-Morss, Susan. *The Dialectics of Seeing: Walter Benjamin and the Arcades Project*. Cambridge, MA: MIT Press, 1989.

Bureau, Jérome and Bennoît Heimermann. Interview with Jean-Luc Godard. First published in *L'Équipe*, May 9, 2001. Reprinted in Jean-Luc Godard. *The Future(s) of film: three interviews, 2000-01*. Bern: Verlag Gachnang & Springer AG, 2002.

Burrell, Harry. *Narrative Design in* Finnegans Wake: *The Wake Lock Picked*. Gainesville, FL: University Press of Florida, 1996.

Chesterton, GK. *St. Thomas Aquinas*. Mineola, New York: Dover, 2009.

Comay, Rebecca. *Mourning Sickness: Hegel and the French Revolution*. Stanford: Stanford University Press, 2011.

Connors, Jimmy. *The Outsider: A Memoir*. New York: Harper, 2013.

Critchley, Simon. *Ethics-Politics-Subjectivity: Essays on Derrida, Levinas & Contemporary French Thought*. London: Verso, 1999.

Davies, Brian. *The Thought of Thomas Aquinas*. Oxford: Clarendon Press, 1992.

de la Durantaye, Leland. *Giorgio Agamben: A Critical Introduction*. Stanford: Stanford University Press, 2009.

Deleuze, Gilles. *Expressionism in Philosophy: Spinoza*. Preface and trans. Martin Joughin. New York: Zone, 1990.

—. *Spinoza: Practical Philosophy*. Trans. Robert Hurley. San Francisco: City Lights, 1988.

—. *The Fold: Leibniz and the Baroque*. Foreword and trans. Tom Conley. Minneapolis: University of Minnesota Press, 1993.

Deleuze, Gilles and Claire Parnet. *Dialogues*. Trans. by Hugh Tomlinson and Barbara Habberjam. London: Athlone, 1987.

Deleuze, Gilles and Félix Guattari. *What is Philosophy?* Trans. Hugh Tomlinson and Graham Burchell. New York: Columbia University Press, 1994.

Derrida, Jacques. *Le toucher, Jean-Luc Nancy*. Paris: Galilée, 2000.

—. *On Touching—Jean-Luc Nancy*. Trans. Christine Irizarry. Stanford: Stanford University Press, 2005.

Dupuy, Jean-Pierre. *Economy and the Future: A Crisis of Faith*. Trans. MB DeBevoise. East Lansing: Michigan State University Press, 2014.

— . *The Mark of the Sacred*. Trans. MB DeBevoise. Stanford: Stanford University Press, 2013.

Dwyre, Bill. "Lendl Lets Everyone in On Jokes". *Los Angeles Times*. 29 August 2007.

Ellison, Ralph. *Invisible Man*. New York: Vintage, 1952.

Esposito, Roberto. *Communitas: The Origin and Destiny of Community*. Trans. Timothy Campbell. Stanford: Stanford University Press, 2010.

—. *Immunitas: The Protection and Negation of Life*. Trans. Zakiya Hanafi. Cambridge, UK: Polity, 2011.

Fein, Paul. *You Can Quote Me on That: Greatest Tennis Quips, Insights, and Zingers*. Washington DC: Potomac, 2005.

Fenves, Peter. *The Messianic Reduction: Walter Benjamin and the Shape of Time*. Stanford: Stanford University Press, 2011.

Ferris, David S. *The Cambridge Introduction to Walter Benjamin*. Cambridge, UK: Cambridge University Press, 2008.

Fichte, JG. *Early Philosophical Writings*. Trans. and ed. Daniel

Breazeale. Ithaca: Cornell University Press, 1988.

Fisher, Mark. *Capitalist Realism: Is There No Alternative?* Winchester, UK: Zero Books, 2009.

Fynsk, Christopher. "Foreword". *The Inoperative Community: Theory and History of Literature, Volume 76.* By Jean-Luc Nancy. Ed. Peter Connor. Trans. Peter Connor, Lisa Garbus, Michael Holland, and Simona Sawhney. Minneapolis: University of Minnesota Press, 1991.

Gracián, Baltasar. *The Pocket Oracle and Art of Prudence.* Trans. with an intro. and notes Jeremy Robbins. London: Penguin, 2011.

Gumbrecht, Hans. *In Praise of Athletic Beauty.* Cambridge, MA: Harvard University Press, 2006.

Hanssen, Beatrice. *Walter Benjamin's Other History: Of Stones, Animals, Human Beings, and Angels.* Berkeley: University of California Press, 1998.

Hart, Kevin. *The Dark Gaze: Maurice Blanchot and the Sacred.* Chicago: University of Chicago Press, 2004.

Hegel, Georg Wilhelm Friedrich. *Lectures on the Philosophy of World History, Introduction: Reason in History.* Trans. HB Nisbet with an intro. Duncan Forbes. Cambridge, UK: Cambridge University Press, 1975.

Heidegger, Martin. *Being and Time: A Translation of 'Sein und Zeit'.* Trans. Joan Stambaugh. Albany: SUNY Press, 1996.

—. *What is Called Thinking?: A Translation of 'Was Heisst Denken?'.* Intro. J. Glenn Gray. New York: Harper, 1968.

Hodgkinson, Mark. *Ivan Lendl: The Man Who Made Murray.* London: Aurum, 2014.

Horkheimer, Max. "The End of Reason." In *The Essential Frankfurt School Reader.* Ed. Andrew Arato and Eike Gebhardt. Intro. Paul Piccone. New York: Continuum, 1982. 26–48.

Jacobs, Carol. *In the Language of Walter Benjamin.* Baltimore: Johns Hopkins University Press, 1999.

Jappé, Anselm. *Guy Debord.* Trans. Donald Nicholson-Smith

with a foreword TJ Clark and a new afterword by the author. Berkeley: University of California Press, 1999.

James, Henry. *The Ambassadors.* Ed. with an intro. Harry Levin. London: Penguin, 1986.

Janoušek, Jiři and Pavel Vitous. *Ivan Lendl.* Praha: Lidové nakladatelství, 1990.

Jaspers, Karl. *Spinoza.* From *The Great Philosophers: The Original Thinkers, Volume II.* Ed. Hannah Arendt. Trans. Ralph Mannheim. New York: Harcourt Brace Jovanovich, 1966.

Jay, Martin. *Refractions of Violence.* London: Routledge, 2003.

Joris, Pierre. Translator's preface. *The Unavowable Community.* By Maurice Blanchot. Barrytown, NY: Station Hill, 1988.

Joyce, James. *Finnegans Wake.* Intro. John Bishop. London: Penguin, 1999.

Kempis, Thomas à. *The Imitation of Christ.* Trans. with an intro. Leo Sherley-Price. London: Penguin, 1952.

Khayati, Mustapha. "Captive Words (Preface to a Situationist Dictionary)." Trans. Tom McDonough. In *Guy Debord and the Situationist International: Texts and Documents.* Ed. Tom McDonough. Cambridge, MA: MIT Press, 2002.

Kierkegaard, Søren. *Papers and Journals: A Selection.* Trans. with intro. and notes Alastair Hannay. London: Penguin, 1996.

Kishik, David. *The Power of Life: Agamben and the Coming Politics (To Imagine a Form of Life, II).* Stanford: Stanford University Press, 2012.

Koepnick, Lutz. "Aura Reconsidered: Benjamin and Contemporary Visual Culture." In *Benjamin's Ghosts: Interventions in Contemporary Literary and Cultural Theory.* Ed. Gerhard Richter. Stanford: Stanford University Press, 2002. 95–120.

Kristeva, Julia. *The Sense and Non-Sense of Revolt: The Powers and Limits of Psychoanalysis, Volume 1.* Trans. Jeanine Herman. New York: Columbia University Press, 2000.

—. *This Incredible Need to Believe.* Trans. Beverley Bie Brahic. New York: Columbia University Press, 2009.

Lambert, Gregg. *The Return of the Baroque in Modern Culture*. London: Continuum, 2004.

Lehman, Robert S. *Impossible Modernism: T.S. Eliot, Walter Benjamin, and the Critique of Historical Reason*. Stanford: Stanford University Press, 2016.

Lendl, Ivan and George Mendoza. *Ivan Lendl's 14-Day Tennis Clinic: Hitting Hot*. Photographs Walter Iooss, Jr. London: Star, 1986.

Leupin, Alexandre. *Lacan Today*. New York: Other, 2004.

Lorge, Barry. Contributing Editor. "Why You Should Like Ivan Lendl." *Tennis*. Vol. 22, No. 10, February 1987. 38–43.

Löwy, Michael. *Fire Alarm: Reading Walter Benjamin's 'On the Concept of History'*. Trans. Chris Turner. London: Verso, 2005.

Luhmann, Niklas. *Art as a Social System*. Trans. Eva M. Knodt. Stanford: Stanford University Press, 2000.

—. *Observations on Modernity*. Trans. William Whobrey. Stanford: Stanford University Press, 1998.

—. *The Reality of the Mass Media*. Trans. Kathleen Cross. Stanford: Stanford University Press, 2000.

McEnroe, John. *But Seriously*. New York: Little, Brown and Company, 2017.

McEnroe, John with James Kaplan. *You Cannot Be Serious*. New York: Berkley, 2002.

Macherey, Pierre. *A Theory of Literary Production*. Trans. Geoffrey Wall. With a new intro. Terry Eagleton and a new afterword by the author. London: Verso, 2005.

Maly, Kenneth. *Heidegger's Possibility: Language, Emergence—Saying Be-ing*. Toronto: University of Toronto Press, 2008.

Marchesi, Simone. *Dante & Augustine: Linguistics, Poetics, Hermeneutics*. Toronto: University of Toronto Press, 2011.

Mendes, Valerie Mendes and Amy de la Haye. *Fashion Since 1900, New Edition*. London: Thames & Hudson World of Art, 2010.

Miller, J. Hillis. *Communities in Fiction*. New York: Fordham University Press, 2015.

— . *The Conflagration of Community: Fiction Before and After Auschwitz*. Chicago: University of Chicago Press, 2011.

Missac, Pierre. *Walter Benjamin's Passages*. Trans. Shierry Weber Nicholsen. Cambridge, MA: MIT Press, 1995.

MLA Handbook. Eighth Edition. Foreword Rosemary G. Feal. Preface Kathleen Fitzpatrick. New York: The Modern Language Association of America, 2016.

Moeller, Hans-Georg. *The Radical Luhmann*. New York: Columbia University Press, 2011.

Mondor, Henri. *Vie de Mallarmé*. Paris: Gallimard, 1941. 687. As cited by Vincent Kaufman from his essay "Angels of Purity" trans. John Goodman in *Guy Debord and the Situationist International: Texts and Documents*, ed. Tom McDonough. Cambridge, MA: MIT Press, 2002.

Montag, Warren. *Bodies, Masses, Power: Spinoza and His Contemporaries*. London: Verso, 1999.

Montale, Eugenio. "Introduction". *The Divine Comedy*. By Dante Alighieri. Notes Peter Armour. New York: Knopf, 1995.

Nancy, Jean-Luc. *The Experience of Freedom*. Trans. Bridget McDonald. Foreword Peter Fenves. Stanford: Stanford University Press, 1993.

— . *L'Experience de la liberté*. Paris: Galilée, 1988. Uncited.

— . *Being Singular Plural*. Trans. Robert D. Richardson and Anne E. O'Byrne. Stanford: Stanford University Press, 2000.

— . Preface. *The Inoperative Community: Theory and History of Literature, Volume 76*. Foreword Christopher Fynsk. Ed. Peter Connor. Trans. Peter Connor, Lisa Garbus, Michael Holland, and Simona Sawhney. Minneapolis: University of Minnesota Press, 1991.

Negri, Antonio and Michael Hardt. *Multitude: War and Democracy in the Age of Empire*. New York: Penguin, 2004.

Pichené, Julien. *Carnets de balles: De Laver à Federer en passant par McEnroe, 250 matches indispensables*. Préface de Patrice Dominguez. Paris: Publibook, 2010.

Plotinus. *The Enneads*. Trans. Stephen MacKenna. Abridged with an intro. and notes John Dillon. London: Penguin, 1991.

Polanyi, Michael. *Knowing and Being: Essays by Michael Polanyi*. Ed. Marjorie Grene. Chicago: University of Chicago Press, 1969.

—. *Personal Knowledge: Towards a Post-Critical Philosophy*. Enlarged edition with a New Foreword by Mary Jo Nye. Chicago: University of Chicago Press, 2015.

Pound, Ezra. "Henry James". In *Literary Essays of Ezra Pound*. Ed. with an intro. TS Eliot. New York: New Directions, 1918. 295–338.

Pound, Marcus. *Žižek: A (Very) Critical Introduction*. Grand Rapids, MI: William B. Eerdmans Publishing Company, 2008.

Powell, Jason. *Jacques Derrida: A Biography*. London: Continuum, 2006.

Rancière, Jacques. *Short Voyages to the Land of the People*. Trans. James B. Swenson. Stanford: Stanford University Press, 2003.

—. *The Ignorant Schoolmaster: Five Lessons in Intellectual Emancipation*. Trans. with an intro. Kristin Ross. Stanford: Stanford University Press, 1991.

Rapaport, Herman. *Heidegger & Derrida: Reflections on Time and Language*. Lincoln: University of Nebraska Press, 1989.

Richardson, Michael. *Georges Bataille*. London: Routledge, 1994.

Roraback, Erik S. *The Dialectics of Late Capital and Power: James, Balzac and Critical Theory*. Newcastle-upon-Tyne: Cambridge Scholars, 2007.

—. *The Philosophical Baroque: On Autopoietic Modernities*. Leiden, The Netherlands: Brill, 2017.

Ruti, Mari. *The Call of Character: Living a Life Worth Living*. New York: Columbia University Press, 2014.

Said, Edward. *Beginnings: Intention and Method*. Intro. Michael Wood. London: Granta, 1985.

Sartre, Jean-Paul. *Critique of Dialectical Reason, Volume 1, Theory of Practical Ensembles*. Trans. Alan Sheridan-Smith. Ed. Jonathan

Rée. Foreword Fredric Jameson. London: Verso, 2004.

Scala, André. *Silences de Federer*. Paris: Les Essais, Éditions de la Différence, 2011.

Serres, Michel. *The Five Senses: A Philosophy of Mingled Bodies (I)*. Trans. Margaret Sankey and Peter Cowley. London: Continuum, 2008.

—. *The Troubadour of Knowledge*. Trans. Sheila Faria Glaser and William Paulson. Ann Arbor: University of Michigan Press, 1997.

—. *Times of Crisis: What the Financial Crisis Revealed and How to Reinvent our Lives and Future*. Trans. Anne-Marie Feenberg-Dibon. New York: Bloomsbury, 2014.

Sloterdijk, Peter. *Critique of Cynical Reason*. Trans. Michael Eldred. Foreword Andreas Huyssen. *Theory and History of Literature, Volume 40*. Minneapolis: University of Minnesota Press, 1987.

—. *In the World Interior of Capital: For a Philosophical Theory of Globalization*. Trans. Wieland Hoban. Cambridge, UK: Polity, 2013.

—. *Nietzsche Apostle*. Trans. Steven Corcoran. Los Angeles, CA: Semiotext(e), 2013.

—. *Spheres I: Bubbles, Microspherology*. Trans. Wieland Hoban. Los Angeles: Semiotext(e), 2011.

—. *Spheres, Volume 3: Foams, Plural Spherology*. Trans. Wieland Hoban. South Pasadena, CA: Semiotext(e), 2016.

—. *You Must Change Your Life: On Anthropotechnics*. Trans. Wieland Hoban. Cambridge, UK: Polity, 2013.

Smith, Daniel W. "Introduction, 'A Life of Pure Immanence': Deleuze's 'Critique et Clinique' Project". In *Essays: Critical and Clinical*. By Gilles Deleuze. Trans. Daniel W. Smith and Michael A. Greco. Minneapolis: University of Minnesota Press, 1997. xi–liii.

Smith, Steven B. *Spinoza's Book of Life: Freedom and Redemption in the 'Ethics.'* New Haven: Yale University Press, 2003.

Spinoza, Benedictus de. *The 'Ethics'* from *A Spinoza Reader: The 'Ethics' and Other Works*. Ed. and trans. Edwin Curley. Princeton: Princeton University Press, 1994.

Stehr, Nico and Gotthard Bechmann. "Introduction". *Risk: A Sociological Theory*. By Niklas Luhmann. New Brunswick, NJ: Aldine Transaction, 2002.

Stevens, Rex P. *Kant on Moral Practice: A Study of Moral Success and Failure*. Macon, GA: Mercer University Press, 1981.

Stiegler, Bernard. *Taking Care of Youth and the Generations*. Trans. Stephen Barker. Stanford: Stanford University Press, 2010.

Sutil, Nicolás Salazar. *Motion and Representation: The Language of Human Movement*. Cambridge, MA: MIT Press, 2015.

Taylor, Charles. *Sources of the Self: The Making of the Modern Identity*. Cambridge, MA: Harvard University Press, 1992.

Vighi, Fabio. *On Žižek's Dialectics: Surplus, Subtraction, Sublimation*. London: Continuum, 2010.

Welsch, Wolfgang. "Sport Viewed Aesthetically, and Even as Art?" *The Aesthetics of Everyday Life*. Ed. Andrew Light and Jonathan M. Smith. New York: Columbia University Press, 2005. 135–155.

Wallace, David Foster. *Both Flesh and Not: Essays*. London: Penguin, 2012.

Wittgenstein, Ludwig. *Culture and Value*. Ed. GH von Wright in collaboration with Heikki Nyman. Trans. Peter Winch. Chicago: University of Chicago Press, 1980.

Wolin, Richard. *Walter Benjamin: An Aesthetic of Redemption*. With a new Introduction by the Author. Berkeley: University of California Press, 1994.

Žižek, Slavoj. *Absolute Recoil: Towards a New Foundation of Dialectical Materialism*. London: Verso, 2014.

— . *Antigone*. London: Bloomsbury Academic, 2016.

—. *Did Somebody Say Totalitarianism? Five Interventions in the (Mis)use of a Notion*. London: Verso, 2002.

— . *Disparities*. London: Bloomsbury Academic, 2016.

—. *First as Tragedy, Then as Farce.* London: Verso, 2009.

—. *Less than Nothing: Hegel and the Shadow of Dialectical Materialism.* London: Verso, 2012.

—. *Living in the End Times.* London: Verso, 2010.

—. *Organs without Bodies: On Deleuze and Consequences.* New York: Routledge, 2004.

—. *The Fragile Absolute: Or, Why Is The Christian Legacy Worth Fighting For?* London: Verso, 2000.

—. *The Indivisible Remainder: On Schelling and Related Matters.* London: Verso, 1996.

—. *The Parallax View.* Cambridge, MA: MIT Press, 2006.

—. *The Puppet and the Dwarf: The Perverse Core of Christianity.* Cambridge, MA: MIT Press, 2003.

Žižek, Slavoj and Boris Gunjević. *God in Pain: Inversions of Apocalypse.* Boris Gunjević's chapters translated from the Croatian by Ellen Elias-Bursać. New York: Seven Stories, 2012.

Žižek, Slavoj and John Milbank. *The Monstrosity of Christ: Paradox or Dialectic?* Ed. Creston Davis. Cambridge, MA: MIT Press, 2009.

Index of Names and Subjects

Note: Page numbers in italics refer to illustrations/photos. The letter 'n' following locators refers to notes. Mentions of names and subjects in the pre-introduction matter, and in the select bibliography, are not included in the index; names and subjects in the notes are indexed where there is some substantive amplification or extension of the discussion in the text. Please note that notions indexed here are sometimes questioned or rejected in the text.

Agamben/Benjamin), 186

"Eiffel Tower, the": 257
(Collins on McEnroe's
confidence); la Tour Eiffel,
290
elated, 275 (Lendl); elation,
275 (Kimmage)
Epicureanism, 35; "'epicurean'
endorsement of joy", 59 (S.
Smith on Spinoza)
equality, 40, 44, 52, 64, 72, 290;
113 (Nancy)
everyday, the, 14, 75, 264
examples, 31, 38, 64, 94,
109, 120, 279; concrete,
11; "*Examples*", 30 (de le
Durantaye); 'examples',
30 (Agamben via de
la Durantaye). *See also*
exemplary
exemplary, 11, 23, 48, 120, 212,
227; cases, 120; "causality",
52 (Deleuze on Spinoza);
cultural figure, 31; "figures
and forms", 30 (de la
Durantaye on Agamben); of
the inoperative community
(McEnroe and Lendl),
259; "Jimmy vs. Ivan
as exemplary occasion,
224;   paradigm, 31;
situation—1984 French
Open Men's Singles Final,

238; of the spectacle society,
219; Strether an exemplary
figure, 118; "'exemplars
[*gli esemplari*]'", 30 (de la
Durantaye on Agamben); the
exemplar's, 31; the example
of Lendl's career, 228; of
Strether, 106; "*The example*",
30 (de la Durantaye on
Agamben)
existence and creation, 21,
44, 93, 147, 174, 179, 186,
188 passim, 202, 207, 280,
287. *See also* aesthetics of
existence
experience, 15, 20, 24, 29, 35–
37, 41–42, 48, 57, 70, 72–75,
78, 80, 82, 85, 87–88, 91, 99,
106, 109, 111–13, 118, 128–29,
148 passim, 150, 152, 154–55,
157, 165, 172–73, 178, 184,
196, 201, 223, 229, 235, 240,
264, 266, 279–80, 286; 281
(Barthes); 142, 182 (Bersani);
154 (Blanchot); 56 (Deleuze
on Spinoza); 136 (Hanssen
on Benjamin); 88, 112 passim
(Nancy); 63 (Spinoza);
Benjamin's experience
(*erfahrung*), 20; bitterest,
222; classic American,
201; collective, 160, 237;
collective-communal, 36;
commodification of, 200;

194, 214, 258, 283; 22 (de la
Durantaye on Agamben/
Benjamin); exemplary,
31; "—or model—for our
action", 22 (de la Durantaye
on Agamben/Benjamin);
Ivan Lendl as "—or
model—for our action", 23;
"for understanding", 22
(Benjamin via Agamben/de
la Durantaye); paradigmatic,
214; paradigmatic power
of tennis, 264; paradigms,
85, 194; *paradigms*, 30 (de la
Durantaye on Agamben)

Paris, France, 240, 250–51,
267–68, 273, 281, 284; 274
(Enberg); 274 (Lendl); "Paris
arcades", 125 (Adorno on
Benjamin); EHESS, 187;
Parisian, 241, 251, 262

passion, 60, 72, 74, 102, 139,
246, 280; 206 (Kishik); 115
(E. Pound); Aquinas's, 162;
athletic, 219; blissful, 55;
of (de)creative writing,
152; immunizing, 152;
"intellectual", 128 (Arendt
on Benjamin); "of patience",
152 (Blanchot); "of patience",
152; of reading, 152;
'passion', 206; *passion*, 102
(Nancy); James's passional
investigations, 118; James's

passional writing life, 102;
passionless, 215; passionate,
26, 290; passionately, 102,
192; "passionate energy",
247 (Serres); sartorial
and athletic, 219; "search
passionately for what
you are", 194 (Serres);
impassioned, 32. *See also*
passions

passions, 65, 67, 117, 250–51;
46 (Deleuze on Spinoza);
"'passions'", 88 (Nancy);
"*passions*", 65 (Spinoza);
active, 55; 'sad', 47 (Deleuze
on Spinoza); "'unleashing
of'", 102 (Bataille via Nancy);
"unrefined", 72 (S. Smith
on Spinoza). *See also* joyful
passions

patience, 145–53 passim,
154–55, 157–60 passim; 182
(Bersani); 157–59 (Blanchot);
147 (*Finnegans Wake*); 146,
148 (Kempis); 76 (Nancy);
strange, 160; "Thought's",
76 (Blanchot); "*patience*",
158 (Blanchot); Patience,
158; "Patience", 151, 275
(Blanchot); patiences,
immunizing, 145; the
patient, 146

physical training, 18, 23

politics of the *flash*: Benjamin's

"of past", 142 (Wolin);
sublational force and magic,
292
substance, 54 passim, 60
(Deleuze on Spinoza);
collective social symbolic
(in post-Žižekese), 30;
collective symbolic, 164;
of creative existence and
the innovative commons,
29; "encompassing global
Substance ('humanity')", 213
(Žižek); immanent, 80; life,
173, 289; Lendl's symbolic,
228; "'organic' ethnic", 213
(Žižek); our common social,
29; "relation *of a substance* to
itself", 103 (Nancy); social
symbolic, 262; spirit and, 58;
symbolic, 237; true, 15, 29;
value and, 46
success, 25 (Brooks); "alone
endures", 40 (Gracián);
Benjamin's lifetime, 128;
of James's late novels, 99;
Lendl desirous of, 259; *true*
(cf. *The Tragic Muse*), 102;
309n8 (Folley on Murray-
Djokovic). *See also* successful
successful: Connors and
Lendl, 211; most from the
1980s men, 231; Murray
and Lendl partnership end
because they were so, 287

surveillance, 45

technology, 68, 77, 170, 183,
200; 261 (Welsch); "art and",
134 (Buck-Morss); digital, 30,
34, 52, 56, 77–78, 80, 83, 129,
133, 139, 166, 177, 188, 213,
291; "latest", 261 (Mendes
and de la Haye); new tennis,
287
Tonite Show, The (TV program),
220
transformative agent, 31, 45,
49, 140, 228; transformative
agents, 279
transindividual, 109;
athletic identity is, 266;
becoming, 48; the Dante
and Virgil transindividual
relation, 198; McEnroe's
transindividual victory at
the 1984 French Open, 265;
and transnational monads,
29; and transnational
subjectivity Lendl and
Murray, 26; transformation,
43; understanding of the
being of identity, 266. *See
also* transindividuality;
transindividually;
"transindividuation,
fields of"; transnational;
transpersonal
transindividuality, 174, 267;

Index of Premodern and Modern Authors and Athletes

Note: Page numbers in italics refer to illustrations/photos, and the letter 'n' following locators refers to notes. Mentions of authors and athletes in the pre-introduction matter and in the select bibliography are not included in the index.

Index of Sources

Note: Page numbers in italics refer to illustrations/photos, and the letter 'n' following locators refers to notes. Mentions of sources in the pre-introduction matter and in the select bibliography are not included in the index.

BOOKS

Iff Books

ACADEMIC AND SPECIALIST

Iff Books publishes non-fiction. It aims to work with authors and titles that augment our understanding of the human condition, society and civilisation, and the world or universe in which we live.
If you have enjoyed this book, why not tell other readers by posting a review on your preferred book site.

Recent bestsellers from Iff Books are:

Why Materialism Is Baloney
How True Skeptics Know There is no Death and Fathom Answers
to Life, the Universe, and Everything
Bernardo Kastrup
A hard-nosed, logical, and skeptic non-materialist metaphysics,
according to which the body is in mind, not mind in the body.
Paperback: 978-1-78279-362-5 ebook: 978-1-78279-361-8

The Fall
Steve Taylor
The Fall discusses human achievement versus the issues of war,
patriarchy and social inequality.
Paperback: 978-1-90504-720-8 ebook: 978-184694-633-2

Brief Peeks Beyond
Critical Essays on Metaphysics, Neuroscience, Free Will,
Skepticism and Culture
Bernardo Kastrup
An incisive, original, compelling alternative to current mainstream
cultural views and assumptions.
Paperback: 978-1-78535-018-4 ebook: 978-1-78535-019-1

Framespotting
Changing How You Look at Things Changes How
You See Them
Laurence & Alison Matthews
A punchy, upbeat guide to framespotting. Spot deceptions and
hidden assumptions; swap growth for growing up. See and be free.
Paperback: 978-1-78279-689-3 ebook: 978-1-78279-822-4

Is There an Afterlife?

David Fontana

Is there an Afterlife? If so what is it like? How do Western ideas of the afterlife compare with Eastern? David Fontana presents the historical and contemporary evidence for survival of physical death.

Paperback: 978-1-90381-690-5

Nothing Matters

A Book About Nothing

Ronald Green

Thinking about Nothing opens the world to everything by illuminating new angles to old problems and stimulating new ways of thinking.

Paperback: 978-1-84694-707-0 ebook: 978-1-78099-016-3

Panpsychism

The Philosophy of the Sensuous Cosmos

Peter Ells

Are free will and mind chimeras? This book, anti-materialistic but respecting science, answers: No! Mind is foundational to all existence.

Paperback: 978-1-84694-505-2 ebook: 978-1-78099-018-7

Punk Science

Inside the Mind of God

Manjir Samanta-Laughton

Many have experienced unexplainable phenomena; God, psychic abilities, extraordinary healing and angelic encounters. Can cutting-edge science actually explain phenomena previously thought of as 'paranormal'?

Paperback: 978-1-90504-793-2

The Vagabond Spirit of Poetry

Edward Clarke

Spend time with the wisest poets of the modern age and of the past, and let Edward Clarke remind you of the importance of poetry in our industrialized world.

Paperback: 978-1-78279-370-0 ebook: 978-1-78279-369-4

Readers of ebooks can buy or view any of these bestsellers by clicking on the live link in the title. Most titles are published in paperback and as an ebook. Paperbacks are available in traditional bookshops. Both print and ebook formats are available online.

Find more titles and sign up to our readers' newsletter at
http://www.johnhuntpublishing.com/non-fiction

Follow us on Facebook at
https://www.facebook.com/JHPNonFiction
and Twitter at https://twitter.com/JHPNonFiction